THE FRANCIS FACTOR

John Littleton and Eamon Maher

editors

The Francis Factor

A New Departure

the columba press

First published in 2014 by
the columba press
55A Spruce Avenue,
Stillorgan Industrial Park,
Blackrock, County Dublin

Cover artwork, *Unfinished Agenda*, by Gerry Carew
Cover design by Dave Mc Namara
Origination by The Columba Press
Printed by ScandBook AB, Sweden

ISBN 978 1 78218 146 0

Contents

Acknowledgements

Our sincere thanks go to all the contributors to this book, who worked assiduously to produce such a rich compendium of views on the first year of Francis' papacy.

We are also particularly grateful to Patrick O'Donoghue, Managing Editor at The Columba Press, who first approached us with the idea of editing this book, and to his colleagues, with whom it has been a pleasure to work on several books to date.

The cover artwork, *Unfinished Agenda*, is by Gerry Carew, to whom we are greatly indebted.

List of Abbreviations

BBC	British Broadcasting Corporation
CDF	Congregation for the Doctrine of the Faith
ed.	Editor
eds	Editors
EG	*Evangelii Gaudium*
EWTN	Eternal Word Television Network
IOR	*Istituto per le Opere di Religione* – 'The Institute for the Works of Religion' (commonly referred to as the Vatican Bank)
LGBT	Lesbian, Gay, Bisexual and Transgender
RCIA	Rite of Christian Initiation of Adults
St	Saint
trans.	Translated

List of Abbreviations of Biblical Books

1 Cor	1 Corinthians
1 Pet	1 Peter
1 Sam	1 Samuel
Eccl	Ecclesiastes
Gal	Galatians
Gen	Genesis
Jn	John
Lk	Luke
Mk	Mark
Mt	Matthew
Ps	Psalms
Rom	Romans
Zeph	Zephaniah

List of Contributors

TINA BEATTIE is Professor of Catholic Studies and Director of the Digby Stuart Research Centre for Religion, Society and Human Flourishing at the University of Roehampton in London, UK.

SEÁN BRADY is the Catholic Cardinal Archbishop of Armagh and Primate of All Ireland.

PATRICK CLAFFEY is a member of the Society of the Divine Word. He is currently working as a priest in the Archdiocese of Dublin and is an adjunct assistant professor in the Department of Religions and Theology at Trinity College.

RICHARD CLARKE became the Church of Ireland Archbishop of Armagh and Primate of All Ireland in 2012, having previously served as Bishop of Meath and Kildare.

MICHAEL COLLINS is a priest of the Archdiocese of Dublin and author of several books, including *Francis: Bishop of Rome* (2013).

JIM CORKERY is a Jesuit priest who is an associate professor of theology at the Milltown Institute of Theology and Philosophy, Dublin. He is co-editor of *The Papacy since 1500: From Italian Prince to Universal Pastor* (2010).

DONALD COZZENS is a priest and writer-in-residence at John Carroll University in Ohio, USA, and has written several award-winning books.

BRIAN D'ARCY is a Passionist priest, journalist and broadcaster who is currently superior of Saint Gabriel's, The Graan, Enniskillen, Northern Ireland. He writes a weekly column for the *Sunday World* newspaper.

LOUISE FULLER is author of the acclaimed *Irish Catholicism since 1950: The Undoing of a Culture* (2002, 2004) and co-editor, with John Littleton and Eamon Maher, of *Irish and Catholic? Towards an Understanding of Identity* (2006).

MICHAEL KELLY is Editor of *The Irish Catholic* newspaper and a writer and broadcaster on religious and social affairs, contributing to various Irish and international newspapers, magazines, radio and television programmes.

COLUM KENNY is Professor of Communications at Dublin City University and a member of the Broadcasting Authority of Ireland. He has written several books and is a columnist with the *Sunday Independent* newspaper.

LEN KOFLER is an Austrian Mill Hill Missionary priest who is Director of the Institute of St Anselm, Kent, UK. He has written several books.

BRENDAN LEAHY is Catholic Bishop of Limerick since 2013. Prior to that, he was Professor of Systematic Theology at St Patrick's College, Maynooth, Ireland.

SARAH MAC DONALD writes for the *Irish Independent*, *The Catholic Times*, *The Tablet* and the Catholic News Service. She researched and produced the documentary, *Mary Ward: Dangerous Visionary*.

ALFRED MCBRIDE is a Norbertine priest and member of St Norbert Abbey in De Pere, Wisconsin, USA. He is the founder of the department of religious education at the National Catholic Education Association and has written numerous books.

PETER MCVERRY is a Jesuit priest who has been working with homeless people and drug users for more than thirty years in Dublin, Ireland. He writes regularly on social issues in Irish society.

MARY T. MALONE retired to Ireland in 1997 after almost forty years in Canada where she taught in Toronto's St Augustine's Seminary and in the University of St Jerome's, the Catholic College on the campus of the University of Waterloo. Mary lives in her home county of Wexford.

LOUISE NELSTROP is Director of spirituality programmes and Lecturer in Christian Spirituality at Sarum College, Salisbury, UK. She is also an associate member of the Theology Faculty at Oxford University.

John O'Connor is a member of the Society of the Catholic Apostolate (better known as the Pallottines) and a parish priest in Shankill, County Dublin. Previously he worked in Argentina for over thirty years with, among others, Cardinal Jorge Bergoglio in Buenos Aires.

Daniel O'Leary is a priest of the Diocese of Leeds, UK, and an author and teacher. He is a well-known conference speaker and retreat director.

Timothy Radcliffe is a Dominican priest who was Master of the Order of Preachers from 1992 until 2001. Since then, he has been an itinerant preacher and lecturer, based at Blackfriars, Oxford, UK. He spends two thirds of the year travelling.

Richard Rohr is a Franciscan of the New Mexico Province, USA, and a globally recognised teacher and writer. He is founder of the centre for Action and Contemplation in Albuquerque, New Mexico.

Fáinche Ryan is Assistant Professor in Systematic Theology at the Loyola Institute, Trinity College, Dublin. Among her recent publications is *The Eucharist: What Do We Believe?* (2012).

Aidan Troy is a Passionist priest who has been parish priest in Mission Anglophone, Paris, France for the past six years. He was previously parish priest at Holy Cross, Ardoyne, Belfast, Northern Ireland during a time of often turbulent protest at Holy Cross School.

Willie Walsh was Catholic Bishop of Killaloe in Ireland from 1994 until his retirement in 2010. He was a regular contributor to Church issues at national level. In retirement, he continues to write on topical issues.

John Waters is a playwright, author of numerous books about politics, culture and transcendence, and newspaper columnist.

Pope Francis: A Biographical Timeline

1936

- 17 December: Jorge Mario Bergoglio born in Flores, Buenos Aires, Argentina.
- Parents: Mario José Bergoglio, an Italian immigrant, and Regina María Sívori.
- Eldest of five children.

1954

- Qualified as a chemical technician.

1957

- Diagnosed with pneumonia, and cysts on his right lung. A portion of the lung was surgically removed to save his life.

1958

- 11 March: Entered the Jesuit novitiate in Córdoba, Argentina.

1960

- 12 March: First vows as a member of the Society of Jesus.

1960–3

- Studied philosophy and humanities as part of his training for the priesthood.

1964–6

- Taught literature and psychology to secondary school students in Santa Fe and Buenos Aires.

1967–70

- Studied theology at the Colegio de San José in San Miguel, Argentina.

1969

- 13 December: Ordained priest by Archbishop Ramón José Castellano.

1970

- Jesuit tertianship programme in Spain.

1972–3

- Served as Novice Master for the Jesuits in Argentina.

1973

- 22 April: Perpetual vows as a member of the Society of Jesus.
- 31 July: Elected Provincial of the Jesuits in Argentina, serving until 1979.

1976

- During Argentina's Dirty War, two Jesuit priests, Fr Franz Jalics and Fr Orlando Yorio, were arrested, tortured and illegally imprisoned by the military. It is suggested that Bergoglio had not supported and protected them – although he worked to have them released.

1979–85

- Served as Rector of the Colegio Máximo de San Miguel.

1980

- June–July: Spent two months in Ireland learning English.

1986

- Went to Germany for doctoral studies.

1992

- 20 May: Appointed Auxiliary Bishop of Buenos Aires (and Titular Bishop of Auca).
- 27 June: Ordained bishop by Cardinal Antonio Quarracino.

1994

- 2–29 October: Attended the ninth ordinary assembly of the Synod of Bishops in Rome.

1997

- 3 June: Appointed Coadjutor Archbishop of Buenos Aires.
- 16 November – 12 December: Attended the special assembly for America of the Synod of Bishops in Rome.

1998

- 28 February: Appointed Archbishop of Buenos Aires, after Cardinal Quarracino's death.

2001

- 21 February: Created Cardinal by Pope John Paul II.
- 30 September – 27 October: Attended the tenth ordinary assembly of the Synod of Bishops in Rome.

2005

- Participated in the conclave that elected Pope Benedict XVI. (It is rumoured that Bergoglio received the second highest number of votes.)
- 2–23 October: Attended the eleventh ordinary assembly of the Synod of Bishops in Rome.
- 9 November: Elected President of the Argentinian Bishops' Conference (re-elected from 2008 until 2011).

2007

- Participated in the fifth general conference of the Latin American Bishops in Aparecida, Brazil.

2010

- Unsuccessfully opposed the government's legalisation of same-sex marriage.

2013

- 13 March: Elected Pope, the 265th successor to St Peter. He took the name Francis, in honour of St Francis of Assisi.
- 19 March: Inauguration Mass for the official start of his pontificate.
- December: Named Person of the Year by *Time* magazine.

Foreword

These are historic days for our Church. The conclave of last March was historic in more ways than one. I will never forget the thrill of being present at, and part of, a conclave which saw one pope resign and his successor elected, and the joy of hearing Pope Francis ask all listening to him to pray that God might bless him before he blessed the world.

The cardinals had gathered in general congregations to seek the guidance of the Holy Spirit. We knew that we were coming together at a critical moment for the Church and for humankind. We knew that, in discerning the person God had chosen to be the next pope, we were not engaged in a merely human assessment but in an act of historical significance for the world.

Fortunately we decided to take sufficient time to first draw near to the Lord in prayer and, in so doing, to draw closer to each other. We listened respectfully to each other's experience, in the sure knowledge that respect for diversity inevitably leads to deeper and more perfect communion.

The conclave opened in a great spirit of gratitude and hope – gratitude for the seeds of renewal planted by the Second Vatican Council; gratitude for the course of authentic continuity between the Council and renewal set by the outstanding patrimony of teaching bequeathed to us by the successors of Peter since the Council.

We came together in the hope that, with the help of the Spirit, we could identify the man, chosen by God, to lead the New Evangelisation, rejoicing in the fact that the next Successor of Peter has never been better placed to do so.

We were hopeful that the man we would elect would avail fully of the modern means of social communications to speak to the hearts and minds of people instantaneously and on a global scale.

We were hoping too that, at this time, the Lord was calling to be Bishop of Rome one who can not only enlighten the minds but also set hearts on fire by his witness to practical Christian love, especially love for the poor.

The rest is history. The Lord, in his mercy, has, once more, heard the cry of the poor. He has given to the Church and to the world a pope who never tires of telling us that God never tires of showing mercy. It is we who tire of asking for that mercy.

I congratulate the editors and contributors to this volume, marking the first year in office of Pope Francis. I know that it will spur us all to become better, and more zealous, missionary disciples of the Lord. I wish it great success.

+ Seán Brady
Cardinal Archbishop of Armagh
February 2014

Introduction

John Littleton and Eamon Maher

It is often said that a week is a long time in politics, but in terms of a worldwide institution like the Catholic Church, a week, or a year for that matter, is almost nothing. Change comes very, very slowly in the monolithic structure that is the Vatican. Doctrine, formed over centuries, reaffirmed in various conciliar documents and papal encyclicals, debated, parsed and analysed in numerous committees, preached about from altars across the globe, tends to take root gradually in people's consciousness, and is difficult to change.

So it is that people, who were reared as Catholics and have long since strayed from the fold, can sometimes think back with wistfulness to the ceremonies and rituals of the Church. Equally, they can on occasion still feel residual guilt about missing Mass on Sunday, dishonest dealings with others, sexual activity outside of marriage, or a lack of charity, because of the repeated warnings they received about what they were told constituted sinful activity. Graham Greene, in *The End of the Affair*, mentioned that Catholicism is sometimes 'caught like a disease', by which he meant that it can lie in the subconscious for many years just awaiting the spark that might reignite it. One never knows from whence that spark might come.

So you may ask what is so special about the election of Jorge Mario Bergoglio as Pope Francis on the 13 March 2013 apart from him being the first pope to be elected from the Americas, the first Jesuit to assume the role and the first Bishop of Rome to take the name Francis? What is the Francis factor? What is the secret of his astonishing and unexpected appeal? Why do people warm to him so much? How has he changed people's perception of the Catholic Church in such a short space of time? Is his Papacy more about style than substance? Is he all that different in essence from his predecessors John Paul II and Benedict XVI?[1]

---

[1]   It should not be forgotten that Benedict himself created a huge precedent by being the first pope to resign from office in over seven hundred years, thus paving the way for Francis' election.

These are the sort of questions this book seeks to explore. The different chapters will examine numerous aspects of the new pontiff's background, spirituality, theological writings, interviews and personality in order to sketch a clearer picture of how a seventy-seven-year-old man can, within months of coming to the highest office in a Church that has suffered massive damage in the developed world – particularly because of the clerical sex abuse scandals and what are commonly perceived to be antiquarian views in relation to women and sexuality – be designated by *Time* magazine as its Person of the Year for 2013?

Clearly, it is difficult to gauge in quantifiable terms precisely what Francis has done to generate new enthusiasm within an ailing institution that seemed intent on circling the wagons and waiting until the fallout from the various controversies in which it was embroiled might pass by. Retrenchment, fear of change, a concentration on reiterating certain core values at the expense of losing the Gospel message of love and compassion, doctrinal conservatism: Francis, in one detailed interview for Jesuit publications, illustrated how this was not the way forward. Instead, he began by declaring himself a 'sinner' like everyone else, an imperfect vessel, a man who had made mistakes and would continue to do so. He emphasised a central Vatican II principle of the Church being the People of God: 'We should not think, therefore, that "thinking with the Church" means only thinking with the hierarchy of the Church.'[2] With this short sentence, he summed up what is a common problem for many Catholics, the perception that the Church *is* solely the hierarchy and its pronouncements. There is a whole other dimension to the institution, as Francis points out:

> I see the holiness ... in the patience of the People of God: a woman who is raising children, a man who works to bring home the bread, the sick, the elderly priests who have so many wounds but have a smile on their faces because they served the Lord, the sisters who work hard and live a hidden sanctity.

The essence of Francis' theology is formed by a commitment to the poor and the marginalised, an unwillingness to pass moral judgements on others, a dislike of legalism and decrees from on high, and a distrust of monolithic institutions. People can identify with him,

---

[2] The full text of this interview with Antonio Spadaro, SJ, was published in *America*, September 2013, and it is from this interview that the quotations from Pope Francis are taken.

because they have the intuitive conviction that he wants to walk in the footsteps of Christ, reaching out to those in pain – whether it is psychological, material or physical – to bring healing. 'I see clearly', the Pope continues in his interview, 'that the thing the Church needs today is the ability to heal wounds and to warm the hearts of the faithful; it needs nearness, proximity.' It is difficult to argue with this assessment, but one wonders if it would have been accepted to the same degree if it had come from either of Francis' two immediate predecessors. The fact that during his career he has demonstrated a genuine commitment to the disadvantaged of Buenos Aires, for example, and that he studiously avoids the trappings of power (insisting on driving a simple car and dressing in a less ostentatious manner), that he chooses not to condemn those whose sexual orientation or lifestyles are at variance with Church teaching, but to 'seek a new balance' in order that the Church might not fall like 'a house of cards', imbues Francis' pronouncements with real moral authority. People feel that he *genuinely* believes what he is saying – which is a new departure.

Francis' love of literature may not yet have extended to his encountering the work of the French priest-writer Jean Sulivan (1913–80), but there is significant convergence in some of the opinions expressed by both. For example, the following words from Francis' interview have a genuine resonance with Sulivan's world view: '[T]he Church's pastoral ministry cannot be obsessed with the transmission of a disjointed multitude of doctrines to be imposed insistently.' Indeed not. Christianity cannot be reduced to a list of prescriptions and laws that must be observed obsessively: it is also about love and joy, committing sins, sometimes out of charitable motives (like Graham Greene's police officer in *The Heart of the Matter*, who commits adultery out of a sense of compassion for a lonely, abandoned woman), taking risks, being ready to uproot and go where the need is greatest. Jean Sulivan was dubious of authoritarianism and believed that the institutional Church was in danger of becoming a mere caricature of what its founder had intended. We read in his spiritual journal, *Morning Light*: 'It is impossible not to grasp the contradiction between the speech of Jesus and ecclesiastical phraseology, mitres, capes, the whole show.'[3] Is this not what Francis is also saying, that it is time to rediscover the type of Church that Jesus intended, a Church

---

3   Jean Sulivan, *Morning Light: The Spiritual Journal of Jean Sulivan*, trans. by Joseph Cunneen and Patrick Gormally (New York/Mahwah: Paulist Press, 1976), p. 10.

based, not on fancy vestments and infallible pronouncements, but on love of God and love of others?

In his spiritual journal, Sulivan also wrote:

> Before acting politically, faith acts poetically. It creates a new way of seeing, it sings the Magnificat – that is, it overturns the powerful, lifts up the lowly, not because it needs to but out of a sudden realization. It sees strength in weakness, glory in the things that are ridiculed. The enormous absurdity of the cross shatters what the world calls reality.[4]

Pope Francis appears to have a similar view of faith and how it operates. He insists that it is a way of being in the world, a way of providing witness to the core Gospel message of caring for the helpless and the wounded, of finding strength in weakness. And the cross is a constant reminder that no one is any better than the next person, that death abolishes all difference. He encourages people not to be always harking back to the past, not to be so quick to judge others:

> If the Christian is a restorationist, a legalist, if he wants everything clear and safe, then he will find nothing. Tradition and memory of the past must help us to have the courage to open up new areas to God. Those who today always look for disciplinarian solutions, those who long for an exaggerated doctrinal 'security', those who stubbornly try to recover a past that no longer exists – they have a static and inward-directed view of things. In this way, faith becomes an ideology among other ideologies … Although the life of a person is a land full of thorns and weeds, there is always a space where the good seed can grow. You have to trust God.

What we encounter in Francis' writings and personality is not any real doctrinal innovation (he upholds the Church's stance on celibacy, same-sex marriage, abortion and the ordination of women), but rather a change in tone and in emphasis. Almost all of the contributors to this book welcome his election, which they dare to hope will mark a new dawn in the history of Catholicism and allow many of those who have been the victims of unjust condemnation (including many theologians and priests who have given years of loyal service to the Church) to envisage a more caring Church, one which encourages dialogue and is open to the possibility of change. Francis calls on

---

4   *Ibid.*, p. 78.

people to glimpse the ground 'where the good seed can grow', while acknowledging that life can also be 'full of thorns and weeds'. His message is one of hope, of unconditional love for the marginalised, of patience and understanding for those who do not share the same opinions. In its editorial of 21 September 2013, *The Irish Times* compared the election of Francis to the fall of the Berlin Wall:

> Something of the spirit of 1989 appears to be afoot in the Catholic Church since the election of Pope Francis last March. Walls are coming down, or appear likely to. Windows wrenched shut in Rome over recent decades are being prised open and a church which had turned in on itself is again facing the city and the world, and with a smile on its face.[5]

These words echo those of several other mainstream publications across the world, which sense the seismic shift that has accompanied Francis' arrival as Bishop of Rome. In just one year, he has transformed how people view the Catholic Church. He has restored hope and injected enthusiasm in what was a tired institution. By any standards, his first year in office has been an astonishing success. In the chapters that follow, many wonder whether a rather elderly man will have sufficient time to continue what he has begun. Will he be overcome by the magnitude of the task with which he is confronted? Will conservative elements within the Curia, or the Church at large, conspire to undermine his mission? Will he flatter to deceive and end up being viewed as a pope who made a promising start, but ultimately succumbed to forces beyond his control? The opinions expressed about his contribution to date are almost all laudatory, some even lyrical. Paddy Agnew, the Rome correspondent for *The Irish Times*, quotes the cautionary note struck by the dissident theologian and astute reader of Vatican politics, Hans Küng, who wrote in a recent article:

> The credibility of Pope Francis will be immensely damaged if Vatican reactionaries stop him from soon translating his words into actions … The huge capital of trust that Francis has built up in these opening months of the pontificate must not be squandered by the Curia.[6]

---

5 'A Church More Open to All', editorial, *The Irish Times*, 21 September 2013.
6 Paddy Agnew, 'The Papal Spring', *The Irish Times*, Weekend Review, 28 December 2013, p. 5.

Küng highlights the big fear that is expressed by many in this book, namely that Francis may not be able to translate his words into actions. One might take some solace from the fact that he is an experienced campaigner, a Jesuit also, who knows the politics of his role and would be well aware of the unrest his pronouncements have aroused in reactionary circles.

This is a man with a mission, a mission whose importance is highlighted by the wave of secularism that has been sweeping the developed world for quite some time. Francis is intensely aware of the huge responsibility he has assumed. He also knows that, in spite of the unprecedented popularity he currently enjoys, one wrong decision, an unguarded comment, even a hint of scandal, has the capacity to undo the good work he has already done. He will not want to be remembered simply as the pope who had a great first year in office. Rather, a more lasting legacy is what he seeks, one marked by a real change of heart and approach within the Church to which he has devoted his life.

This book has been an inspiring undertaking. Dealing with theologians, historians, clergy, journalists, sociologists and commentators from Ireland, the UK and the USA, all extremely busy people, and receiving their reflections on Francis' first year in office, has been a hugely satisfying experience. Their generosity, professionalism, honesty and humility are in some ways a mirror image of the subject of this book. One year on, the Francis factor shows no sign of losing its lustre and one wonders if things will ever be the same again in the Catholic Church.

Francis: A View from the Periphery

Patrick Claffey, SVD

In the week before the conclave that elected Jorge Mario Bergoglio as Francis, Bishop of Rome, I had dinner with a journalist and his partner. They were leaving for Rome the following day to cover the conclave and like many people they seemed to believe that every priest is also something of a Vaticanologist, with a real interest in and knowledge of what are often seen as the arcane goings-on at the centre of the enormous institution that is the Catholic Church. The truth, of course, is often very different since most priests live out their lives with, if not quite indifference to what might be going on in Rome, at least a certain detachment. Even if they read *The Tablet*, they know more or less the same as everybody else, simply what they read in the papers. Those who pretend to know more are almost certainly fooling themselves as they feed off scraps of rumour and engage in more or less futile speculation. The election of Francis was surely a good illustration of this point. While it seems to have been widely known that he had been the 'runner-up' in the previous election, his name had not figured in the shortlists of *papabile* and, when he was referred to, he was dismissed as being too old.

My friend wondered, as a political columnist might, whether the College of Cardinals that would elect the new pope was not somewhat 'stacked' to elect somebody in the image, and the theologically-conservative likeness, of John Paul II and Benedict XVI, who had, after all, appointed most of them. It was a reasonable argument and one I pessimistically shared to some extent.

In a chapter for a previous collection of essays in this series, I wrote of my feeling of living in a Church that often seemed to be obsessed with a desire for dogmatic certainty and doctrinal conformity.[1] It was

---

[1]   See Patrick Claffey, 'The Faith to Change' in John Littleton and Eamon Maher (eds), *Catholicism and Me* (Dublin: The Columba Press, 2012), pp. 96–103.

a Church ill-at-ease with modernity, an increasingly cold place, and out of touch with where many Catholics are at in their lives. The chapter expressed a sense of disempowerment and frustration at the way the Church seemed to have been theologically/ideologically 'taken over'. I was not optimistic about the conclave.

However, I do remember saying to my friend that one could never tell what might happen when one put a large group of men into a room, locked the door, and asked them to take history in their hands. While they may have been appointed by the previous popes, this did not mean that they did not have minds of their own. Besides, I pointed out, we still have our belief in the Holy Spirit and her ability to surprise us.

What was very clear was that events leading up to the resignation of Benedict XVI and the resignation itself were a definite indication of a very deep crisis in the Church. If there was one thing Benedict abhorred it was the idea of any kind of *rupture*, anything that suggested crisis or any kind of radical change. However the *relatio*, or report, drawn up and submitted to Benedict 'for his eyes only' by three of the most senior cardinals, Herranz, Tomko and De Giorgi, was very much on the mind of the 115 cardinals who gathered to choose his successor and they were apparently fully briefed on its contents. From all accounts it left them in no doubt that the Church was in deep crisis and in a situation that needed to be addressed immediately and radically. In casting their eyes around for the man to take on the job, they stopped at Jorge Mario Bergoglio. We will never know what exactly happened but it seems obvious that it was quite a spontaneous decision and Bergoglio, obviously not a man to prevaricate, accepted after only a very brief moment of prayer and reflection.

People talk frequently about his appearance on the balcony immediately after the election and how they were impressed by the body language and the apparent spontaneity in the now famous simple greeting, '*Buona sera*'. I remember my own immediate response was that he reminded me very much of several bishops I had known and worked with. I had the feeling that in some way I had met him and knew him. However, there was still a natural caution, since I was well aware of the papal style in this media driven age, so I would wait to see how things worked out over the following weeks and months.

Tested in the fires of human experience

Interestingly, the moment I began to feel the kind of empathy for Francis that I had never felt for his immediate predecessor was when he began to be questioned on his relationship with the Argentinian junta back in the 1970s. Given the situation that had prevailed in Argentina during that period, this was almost inevitable. It was also likely to have more traction than the questioning of Benedict XVI over his relationship with the Hitler Youth given that Bergoglio was an adult at that time and indeed Provincial of the important Argentine province of the Society of Jesus. It was also clear that there were several genuine questions to be asked and answered and, indeed, a certain amount of ambiguity remains, as is often the case in these messy human situations. I felt a definite empathy for him because as a young missionary in Togo (West Africa) in the late 1970s I had also lived under a similarly ugly, authoritarian and often brutal national security regime. At the same time I was part of a local church that often appeared, and indeed was, sycophantic at the highest level in its relationship with that regime. There was what the French political scientist Jean-François Bayart, writing about Togo at that time, described as 'a reciprocal assimilation of elites' between an often fawning, clientelist clergy and the patrimonial elite of a repressive regime. There was certainly very little in terms of any kind of contestation or prophetic witness.

In this situation I was often angered and frustrated by what I saw, and found myself at loggerheads with the local political authorities on several occasions, being called in for questioning a number of times – but never pushing my protests beyond the point that would surely get me expelled. For practical reasons, I didn't want that and neither did the local district commissioner who represented both the State and the party – so we compromised! It was not the stuff of radical liberation theology, but what these often somewhat tense encounters, with their frisson of dissidence, gave me was some insight into the moral dilemmas that exist in these situations. There was little of the Becket in me and, while I might have been something of a minor irritant, I was not a particularly 'troublesome priest'.[2] While it is relatively easy to ask questions about this from a safe distance, it was

2   See Mike Ibeji, 'Becket, the Church and Henry II: "Troublesome Priest" or Tormented Soul – Was Becket Henry's Nemesis?' http://www.bbc.co.uk/history/state/church_reformation/becket_01.shtml [accessed, 5 January 2014].

quite different on the ground. Martyrdom cannot be written into any job description and life in such a situation is indeed often about compromise – and survival.

Paul Vallely, in his recent book, has given quite a detailed account of Francis' role in Argentina at this time, and it is indeed complex and marked by a definite ambivalence.[3] However, what is most convincing is Francis' own narrative, which Vallely describes as 'penitential', saying that his judgement of himself was probably more severe than that of anybody else. His behaviour was at best pragmatic and certainly not overtly heroic, whatever his more or less discreet efforts at mitigation and helping people in trouble with the regime might indicate. Reflecting on that time he has, however, acknowledged his failings in quite striking terms:

> I don't want to mislead anyone – the truth is that I am a sinner who God in his mercy has chosen to love in a privileged manner. [...] I made hundreds of errors. Errors and sins. It would be wrong of me to say that these days I ask forgiveness for the sins I might have committed. Today I ask forgiveness for the sins that I did indeed commit.[4]

This is quite a remarkable, spin-free, confession that leaves me in little doubt about the human and spiritual qualities of the man. He belongs to a Church of sinners rather than a Church of saints and in my view this is what will define his pontificate.

A change in Christianity's centre of gravity

It has long been obvious that, as the American scholar of religion Phillip Jenkins has noted, the centre of gravity of Christianity has been shifting south over the past century.[5] Religious decline in the traditional Euro-centre has been demographically compensated for by an often spectacular expansion on what up to recently had been considered the peripheries: Asia, Africa and, perhaps most signifi-cantly, Latin America where several shifts have been going on at the same time, notably the remarkable rise of evangelical Pentecostalism, leading the American scholar David Stoll to wonder, as far back as

---

3   Paul Vallely, *Pope Francis: Untying the Knots* (Bloomsbury, London, 2013).

4   Cited by Vallely, *Pope Francis*, p. 94.

5   Phillip Jenkins, *The Next Christendom: The Coming of Global Christianity* (Oxford: Oxford University Press, 2011), p. 1.

the 1990s, if Latin America was not 'turning Protestant'.[6] With the demographic shift there is an inevitable theological shift as contextualised theologies give voice to more local and immediate preoccupations. In attempting to come to terms with the phenomenon that is Pope Francis it is essential to understand this since it is clear that his own election marks probably the most significant symbolic step to date in this process.

One of the qualities I most admired in the two 'missionary bishops' I worked closely with in West Africa was their pragmatism. Following the recent apostolic exhortation, *Evangelii Gaudium (EG)*,[7] I see Francis as belonging to this tradition within the Church, a tradition that has now hopefully come into its own and one from which the Church is currently drawing its life. This Church tended to see the broad picture and was usually reluctant to get involved with the kind of theology that might prove to be 'a burden to the lives of the faithful' (*EG*, n. 43) and ultimately an obstacle to faith (*EG*, n. 24). There was, rather, a great emphasis on simply getting the Word *out there*, into the towns and villages and into people's lives, and a belief that the rest would look after itself at 'harvest time' (Mt 13:30) and as faith reflection deepened. One was usually told simply to get on with the task in hand: preach, teach, and, perhaps above all, *build*, both infrastructure and communities. The suggestion was that requests for permission to do things were best left, as it was much easier to grant forgiveness in the case of a mistake than it was to grant a permission that might later cause embarrassment in the higher echelons during the *ad limina*. So no *nihil obstat*, no *imprimatur*, just get on with it once it seemed right in the situation. My own experience of this came in translation work when I asked the bishop for permission to publish texts for use in a small edition of two hundred copies for the villages speaking a small minority language. He simply smiled and waved his hand. I am happy to say my undoubtedly very ropey translations into a local language are apparently still serving their initial purpose of, as Lamin Sanneh has put it, 'translating the message',[8] getting the story out

---

[6] David Stoll, *Is Latin America Turning Protestant?* (Berkeley: University of California Press, 1990).

[7] Pope Francis, *Evangelii Gaudium* (The Joy of the Gospel), Apostolic Exhortation on the Proclamation of the Gospel in Today's World, 2013. Subsequent references will be denoted by *EG*, followed by the paragraph number(s).

[8] Lamin Sanneh, *Translating the Message: The Missionary Impact on Culture* (New York: Orbis Books, 1989).

there, still without an *imprimatur*, but now with the legitimacy of being 'the book' of the people for whom it was translated – the stylistic and theological niceties left till later!

Evangelii Gaudium – *Vatican II reclaimed*

It has taken Francis less than a year, albeit with some help,[9] to articulate his thinking in the recent letter of encouragement to the missionary Church *Evangelii Gaudium*. Probably the most striking thing about this innovative text is the freshness and immediacy of the language, leading one southern theological commentator to enthusiastically describe it as 'a magna carta for Church reform'.[10] The *locus theologicus* here is certainly very different. The exhortation is very attentive to the voices of the south, with numerous references to the documents of local bishops' conferences in Latin America, Africa, Asia and Oceania. While keeping the tradition and his predecessors in mind, the theological footsteps in the sand are often those left by liberation theology, as well as many aspects of the evangelical Christianity that has become so influential in Latin America, not least in Argentina which has one of the highest rates of evangelical growth.[11]

Even reading it in English, one can almost hear the Spanish as he refers repeatedly to *la Palabra de Dios* and *los pobres*, both as being at the heart of *la misión* (*EG*, nn. 13, 21). There is also a strong emphasis on *joy* and 'a renewed personal encounter with Jesus Christ, or at least an openness to letting him encounter [us]' (*EG*, n. 3) that is quite evangelical in tone and reflective of *la realidad latinoamericana*. While he appears to have had little sympathy with liberation theology in its earlier articulations, Francis lived through the neo-liberal destruction

---

9   In an excellent piece in *The Irish Times*, respected commentator Paddy Agnew notes the influence of the Pope's 'trusted advisor Víctor Manuel Fernández, the current rector of Argentina's Pontifical Catholic University'. While there is little doubt that the work carries his personal stamp, one may also assume that there was other considerable theological backup, quite probably Jesuit, in writing a relatively long text of 50,000 words while carrying out a heavy papal schedule. See Paddy Agnew, 'The Papal Spring' *The Irish Times*, 28 December 2013, http://www.irishtimes.com [accessed, 3 January 2014].

10   Suresh Matthew, '*Evangelii Gaudium*: Pope Francis' Magna Carta for Church Reform', *Sedos Bulletin*, 45 (11/12), 2013, pp. 261–4.

11   See Pew Research: Religions and Public Life Project, 'Overview: Pentecostalism in Latin America', http://www.pewforum.org [accessed, 3 January 2013]. See also Jamie Manson 'Is Pope Francis Ecumenical, Evangelical or Both?' *National Catholic Reporter*, 22 March 2012. See http://www.ncronline [accessed, 2 January 2013].

of his country that left honest and hard-working families in penury and this too is part of his *realidad* and one which he brings to the exhortation in his critique of 'the structural causes of poverty' (*EG*, n. 188) and 'the absolute autonomy of markets and financial specu-lation'. This led the neo-con American commentator Rush Limbaugh, not surprisingly, to describe him as a Marxist, something he appar-ently refuted quite lightly simply saying 'I have known plenty of good Marxists'.

What is clear from the text is that it reflects a desire to re-engage with the world, to take up the truncated project of Vatican II and move it on. He sees a Church that 'never closes itself off, never retreats into its own security, never opts for rigidity and defensiveness' (*EG*, n. 45). It is, one imagines, part of what he describes as getting 'bruised, hurting and dirty because it has been out on the streets' (*EG*, n. 49). He opts for this 'rather than a Church which is unhealthy from being confined and from clinging to its own security' (*EG*, n. 49). Even more pointedly he writes: 'I do not want a Church concerned with being at the centre and then ends by being caught up in a web of obsessions and procedures' (*EG*, n. 49). This is nothing if not a new opening of the windows.

Popes do not simply repudiate the style and, even less, the teaching of their predecessors and neither does Francis as this text makes generous use of the writings of both John Paul II and Benedict XVI. However, there is a definite shift of emphasis and language that cannot be described as subtle, a stepping back from a magisterial articulation to a more maternal concern for the faith that echoes John XXIII's vision of the Church as *mater et magistra*,[12] and seeks to renew the links with this movement in Church thought. This is well reflected when he speaks of the Church as 'a mother with an open heart' and emphasises 'a mother's conversation' (*EG*, nn. 76–109, 135–44). This is surely at least a marked difference from the magisterial authori-tarianism of his immediate predecessors. He is certainly wary of those 'who long for a monolithic body of doctrine guarded by all and leaving no room for nuance ...', concluding rather that '[d]iffering currents of thought in philosophy, theology and pastoral practice, if open to being reconciled by the Spirit in respect and love, can enable the Church to grow [...] in fact such variety serves to bring out and develop different facets of the inexhaustible riches of the Gospel'.

---

12   Pope John XXIII, *Mater et Magistra*, 1961.

Maintaining the momentum

Commentators have been more or less unanimous in lauding Francis' first nine months in office; the faithful, and less faithful, have seen it as a breath of fresh air and, indeed, a breath of the Spirit. It has been a time marked by a genuine sense of joy and even perhaps a sense of liberation. However, the professional observers also point to the possibility of a kind of 'Obama effect'; lots of hope and promises but less in terms of delivery as conservative forces start to react. All agree that 2014 will be a big test. Paddy Agnew, the Rome correspondent of *The Irish Times*, notes that the positive signs for reform are all there in *Evangelii Gaudium*[13] and in the extensive interviews he has given. Robert Mickens, writing in *The Tablet*, sets out the 'urgent challenges to the Church's credibility' which have to be addressed if it is not to risk 'losing the trust and confidence he has so successfully garnered up to now'.[14] Although it has somewhat faded from the headlines in the wave of enthusiasm and media attention given to Francis, Mickens puts 'the ongoing sexual-abuse, including the lack of accountable bishops that mishandle or cover up such crimes' as still the most urgent priority.[15] In my view, part of the changing centre of gravity of the Church will also mean bringing the spotlight to bear on other parts of the world, including Latin America. The question will not simply go away. Significantly perhaps, one of the first headlines of the New Year refers to a new document where Francis addresses the issue in response to the findings of an expert group he set up last year to look into the matter with a view to articulating an adequate response to an issue that in the view of many has almost broken the Church.[16]

I share Mickens' view that the second issue that requires a meaningful rather than simply symbolic response is that of the role of women in the Church and the need, as Mickens puts it, 'to bring [...] them into all areas of Church governance and decision-making'.[17] This touches on the question of clericalism and power which have been so central to the Church's difficulties with modernity and it seems likely to be the most intractable of problems in what must be the most masculine hundred acres in the world.

---

[13]   Agnew, 'The Papal Spring'.
[14]   Robert Mickens, 'Can Francis of Rome Answer the Summons of Christ to Rebuild His Church?' *The Tablet*, 4 January 2014, p. 12.
[15]   *Ibid.*
[16]   Paddy Agnew, 'Pontiff Addresses Issue of Clerical Sex Abuse in New Paper Document', *The Irish Times*, 4 January 2013.
[17]   Robert Mickens, 'Can Francis'.

As he will know, none of this will be easy, since even a robust seventy-seven-year-old cannot hope to beat the psalmist's time constraint of 'eighty, if we are strong' (Ps 90:10), at least in terms of the reforms he can achieve. After the photo-opportunities and the positive media reports there will be an Everest of hard, detailed work and endless discussions that will no doubt test him. While the media have tended to present him as someone who will unite the Church, it is inevitable that he will face determined opposition and even dirty tricks from within. There is and will be mischievous, even nefarious, briefings in the corridors of an atrophied but strongly entrenched clerical/curial power anxious to protect its privilege and its conservative agenda. There is a certain amount of evidence of this already. In the wider Church there is already opposition from people who have built their vision of Catholicism on a neo-orthodox conservative agenda, with a strong, often single-issue, emphasis on opposition to abortion, little acceptance or understanding of homosexuality, and a wider conservative socio-political and economic platform which is clearly at odds with Francis' vision. These two interdependent elements make a powerful coalition that has been favoured and seen as close to power for a long time and it will be reluctant to relinquish its hold on power and privilege.

In tackling the financial institutions, he is taking on a hydra with many very dangerous heads, some of which, one fears, would not hesitate to do him bodily harm. There has been evidence of this in the past, and suggestions that there have already been serious dirty tricks as Francis has started to tackle the issue in appointing a news head of the IOR (Institute of Religious Works), more commonly referred to as the Vatican Bank.[18]

Finally, Francis is probably the most prominent representative of the south on the world stage, a sometimes disturbing, perhaps even subversive, voice as he challenges the interests of the global economic system. While one is loath to get involved in conspiracy theories, his predecessor John Paul II was not safe from attack by shadowy forces, and Francis' security must be a matter of some concern, especially since he seems so personally indifferent to it.

There is, however, plenty of reason to hope. There is an increasingly popular belief that 'he was put there by God' for a purpose and that he is a man who clearly means business. He has had

---

[18] Agnew, 'Papal Spring'.

a Jesuit formation and surely has both the spiritual and the intellectual qualities needed to see his mission through, or at least make a significant start on reform in whatever time is given to him. Indeed quite an amount has already been delivered if one looks at the establishment of the C8 group of cardinals, a significant 'reshuffle' in the Curia and what is manifestly an attempt at a root and branch reform, or even a dismantling, of the Church's financial institutions.[19] In purely political terms this would have been a significant achievement in a first year. But as the Pope would be the first to point out, this is not about Francis, but rather about the Church and its place in the modern world. Robert Mickens puts it very concisely but eloquently when he writes: 'It all comes down to one simple question: can Francis of Rome, like his sainted namesake of Assisi, answer the summons of Christ to rebuild his Church?'[20] I, like so many others, dare to hope he can.

---

[19] Paddy Agnew, 'Pope's New Broom Sweeps Vatican Bank', *The Irish Times*, 31 December 2013.
[20] Robert Mickens, 'Can Francis'.

Bergoglio and the Buenos Aires Connection

John O'Connor, SAC

My first encounter with Jorge Bergoglio was far from inspiring. I met him when we concelebrated at the wedding of his nephew, Pablo, in the early 1980s. I knew his sister, Martha, very well and was somewhat surprised to see the difference between the two siblings. Martha was a very outgoing, bubbly and happy person but the impression that Jorge gave was very different. He was obviously very intelligent but was very serious looking, shy and not particularly friendly or sociable. I remained very friendly with Martha and her family but didn't meet Jorge again until his appointment as an auxiliary bishop of Buenos Aires in 1992.

His appointment came as a surprise to many people because he wasn't particularly well known in Argentina, but obviously the archbishop, Cardinal Antonio Quarracino, knew what he was capable of. Just a year after his episcopal ordination, Quarracino named him Vicar General of the Archdiocese and Bishop Bergoglio gradually became a familiar face in the Curia. He was always very welcoming and friendly with an eye for detail and a desire to make people feel comfortable. This in itself was quite surprising as the Curia in the archdiocese has always been a very formal, cold and off-putting place. It wasn't surprising when he was appointed coadjutor archbishop in 1997 because he was already making his presence felt in a very positive way, and was bringing his particular style and personality to the job. When he became Archbishop of Buenos Aires in 1998, he was not only well-prepared for the task but also knew exactly what he wished to do in the diocese.

When I was moved from my parish in the province of Buenos Aires in 2000 to the parish of San Patricio in the Buenos Aires suburb of

Belgrano, I once again came in contact with Jorge Bergoglio. He was still the shy and serious looking man I had met twenty years previously but now he was much more open and friendly and very definitely a man with a mission.

The Bergoglio factor in Buenos Aires

The first big change that Bergoglio brought to the Church in Buenos Aires was his *humility*. At that time most of the bishops in Argentina, with a few notable exceptions, looked like and behaved like princes rather than pastors. Bergoglio had no chauffeur-driven car but, instead, used public transport. He was frequently seen walking around the streets of Buenos Aires and was very approachable. He lived in a simple apartment in the Curia building and cooked for himself. He dressed in an austere way, preferring a simple grey suit to the usual robes of bishops or cardinals. He was no lover of ecclesiastical titles and preferred to be known as Padre Jorge. Indeed when he was appointed cardinal he sent the late Cardinal Quaraccino's robes to a tailor to be made to his size rather than spending a fortune on new robes. As the Cardinal Archbishop was living such a humble lifestyle, the priests of the diocese were inspired to follow his example.

The second big change that comes to mind was his *good relationship with his priests*. In most dioceses in Argentina at that time, there was a huge divide between priests and their bishops and, indeed, most priests had little or no contact with their bishop. I remember at one deanery meeting, when he was asked about the ideal relationship between a bishop and his priests, he replied straight away by saying that as far as he was concerned 'his priests were his parish'. These weren't mere words; he really meant it. He was very attentive to the spiritual and temporal needs of his priests and we all knew that he could be easily contacted day or night.

He was also very demanding, however, and didn't bear fools lightly. He was scrupulously fair, communicative and understanding but was also quick to act when there was a need for it. He wasn't afraid to remove a priest from ministry if there was just cause. He was particularly respected and admired by the younger priests of the diocese and vocations flourished. He was very involved in the life of the diocesan seminary in Villa Devoto and expected high academic standards from the seminarians. Under his watch there was strict scrutiny of potential candidates for the priesthood and a large proportion of those seeking admittance into the seminary were turned away.

His choice of auxiliary bishops was also very revealing. He chose men like himself, and some of his choices were courageous and surprising. Most of his auxiliaries went on to become diocesan bishops in their own right and so Bergoglio's influence and style spread throughout the country. It is worth noting that his appointments of bishops in Argentina since his election as Pope have come quickly and continue in the same line.

Another huge change that he brought about was his desire for a *clear separation between Church and State* and he avoided public contact with politicians. This again was a new departure for bishops in Argentina and especially for the primate who, up to that time, had always been very closely associated with the political or military power of the moment. Surprisingly, this separation of Church and State gave him great freedom to exercise his moral authority in word and deed, and he began to earn the respect of the people. As time went by he became more aware of the needs of the poorer members of society especially those who lived in the very numerous shanty towns or Villas de Miseria, as they are called. He strongly supported the priests who worked with the poor, defending and supporting them in a very public way.

In spite of his meek appearance, he showed that he was tough and was willing to stand up to the drug dealers and corrupt politicians. He took a strong stand on social justice issues and wasn't afraid to speak his mind. This made him unpopular with many people in the government and, indeed, the President stopped going to the *Te Deum* celebrations in the cathedral of Buenos Aires on national feast days, in order to avoid listening to his sermons. I believe that it also made him unpopular with many of his brother bishops and the more conservative sectors of the Church. He became visibly more at ease with the people through his increasingly frequent visits to the villas. As time went by, his concerns for social justice grew and he sought concrete ways and means to improve the living and educational needs of the poor.

He also had a *clear pastoral programme* for his diocese and his pastoral letters and sermons were always well thought-out and profound, yet clear and easy to understand. It was particularly interesting to listen to his sermons at the Chrism Mass each Holy Thursday and it was as if he was using them to set out his pastoral plan for the year.

On a personal level, he maintained a low profile and he wasn't particularly sociable; yet he visited his parishes frequently, made himself available to all the parishioners and he certainly didn't stand on ceremony. There was no pomp with him and his celebration of the liturgy was simple and relaxed, but also meaningful and profound. When he preached he would begin speaking in a low voice and slowly raise the volume as he went on. His sermons were always worth listening to and showed his deep faith in the Eucharist and his love for Mary. I was always struck by his signature because it was the tiniest I have ever seen.

He listened to the opinions of others but made up his own mind. Some said that he was controlling, and this may be true; but he was always attentive to and interested in the opinions of others, especially those of his auxiliary bishops. However, the final word and decision was always his. Unlike now as Pope Francis, he didn't give press conferences. Yet he always had a short and very clear television message for Christmas and Easter. He led by example and didn't expect anybody to do what he himself wasn't prepared to do. While he never asked others to imitate his lifestyle, his example certainly inspired his priests to be more humble, outgoing and listening.

Another subject that I must mention is that of *human rights*. One of the saddest chapters in Argentina's history was that of the military dictatorship of the 1970s and early 1980s. The violence, terror and injustices that we all experienced during that period are too numerous to be spoken of here. Bergoglio has been accused of acting unjustly towards two of his priests who were working with the poor during his term as a Jesuit provincial. Indeed, the Jesuits in Argentina are still divided in their opinion on this matter. Having lived through this terrible period, I must point out that it was a time of great fear and confusion, and the law courts in Argentina have declared Bergoglio innocent of any wrong doing. Whatever the truth may be, he certainly came to terms with the matter and, with time, became more outspoken.

The one incident that I must mention, because of the way it affected me personally, is that of the horrendous murder of five of my

Pallottine brothers on the night of 4 July 1976. The five, three priests and two seminarians, were killed by the military in the living room of the parish house of San Patricia in Buenos Aires. Like so many people in Argentina, we had always felt let down by the institutional Church. Most bishops refused to condemn the violence and injustice and did nothing to defend the people. Indeed, the whole theme of the Dirty War had always been avoided by the hierarchy. In the case of the murdered Pallottines, the institutional Church did nothing and said less. When we celebrated the twenty-fifth anniversary of the murders in 2001, I invited Cardinal Bergoglio to be the principal celebrant at the Mass. He accepted the invitation and during the Mass preached a very strong sermon, speaking of the terrible injustices that had been committed during the dictatorship and he referred to our murdered brothers as martyrs. This was the first time that the term 'martyrs' was used in reference to them by an Argentinian bishop. The Cardinal had been spiritual director to one of the victims, Fr Alfie Kelly, and was most conscious of the dreadful horrors of the 1970s. He was not afraid to address the issue and his words and his attitude on the occasion of the jubilee Mass brought much consolation and healing to me and to my fellow Pallottines, and I remain very grateful to him for that. Up to the present day, he has encouraged us to press for the beatification of our five brothers and, please God, that will soon come about.

Cardinal Bergoglio was also very active in *inter-faith dialogue*, especially with the Jewish and Anglican communities, and demonstrated that he deeply valued and respected their beliefs and traditions. He did much to reach out to other beliefs also and to popular religious practices.

I believe that there is a very significant 'before and after Bergoglio' reality in the Church in Argentina. He grew into his role and, as time went by, he became more and more sure of and comfortable with his mission. With time, his influence also grew and he became a strong leader, not only in the Church in Buenos Aires, but also throughout Argentina and Latin America.

This confidence is now clearly seen in his new role as leader of the universal Church. Nothing he has done since his election has surprised those of us who witnessed him in action in Buenos Aires. The only surprising thing is that he is so happy. His smile has now become famous throughout the world but this is something we never saw in Buenos Aires. His successor in Buenos Aires, Archbishop Poli, speaks of the 'Bergoglio cemetery face'. The only explanation that I can give for this change is that he is now a really happy man. I believe that he was born to be Pope. He is now happy to be able to do the things that he is doing, and free to say the things that he is saying. It would appear that his life up to now, as a Jesuit and as a bishop in South America, was a preparation for his present mission. The changes that he brought to the Church in Argentina are those which he is now bringing to the universal Church. He is leading the Church in a new direction. He is inspiring all baptised people to be more humble and attentive: to be a Church that responds to the needs of those who are suffering in any way. A Church that respects and dignifies every human being, a Church which is at the service of others, a Church that does not judge, a Church that condemns the sin but not the sinner, a Church that is more Christlike.

Jorge Bergoglio is now seventy-seven years old and only God knows how long more he will be with us. There is so much to be done – and such expectation rests on his shoulders. We cannot be sure that he will be able to achieve all that he wants to achieve or all that we hope that he can achieve. What we can be sure of, however, is that after Pope Francis there can be no turning back.

Some Definitive 'No's'

Mary T. Malone

For a pope who has offered only an increasingly expansive and inclusive account of Christianity, his definitive 'No' to the priestly ordination of women struck a rather discordant note, according to media accounts. It is, of course, quite unlikely that any pope will so significantly countermand the very definitive, and indeed, quasi-infallible, teachings of his predecessors, but there seems to have been a fairly universal expectation, if only among the media corps, that Pope Francis would be different. His suggestion of a 'new' theology of women is also somewhat startling, since several such papal and other theologies already exist, and we will examine some of these later.

The 'woman' question, however, for the vast majority of believers and commentators is a very minor chord in the phenomenon of Pope Francis. He has uttered some other loud and definitive 'No's', some of which have been noticed with appreciation and approval, others which have been silently ignored. It is part of the complexity of this utterly charming, charismatic and compassionate pope, that he continuously confounds the expectations of his followers and observers, whether believers or simply bystanders. The amazing thing about Pope Francis is that he only says what he believes, and his thoughts and teachings come directly from a deeply compassionate and profoundly committed Christian life. He does not have a philosophical agenda, but a Gospel agenda. As he says himself in his recent apostolic exhortation, *Evangelii Gaudium (EG)*,[1] his intended 'Francis effect', he is not deriving his teaching from a philosophical or theological analysis of the state of the Church or of society, but from the Gospel imperative. And this is a lived imperative and that is what

---

[1]   Pope Francis, *Evangelii Gaudium* (The Joy of the Gospel), Apostolic Exhortation on the Proclamation of the Gospel in Today's World, 2013.

makes all the difference. If there is a 'Francis effect', it is this. The Pope lives joyfully and lovingly the evangelical life, he acts it out, and everybody seems to be waiting for the 'act' to stop, without realising that this is the man. The man is the Gospel and the Gospel is the man.

Whenever there is a public discussion about being a Catholic in the media or elsewhere, it is usually along the lines of 'these are the rules for Catholics'. The whole of the faith is reduced to a superficial version of the catechism, a few 'Catholic' doctrines and a few well-known moral dilemmas. Pope Francis' version of the Catholic faith is so far removed from this that it has taken most people by surprise. The media and many Catholics had become comfortable with what one might call dogmatic popes. They knew what to expect in terms of a constant reiteration of the well-known Catholic beliefs. Pope Francis is not about to diminish these in any way, but he has let it be known, in word, interview and writing, that for him, these things are secondary to a following of Jesus, especially in the care of the poor.

Many of the other definitive 'No's' of Pope Francis have to do with the world economic structures and how they necessarily function to keep the rich rich and the poor poor. He has said a definitive 'No' to the exclusionary nature of these policies, that is, how they function to keep the poor out of the normal social structures (*EG*, n. 53). He has said a definitive 'No' to the idolatry of money, and the greed and consumerism that it generates (*EG*, n. 55). He further denounces this world economic system for ruling rather than serving the ordinary people, and decries in scathing terms the trickle-down theories that have so dominated this system, including, of course, the Irish system, both before and after the financial crisis and subsequent bailout (*EG*, n. 57).

Pope Francis turns his attention inward to the effects of this economic system both on those who are running it and on those who are its victims. He speaks of blunted consciences (*EG*, n. 89) and spiritual worldliness (*EG*, n. 93). Francis writes in everyday language that can be understood by all, and even, unusually in the reading of a papal exhortation, causing one to smile gleefully to oneself at words such as 'sourpuss' (*EG*, n. 85) and 'funeral faces' (*EG*, n. 10). The Pope further rehabilitates the 'signs of the times', one of the Vatican II mantras that had become part of the rhetoric of discontinuity, and points to the massive dehumanisation of people through poverty, neglect, oppression and despair. There is no doubt whatsoever that one of the major effects of the arrival of this pope has been to turn the world's attention to the poor. This is not in order to increase charitable donations, but to effect a total change in society and its perception of itself and in the Church and its perception of itself. He has repeated again and again that he wants the poor to be part of society, part of the Church. And not just a part of the Church. He wants a Church of the poor and a poor Church. It is obvious from the Pope's own lifestyle choices that this is an invitation to all of us, from cardinals to the lowliest believer, as he expresses it himself, in imitation of Augustine of Hippo, to alter our lifestyle and life choices. Sharpness is not characteristic of the utterances of this pope, but his sharpest utterances have been in the direction of those clerics who, it must be said, in a long tradition of the living patterns of the upper clerics, surround themselves with luxuries.

The 'Francis effect' has, most significantly, penetrated the power structures that he inherited. This papal power seemed to cast a pall of anxiety over several of his predecessors. They presented a face of distress and anxiety to the people and, in their analyses of ecclesial problems, they turned to the traditions of papal decisiveness in doctrine, and austerity in their moral teaching. Pope Francis presents a face of joy to the public, in a way that suggests that joy is one of the main motivators of his spiritual life. He speaks more as a spiritual director, probably a result of his life as a Jesuit, than as a papal authoritarian. He has turned to his fellow bishops and set up structures of dialogue. He has recalled the expectations of inclusion that surrounded the original organisation of episcopal conferences, and has suggested that their power and authority should even extend to the doctrinal level. This is definitely not a pope who wishes to retain all teaching authority, whether doctrinal or moral in his own hands. Pope Francis has also resurrected another mantra from the Second Vatican Council, one that had long been hidden away in the hermeneutic of continuity, namely, the 'hierarchy of truths' (EG, n. 36). While lauding the benefits of genuine popular devotion, Pope Francis shows that he has little patience with secondary devotions that haunt people's lives instead of Gospel-based faith. This is where evangelisation comes in. People need to be grounded in a biblical spirituality so that they can discern the essential from the merely frivolous.

As is obvious from various teaching occasions, Pope Francis is very familiar with the revised rites of sacramental initiation. He takes

his teaching on the processes of evangelisation, catechesis and mystagogical catechesis from, one supposes, years of participation in these rites. In his understanding, the 'New Evangelisation' is not rooted in the *Catechism of the Catholic Church*, even though he occasionally quotes from this document, but the new evangelisation is the evangelisation of the poor. And this, the Pope implies, is a two-way process. We evangelise and are evangelised by the poor.

Pope Francis expands the notion of evangelisation to include confrontation, so in that spirit, it is now only just to look at the question of women in the world and theology of the Pope. Even though the Pope says that women are indispensable in society (*EG*, n. 103), he does not extend this to the Church, even though he must be aware that the majority of all Church gatherings, with the exception of clerical gatherings, are composed mainly of women. He denounces machismo and violence against women in very strong terms (*EG*, n. 69), but not so much as a Gospel imperative, but as a social ill. One can therefore say that the 'Francis effect' has not really touched even the borders of women's lives, except in the generic sense of the poor. The Pope speaks of a more incisive female presence in the Church (*EG*, n. 103), which is a vast improvement on the wishy-washy feminine rhapsodies of recent papal documents. Female presence would make a very good starting point for the 'new theology' that the Pope has wished for.

There is nothing of the female in Catholic theology. The female is associated with female carnality, something that marks all our mothers, but this element has always been seen as the female inheritance of the 'daughters of Eve' and furthest removed from the Divine. In the whole of the Catholic tradition, there is not one single reflection on the most foundational of all human experiences, namely the experience of giving birth to and feeding a child from one's own body. Male theologians of necessity, cannot reflect theologically on this experience and female theologians are not, never have been, and never will be part of the Magisterium. The silencing of women – the continued silencing of women – has deprived the Church of a huge range of human experience as the basis for theological reflection. True, there are many female theologians in the Catholic Church today, but none of their theology ever reaches the level of official teaching.

In seeking a new theology, Pope Francis is obviously rejecting or finding unsatisfactory, or is actually unaware of several existing theologies of women. Since he decries all oppression, obviously he is rejecting the millennia-old consequences of the teachings on women's essential inferiority. He also seems to be rejecting the beginnings of a new Christian anthropology of women attempted by Pope Paul VI in the magnificent *Marialis Cultus*,[2] where Paul VI tries to rehabilitate Mary as a model for the modern woman. Pope Francis also seems to be rejecting the agonising attempts of Pope John Paul II to deal with the question of women, ever-present but mysteriously so in their imposed silence in the Church of God. Starting from *Mulieris Dignitatem* (On the Dignity of Women)[3] in 1988, Pope John Paul II made repeated attempts in a stream of documents to theologise the position of these silenced women in the Church. He finally produced what right-wing Catholics called the 'new feminism' in the phrase 'ontological complementarity', which designated women forever into an auxiliary place in the Church. It is true that much of the former pope's writing was in direct opposition to the ordination of women, but nevertheless, it seemed to say that nothing whatsoever was expected of women except obedience.

There are two other areas of official teaching on women that seem to be rejected by Pope Francis. One is the teaching of the four recently proclaimed women Doctors of the Church. Presumably a doctor of the Church now has an official place in the Church's Magisterium, and the writings of Catherine of Siena, Teresa of Avila, Thérèse of Lisieux and Hildegard of Bingen are now part of that Magisterium. But since 1970, when both Teresa and Catherine were declared doctors, there has been barely a ripple of interest. Most certainly no effort to read or understand their teachings has been perceptible.

Another area of women's theology has been the amazing output of teaching by the medieval and later women mystics. This is another area of profound and illuminating theology that has not even touched official teaching. In a Church that is desperately seeking solutions to the crisis of faith and belief, these brilliant writings lie languishing in obscurity, instead of being used to open new doors to faith.

So what about the priestly ordination of women? That women cannot be ordained to a male priesthood is patently obvious. The

---

2   Pope Paul VI, *Marialis Cultis*, Apostolic Exhortation for the Right Ordering and Development of Devotion to the Blessed Virgin Mary, 1974.

3   Pope John Paul II, *Mulieris Dignitatem*, Apostolic Letter on the Dignity and Vocation of Women, 1988.

priesthood, as we have known it through the centuries, was designed by men, inhabited by men, experienced by men, theologised by men and liturgised by men. It is a wholly male priesthood, made even more so by the requirement of mandatory celibacy, which makes the avoidance of women one of the basic elements of a male priesthood. No matter how often mandatory celibacy is spiritualised, this is the fact of the matter. This is not a negative criticism of the male priesthood. It is a statement of fact. I have worked in seminaries all my life and taught hundreds of future priests and worked with dozens of priests in many situations. They have earned my highest regard. Despite the recent horrors, the priests we have known in the last few generations stand out as the best in our history. Even St Vincent de Paul became a priest to feather his own and his family's nest, until, like Pope Francis, he was converted by the poor. So discussion of the ordination of women to this priesthood is a non-starter, and I think Pope Francis knows this. Nor is it a question of employing women at the Vatican, or making them cardinals.

A whole new anthropology and theology is needed, as Pope Francis indicated, and the first step in this new anthropology is to accept women in all their femaleness, and not in some kind of sentimental femininity. Women are sexual beings and all our mothers have engaged in holy sexual activity. The next step is to ask how these fully female and carnal women can possibly be made in the image of a wholly male metaphored God, or, as the vast majority of people think, a male God, familiarly referred to in Ireland as the 'man above'.

As the medieval women mystics knew, their God had to be gendered, as, for example, the favourite name of Doctor Hildegard of Bingen's God was Lady Wisdom. The Catholic Church, as we know it today is so far from these first steps that it is almost superfluous to enumerate any other steps in this new theology of women. One other step, however, which is also brought to mind by the words of Pope Francis, is to make the first creation story (Gen 1:1–2:3) the basis of a theology of women, as all of the women theologians known to us from the past have done. The story of Adam and Eve is not even a starting point for women, nor is the subsequent glorification of Mary, the mother of Jesus, as the antidote to a carnal Eve, through her virginal motherhood. Pope Francis constantly refers to himself as a sinner, a theological reflection coming straight from the second creation story (Gen 2:4–24). The reflection coming from the first creation story suggests that fundamentally we are made in the image of God and that this image is primary and before all sense of sin. Far be it from me to correct the Pope's theology, but I stand in the company of Julian of Norwich, Marguerite Porete and Mechthild of Magdeburg.

A solution to this new theology is to be found in the hermeneutical task Pope Francis has set himself in his analysis of the poor. If the same hermeneutic is applied to women, the silenced poor of the Church, a beginning of a way forward might be found. Pope Francis begins with the plea that the Gospel should not be distorted, and if that had been the case, the biblical witness of the women apostles and disciples would not have been first distorted and then forgotten. Other elements of his hermeneutic include 'time is greater than space' (*EG*, n. 222), which means seeing time, this moment, as *kairos*, a moment of revelation and newness. It is not necessary to enumerate all the ingredients, but one more will suffice, 'realities are more important than ideas' (*EG*, nn. 231–3). The reality of women within the Church of God is so much more important than any theological reflection by male theologians, even by popes, even when that reflection becomes quasi-infallible. Presumably, the new theology that Pope Francis suggested is to be done by male theologians, since women are not allowed to teach such a theology, or use their own experience as a resource for the doing of theology. If that is the case, one hopes that it will not be on the immediate agenda.

The effect of the brief presence of this extraordinary pope is multifaceted. It has changed perceptions of the papacy and of the Catholic Church. It has thrown up an example of a man following the Gospel imperative in his own life, despite generations of activity to the contrary in his place of work. Not that the popes were not following the Gospel, but that the preservation of the Catholic Church as an institution seemed to take pride of place. This pope has also created an atmosphere of joy, similar to the atmosphere in the late 1960s after the Second Vatican Council. It then seemed a joyful thing to be a Catholic. This now again seems to be a possibility. Whether the Pope reforms the Roman Curia or changes specific doctrines is almost irrelevant. He seems to have asked us to stand on our own two feet and follow. He has altered ecclesial boundaries by becoming one of us, a man accessible and available. He has shown that it is possible to bridge boundaries that were thought impassable, by washing feet and embracing the bereft.

All of this, and so much more, has drawn people to him. The centre has become the embodiment of love again, and not the embodiment of authority. In a way, he reminds us of Pope Gregory the Great (*c.*540–604) who was one of the first popes to care about the pastoral well-being of the people. Some people await the proof of all of this in action. But that is not necessary. Even if there is no 'action', the change has already happened. When the world now thinks of the Pope, they have to smile. That in itself is a profound change.

Pope Francis and the Challenge to Catholics

Michael Kelly

If you're a Catholic and you're not challenged or even unsettled by some of the things Pope Francis is saying, then you're not listening. Pope Francis is challenging Catholics – all Catholics – to change the way they think about the Church and their faith and, in so doing, he may well transform the Church beyond recognition. In a media world which relies on sound bites and simple (sometimes simplistic) narratives, the nuance of the Catholic Church in general, and the Argentine Pontiff in particular, is often lost amid the rush to pigeon-hole the Pontiff.

To understand the genesis of the embryonically-transformative papacy of Francis, it is not sufficient to look to his background as a Jesuit in Argentina; one must look back to the circumstances in which a vacancy in the See of St Peter occurred. Monday 11 February 2013 is a day that will loom large when the history of Christendom in the early years of the twenty-first century is written and spoken about. Benedict XVI, in a relatively routine meeting with the College of Cardinals, announced that he was renouncing the papacy in favour of retirement. The news sent shock waves throughout the world and made the front pages of virtually every newspaper in the world: not for the first time, the Catholic Church had captivated the world's attention.

Anyone who doubts the ability of the Catholic Church to adapt to change should marvel at those remarkable events which, having seemed unthinkable for so long, became real very quickly. And Catholics adapted to it with breakneck pace. As a journalist and broadcaster specialising in religious affairs, the announcement catapulted me into a month of constant interviews and commentary about what this means for the Church, what kind of future there would be and what kind of legacy Benedict XVI had left behind.

One Catholic commentator at the time rather unkindly observed that the resignation of Joseph Ratzinger was the greatest moment of his pontificate. History, liberated from the petty likes and dislikes of the moment, will judge Benedict XVI in a more rounded and nuanced fashion. I suspect, for example, he will never get the credit he deserves for his role in forthrightly addressing the clerical abuse scandals after an era when most people in the Vatican simply wanted to turn a blind eye. Nor is he likely to get the credit for beginning much-needed reforms in the Vatican's murky financial landscape.

Perhaps the most profound influence of Benedict XVI on the modern Church will be seen in years and decades to come as a generation of priests and religious are coming of age who were steeped and immersed in the complex thought of Joseph Ratzinger on issues as diverse as the liturgy, Church–State relations and the place of religion in the public square. Benedict's resignation has transformed the shape of the papacy forever. In stepping down, he has removed one of the last great taboos in an understanding that sees the papacy as a monarchy. As a result, it's difficult to see a future pope governing the Church beyond the age of eighty-five years as the role is increasingly seen as leading, guiding and, crucially, serving the universal Church.

I was one of the seven thousand-plus journalists who descended on Rome for what became known as 'papal transition'. As Benedict XVI waved goodbye from the balcony of the papal summer residence of Castel Gandolfo, he spoke without notes: 'I am simply a pilgrim', he said to the crowd, 'beginning the last leg of his pilgrimage on this earth.' 'Thank you and good night', were his last public words as pontiff, sentiments that resonated beautifully with the first public words of his successor, 'Good evening', when Jorge Mario Bergoglio stepped out on the balcony of St Peter's Basilica as Pope Francis.

He was the first pontiff in the Church's history to choose the name Francis – a gesture which immediately endeared him to the Italian crowd given St Francis' status as the nation's patron. He was the first Jesuit Pope – an order dedicated to serving the papacy was now engaging in the ultimate act of service by giving to the Church a Jesuit to lead us. He was the first Latin American pope. Greeting the crowds on that rain-soaked evening he joked that the cardinals have gone 'to the ends of the earth' to get a new pope. It had echoes of Polish Cardinal Karol Wojtyła's observation upon his election as pope in 1978 that the cardinals had called him 'from a faraway country'.

From the moment of his election, Francis signalled that he cherished simplicity. He wore just the simple white cassock and set aside the red papal mozzetta, he boarded the bus with the other cardinals and soon set aside a papal Mercedes for a more modest Ford Focus. To be sure, these are issues of style rather than substance, but it's also true that substance can often be seen in the style.

Pope Francis' first year in office has been remarkable. His evident simplicity and relaxed style have won him widespread admiration. Journalists and the mass media were immediately smitten with him, a love affair which shows no signs of abating. Pope Francis is big news and he sells newspapers. His charisma is infectious and, at a time when people have lost trust and confidence in leaders, he radiates a servant model of leadership. In the Church, he is calling cynics to new hope: after all, most cynics are just disappointed optimists.

From a media perspective, Pope Francis is an interesting case study in how powerful the mass media is in creating and sustaining popular perceptions about public figures. Benedict's previous role as the Vatican's chief doctrinal enforcer meant that he was quickly shovelled into a narrow caricature by the media. In contrast, Pope Francis is almost universally portrayed in a positive light. Utterances that would have had Benedict XVI consigned to the Dark Ages are barely reported when they come from Pope Francis. His challenging words about the need for a more just world are embraced while Benedict's excoriations of dehumanising economic models were ignored.

Why is this? Well, I think one of the main reasons is the fact that most journalists are generalists. They think in black and white, good and evil, left and right. Caricatures become necessary, whatever doesn't fit the caricature is tossed aside like an old cigar butt or explained away. *Time* magazine announced that they had chosen Pope Francis as Person of the Year because of his rejection of Church dogma, this despite the fact that he has rejected none of the Church's dogmas (the magazine later corrected this error). When Pope Francis spoke out about abortion recently, *The New York Times* dismissed his remarks as merely designed to pacify Catholic conservatives!

You can't please everyone as pope: Benedict XVI certainly didn't, and Pope Francis won't either. That said, his evident popularity both within and outside the Church is a golden moment for Catholicism to blossom and show itself as a Church of welcome for the many people who feel estranged. He is also challenging Church leaders to see the Church not merely as a place of ideology, but a place where people experience the mercy and forgiveness of God and feel themselves loved and valued.

In his short time in office, Francis has already ushered in what can only be described as a kind of ecclesiastical *perestroika*. It's a message that may well find resonance in a country like Ireland where many people describe themselves as Catholics but no longer attend Mass regularly, if at all. Not that the Argentine Pontiff has given a signal that the Church is about to take a dramatic lurch to the left: on the contrary, many of his pronouncements on controversial issues like women's ordination and sexuality mirror those of his predecessors.

But Pope Francis understands the art of communication and the golden rule that what is heard is the message. And too often what people have been hearing is a list of negatives: 'The Church is against this', or 'the Vatican opposes that'. The Pope is calling Catholics to concentrate a bit more on what the Church is for, and less about what it is against.

Principally, for Francis, this is about transforming the Church from a place of ideology to a Church where people experience spirituality and where the deep-seated need for transcendence is met. In so doing, he is reaching out to what might be described as the Catholic 'middle ground'. He is moving away from a model of the Church that is 'fewer and truer' to one where all Catholics can find a home.

The remarkable twelve-thousand-word interview with *La Civiltà Cattolica*, in which the Pope excoriates some elements in the Church for being 'obsessed' with abortion and gay marriage, shows that Francis wants some elements of the hierarchy to find a different way of being the Church. It would be wrong to think that he is signalling a seismic shift where the Catholic Church would suddenly start endorsing gay marriage or would approve of abortion. His words on these issues have been firm, and his consistent approach should also serve as a watchword to those who think that the Church's teachings on controversial issues should be set aside. It's not either/or, for Pope Francis, it's both. A consistent pro-life ethic, for example, requires that all human life – born and unborn – is cherished.

Francis makes it clear in the *Civiltà Cattolica* interview that he is a loyal son of the Church and, as such, stands fully behind Church teaching. It's hardly a surprise that the Pope is a Catholic, but he is a Catholic who wants the Church to emphasise more the message of mercy and love. As one theologian put it to me: 'It's about telling people what God can do for them, rather than what they have to do for God.'

Francis is trying to steer a middle ground between those who push a heartless form of Catholicism, based on rigid rules and regulations, and those who would adopt an all-you-need-is-love approach. It's not an easy path and there's been a tendency from many people to emphasise the parts of his message that are palatable. There is an inherent danger in this: in seeking to use quotations from the Pope to hector opponents, one risks making Pope Francis a sign of disunity rather than a sign of unity. He has words of challenge for those 'obsessed' with sexual morality just as much as he has warned priests and religious to 'keep doctrine safe from ideologies and abstract theories'.

The controversial theologian Hans Küng is an example of people trying to spin Pope Francis to suit a particular agenda. Eighty-five-year-old Küng, who is no stranger to picking and choosing what parts of the Church's teaching he thinks worthy of following, penned a lengthy response to the Pope's recent apostolic exhortation, *Evangelii Gaudium*.

Predictably, Küng gushes about the parts of the document where he believes the Pope to be in agreement with his own analysis. Where Francis is at odds with Küng, the Swiss theologian has a formula to explain the Pope away: Francis is 'under pressure' from the Congregation for the Doctrine of the Faith to conform. This, Küng says with bombastic arrogance, shows the 'dogmatic limits of this pope'.

Francis has also provoked the ire of conservatives – particularly in the USA – who have ridiculously accused him of being a Marxist. As a newspaper editor, I take comfort that I am steering a *via media* when I open up the post bag and a letter telling me I am too liberal is followed by a letter telling me that I am too conservative. Catholicism, ever the big-tent faith rather than a sectarian rump, is about steering a *via media*, faithful to the Church's tradition while being able to inculcate the faith in very different circumstances.

So, where will Pope Francis lead us? What has been clear is that he is not a man to be the puppet of anyone. He is a man who simultaneously wants to push radical reform of the Church's structures and life while making it clear that the essence of the faith remains timeless and unchanging. People like Hans Küng are desperate to latch on to anything to try and prove their specious claim that Pope Francis is determined to change the essential teachings of the Catholic Church beyond recognition. They conveniently ignore the fact that Pope Francis has repeatedly reiterated the Church's teaching on the issues that the mainstream media find contentious: abortion, the ordination of women, homosexuality and the traditional family based on marriage between a man and a woman.

But, make no mistake, Pope Francis will transform the Church: he is definitely determined to place the entire Church on a missionary footing. In some circumstances, this will mean leaving old ways and old mindsets behind. Governance is one of the key – and overdue – issues that Pope Francis must address. He has given clear hints that he wants to give more power to local churches in general, and bishops' conferences in particular.

His apostolic exhortation, *Evangelii Gaudium*, is a *tour de force* on evangelisation; it is also a challenging document that calls all members of the Church to move beyond complacency. It is clear that the Pope wants the entire Church to be on a missionary footing, right up to the Pope himself:

> I too must think about a conversion of the papacy … It is my duty, as the Bishop of Rome, to be open to suggestions which can help make the exercise of my ministry more faithful to the meaning which Jesus Christ wished to give it and to the present needs of evangelisation … The papacy and the central structures of the universal Church also need to hear the call to pastoral conversion (*Evangelii Gaudium*).[1]

He clearly wants to breathe life into the concrete idea of collegiality understood as shared co-responsibility between the Vatican and local bishops:

> The Second Vatican Council stated that, like the ancient patriarchal Churches, episcopal conferences are in a position 'to contribute in many and fruitful ways to the concrete realisation of the collegial spirit'. Yet this desire has not been fully realised, since a juridical status of episcopal conferences which would see them as subjects of specific attributions, including genuine doctrinal authority, has not yet been

---

[1] Pope Francis, *Evangelii Gaudium* (The Joy of the Gospel), Apostolic Exhortation on the Proclamation of the Gospel in Today's World, 2013, n. 32. Subsequent references will be denoted by *EG*, followed by the paragraph number(s).

sufficiently elaborated. Excessive centralisation, rather than proving helpful, complicates the Church's life and her missionary outreach (*EG*, n. 32).

There needs to be a lot of reflection on how collegiality can be exercised in the Church in a more collaborative fashion. I would say, however, that the experience of bishops' conferences has been far from universally positive. Too often the bishops' conferences have served as an excuse for individual bishops to hide behind a form of collective responsibility which really leads to a situation where no one is responsible. A bishops' conference can too often lead to a triumph of mediocrity where individual bishops are unwilling to speak or to act, preferring instead to defer to a sometimes unwieldy structure.

Perhaps the most intriguing part of the Pope's text is where he speaks about the Eucharist as 'not a prize for the perfect but a powerful medicine and nourishment for the weak. These convictions have pastoral consequences that we are called to consider with prudence and boldness' (*EG*, n. 47). This is surely a thinly-veiled hint at the debate about the admittance of divorced and remarried Catholics to the Eucharist. He warns that 'the Church is not a tollhouse; it is the house of the Father, where there is a place for everyone, with all their problems' (*EG*, n. 47).

The Pope is trying to reach out to those who have long since drifted away from the practice of their faith or even those who are hostile towards Catholicism. He is likely to get short shrift from the latter, but he may well get a warm reception from lapsed Catholics. This is why he says that the Church needs to find a new balance between upholding rules and demonstrating mercy. Otherwise, he warns in his interview for Jesuit publications, 'even the moral edifice of the Church is likely to fall like a house of cards'. It's a stark warning that rings true in Ireland, where the Church's moral authority has crumbled as a result of revelations about the cover-up of clerical abuse.

The reason that the Catholic Church has survived for two thousand years is because of an ability at moments in history for the Church to recreate and re-present itself. Catholicism survived the Dark Ages by preserving Christian tradition in the monasteries. The Church survived the Reformation by engaging in a massive programme of reform in the sixteenth century. We may be witnessing another such moment when one form of Catholicism dies and a new one is birthed.

Pope Francis' simple style and humility have won him widespread approval. The challenge for bishops and priests across Ireland will be to put flesh on the bones of what the Pope is saying and make real Francis' pledge that the Church will be more open to meeting people with mercy and love. They will need to reassure people that the form of Catholicism Francis criticises – the Church that has 'locked itself up in small things, in small-minded rules' – is also capable of openness and being a place of welcome for many rather than a museum for the saintly few.

If you're a Catholic and you're not challenged or even unsettled by some of the things Pope Francis is saying, then you're not listening.

Pope Francis the Evangelist:
A Parish Priest for the World

Alfred McBride, OPraem*

In Matthew's Gospel, Christ's last words to his followers before he ascended to heaven were about evangelisation. His words were meant for all who would become his disciples. Jesus said:

> All authority in heaven and on earth has been given to me. Go therefore and make disciples of all nations, baptising them in the name of the Father and of the Son and of the Holy Spirit, and teaching them to obey everything that I have commanded you. And remember, I am with you always, to the end of the age (Mt 28:18–20).

Pope Francis calls the baptised to be evangelisers
It is clear that Pope Francis wants all the baptised to hear this call. In various parts of the Church, people who were raised Catholics have stopped practicing the faith. The percentage of ex-Catholics is growing. The number of marriages celebrated in church is decreasing dramatically. Marriage and the family are in crisis. Belief among a number of Catholics in a personal God is decreasing. The Pope wants Catholics to be evangelisers. This means that they first need to be evangelised themselves. Catholics are called to make a conscious choice to follow Jesus. They are invited to know who Jesus is, welcome him into their personal lives and, with joy and energy, share their faith with others. Evangelisation is a process by which a growing union with Christ occurs throughout our lifetime. It causes in people of faith the possibility of attracting others to faith in Jesus.

---

*   I thank Fr Andrew Ciferni, OPraem and Therese Dougherty for their assistance in the writing of this chapter.

By his inspiring words and personal witness, Pope Francis is helping us to be evangelised so we can evangelise others. He has written a letter – an apostolic exhortation entitled *Evangelii Gaudium*[1] (The Joy of the Gospel) – in which he outlines the many aspects of evangelisation: the centrality of a relationship with Jesus, the need to be a joyful Catholic, being familiar with scripture and the Church's teachings, care for the poor and avoidance of the idolatry of money in place of the Church's social teaching. He urges us to be filled with the spirit of mercy and ready to sacrifice ourselves for this essential calling of our faith. In this chapter, I will unfold insights from Pope Francis as he witnesses evangelisation through word, deed, faith, love and hope.

Pope Francis has proved to be a born communicator in word and deed. But he is more than an effective speaker. As a bishop and pope he is an evangeliser. He uses his personal talents and the gift of the papacy to bring Jesus Christ to everyone. He witnesses St Paul's words: 'And it is no longer I who live, but it is Christ who lives in me. And the life I now live in the flesh I live by faith in the Son of God, who loved me and gave himself for me' (Gal 2:20). His pectoral cross signifies the kind of evangelising pope he wants to be. The cross shows the Good Shepherd carrying the lost sheep on his shoulders. Behind him is his flock. In front is the Holy Spirit in the form of a dove.

Evangelisers seek the lost sheep to carry them to Christ
The Pope envisions his calling in the same way. Parish priests are often called to rescue people who have radical needs for a number of reasons. Pope Francis often acts in a similar way even though he occupies a lofty position. It is no secret that the word 'pastor' is synonymous with the word 'shepherd'. Our Pope looks for the lost sheep in the many ways they appear and he will carry them home to Christ. He likes to tell bishops and priests that the call to be shepherds includes acquiring the 'smell of the sheep'.[2] This is why many people have begun saying that Pope Francis is like the world's parish priest.

---

[1]   Pope Francis, *Evangelii Gaudium* (The Joy of the Gospel), Apostolic Exhortation on the Proclamation of the Gospel in Today's World, 2013. Henceforth, this will be referred to as *EG*, followed by paragraph number(s).

[2]   From the homily of Pope Francis at the Chrism Mass in St Peter's Basilica on 28 March 2014.

Pope Francis continues the contributions of recent popes. He has the common touch that people admired in Pope John XXIII. Like Benedict XVI, he upholds the Church's faith when he says, 'I am a son of the Church.'[3] He also prefers a personal and energetic outreach to the world, like John Paul II. As Archbishop of Buenos Aires he was a people person who hit the streets where the poorest of the poor may be met. He was just four months in office as pope when he travelled to Brazil for World Youth Day to address three million young people who roared with joy at his presence and words. In his final homily of the World Youth Day festivities, he urged them to evangelise: 'Go out and spread your faith to the fringes of society, even to those who seem farthest away, most indifferent. The Church needs you, your enthusiasm, your creativity and the joy that is so characteristic of you!'[4]

The Pope evangelises by his deeds

Francis has charmed the secular media. One night while I watched the evening news I was touched that the programme ended with a moving scene at the Vatican. A little boy was clinging to the Pope's cassock. When the Pope finally released him gently, the smiling boy jumped into the papal chair, threw his arms wide open and looked like he was about to give a blessing. The evangelising deeds of Pope Francis are ideal for the social media of Facebook and Twitter which carry his Christian outreach to the world. When he washed and kissed the feet of young prisoners, the pictures flooded the world. When he hugged and kissed the gnarled face of a poor man with such deep disfigurement, a close-up went around the world and was repeated many times. Commentators immediately retold the story of St Francis of Assisi kissing the leper.

What makes these scenes so captivating is their spontaneity, their lack of theatrical control and their absence of manipulation of the viewers. Francis is an exuberant man who speaks a lot about joy and proceeds to show us how to be joyful in opening our arms to welcome the world's unlucky and unfortunate people. Because of his role as

---

[3] From Pope Francis' interview with Antonio Spadaro, SJ, published in *America*, September 2013. The quotations in the remainder of this chapter are, unless otherwise indicated, taken from this interview.

[4] From Pope Francis' homily at World Youth Day in Rio de Janeiro, Brazil on 28 July 2013.

pope, he is automatically a public figure. Because of his being the shepherd of a religion counting over one billion members, he cannot avoid being in the spotlight.

Evangelisers need to witness mercy and forgiveness
So far this papal lifestyle suits the wishes of our new Holy Father. I think he is trying to live the open transparency of Christ during his public ministry. About the only privacy Jesus treasured was his occasional all-night vigils of prayer on a mountain. Otherwise, he strode the towns, villages and cities of Palestine looking for converts, hoping to elicit faith, and was passionate about mercy and forgiveness. Pope Francis is also the champion of mercy, a rare virtue that could heal millions of families and the life of each human being. In thinking of his plea for mercy, I recall Shakespeare's Portia who agreed that 'the quality of mercy is not strained … It becomes the throned monarch better than his crown … It is an attribute to God himself … And earthly power doth then show likest God's when mercy seasons justice'.[5]

Pope Francis encourages us to rely on Christ's forgiveness. Now is the time to say to Jesus: Lord, I have let myself be deceived; in a thousand ways I have shunned your love, yet here I am once more to renew my covenant with you. I need you. Save me once again, Lord, take me once more into your redeeming embrace. How good it feels to come back to him whenever we are lost! Let me state this once more: God never tires of forgiving us; we are the ones who tire of seeking his mercy. Christ, who told us to forgive one another 'seventy-seven times' (Mt 18:22) has given us his example: he has forgiven us seventy-seven times. Time and time again he bears us on his shoulders. No one can strip us of the dignity bestowed upon us by this boundless and unfailing love. With a tenderness that never disappoints, but is always capable of restoring our joy, he makes it possible for us to lift up our heads and to start anew.

Pope Francis has teaching skills as well as preaching ability
Another fascinating fact about Pope Francis is his love of literature. As a young Jesuit he taught high school literature (and psychology) from

---

[5]   *The Merchant of Venice*, Act IV, Scene I.

1964 until 1966. In a recent interview he was asked about his experience with teaching. 'It was a bit risky,' he answered. He continued:

> I had to make sure that my students read *El Cid*. But the boys did not like it. They wanted to read García Lorca. Then I decided they will study *El Cid* at home and that in class I would teach the authors the boys liked the most. Of course, young people wanted to read more 'racy' literary works, like the contemporary *La Casada Infiel* or classics like *La Celestina*, by Fernando de Rojas. But by reading these things, they acquired a taste in literature, poetry, and they went on to other authors.

Pope Francis admires the way Jesus attracted ordinary people by his lofty teachings and demands. He believes that the secret lies in the way that Jesus looked at people, seeing beyond their weaknesses and failings. 'Do not be afraid, little flock, for it is your Father's good pleasure to give you the kingdom' (Lk 12:32). Jesus truly enjoys talking with his people. Preachers should strive to communicate that same enjoyment to their listeners. The Pope describes a way to do this in these words:

> Dialogue is much more than the communication of a truth. It arises from the enjoyment of speaking and it enriches those who express their love for one another through the medium of words. This is an enrichment which does not consist in objects but in persons who share themselves in dialogue. A preaching which would be purely moralistic or doctrinaire, or one which turns into a lecture on biblical exegesis, detracts from the heart-to-heart communication which takes place in the homily and possesses a quasi-sacramental character: 'Faith comes from what is heard, and what is heard comes by the preaching of Christ' (Rom 10:17). In the homily, truth goes hand in hand with beauty and goodness. Far from dealing with abstract truths or cold syllogisms, it communicates the beauty of the images used by the Lord to encourage the practice of good ... [The hearts of the faithful] growing in hope, from the joyful and practical exercise of the love which they have received, will sense that each word of Scripture is a gift before it is a demand (*EG*, n. 142).

Pope Francis evangelises from heart to heart
One way of understanding his success may be found in the words of Blessed John Henry Newman's motto, *Cor ad cor loquitor* ('Heart speaks unto Heart'). Newman explains this in the following way: 'The

heart is commonly reached not through reason, but through the imagination, by means of direct impressions, by the testimony of facts and events, by history, by description. Persons influence us, voices melt us, looks subdue us, deeds inflame us.'

Pope Francis illustrates what Newman means. He agrees that rational arguments do have an essential role, but stories, imagery, poetry, parables and wisdom sayings aim for the heart of the listener and have a considerable impact. Being personal in a prudent and humble sense influences others. Voices that emerge from the sincerity of people's hearts melt us. Deeds that flow from love and concern for everyone, especially the least of our brothers and sisters, melt us. History, when reported as a family album with its memories of good times and bad, but also framed with affection for the humanity and faith of our ancestors infuses a warm glow of forgiveness. It also encourages confidence in the potential of our own experience. Such voices melt us.

The delightful, truthful and comforting joy of evangelising

In paragraphs 9–10 of *Evangelii Gaudium*, Francis – ever practical – advises us not to look like we just came from a funeral. Joyful evangelisers have the proper approach. The secret of joy comes from the Gospel by inviting us to live on a higher plane. My life grows by giving it away and it falters by isolation and comfort. I enjoy life most when I leave the security of home or homeland and become excited by becoming a missionary for the Gospel. My life matures when I use it to give life to others. This is what mission of the Gospel means. St Thomas Aquinas taught that goodness tends to share itself. If we are growing in goodness it will spread to others. If we become ever more truthful that will be contagious and will spread from ourselves to others.

Mary is the Star of Evangelisation

I believe it is fitting to conclude this chapter with a brief reflection on Pope Francis and Mary. During his trip to Brazil for World Youth Day, he made a trip to the shrine of Our Lady of Aparecida. While he prayed to her, he seemed on the point of tears as he dedicated his entire papacy to Our Lady of Aparecida. As I write this chapter, in

January 2014, Francis has made six trips to the Basilica of St Mary Major that houses a shrine of Mary under the title of *Salus Populi Romani* (Protector of the Roman People). It is the most visited shrine outside the Vatican.

Our Blessed Mother Mary is the Star of Evangelisation for the spirituality of Pope Francis. Like the Magi, he has followed the star to meet the living Christ. In every Mass we pray for our Holy Father. Let us keep him in the prayers of our heart every day. As each of us realises our vocation as a Catholic missionary in our given situation, we may find strength and enthusiasm in saying the following prayer of discipleship each day. It was published by Our Sunday Visitor and adapted from a homily of Pope Francis at the Basilica of St Paul Outside the Walls on Easter Sunday, 14 April 2013.

> Loving God, I thank you for choosing me to be your disciple and for the gift of your Son, Jesus.
> Help me to proclaim and bear witness to the Gospel by word and deed, today and every day.
> Open my heart to the outcast, the forgotten, the lonely, the sick, the poor.
> Grant me the courage to think, to choose, and to live as a Christian, joyfully obedient to God.

Affable and Unpredictable

Colum Kenny

It is March 2015. A blue Ford Focus nudges its way into Rome's traffic. From a back window of the small car Pope Francis smiles benignly at two mothers who have held up their babies for him to see. He has just left the Church of the Most Holy Name of Jesus, where he was meeting and praying with some old Jesuit acquaintances.

The pontiff is now late for an appointment at the Vatican. His driver turns onto the Via del Plebiscito but finds himself forced to brake. A truck has stopped abruptly ahead. When a motorcyclist pulls up alongside the car there is a small explosion, followed by two shots. As the motorcycle speeds away, Francis slumps forward, dead.

The media coverage of the assassination is awash with conspiracy theories, with commentators trumpeting 'I-told-you-so'.

*****

What if this affable pope were to exit the world stage before he has had time to establish himself on it? He was no sooner appointed than those who dared to hope that the Holy Spirit had moved the cardinals to make a wise choice were looking nervously over their shoulders at the spectre of John Paul I. That smiling pontiff died after just thirty-three days in office in 1978, and his early death sparked various wild rumours.

People attempt to discern signs of hope in the papacy of Francis, but what are those signs? Every Catholic, and many a non-Catholic, has his/her own secret ambition for whatever cardinal steps forward as a new pope on the balcony of St Peter's. 'But who do you say that I am?' asked Jesus of his disciples (Mk 8:29).

In the first flush of enthusiasm a new leader can seem to promise more than he or she will later deliver. Those who in 2009 awarded

Barack Obama the Nobel Peace Prize 'for his extraordinary efforts to strengthen international diplomacy' must now square that decision with his continuing deployment of deadly drones to kill people convicted of no crime who live in states with which the USA is not at war. Pope John Paul II appeared to be a modernising pontiff as he first flew around the world and took to his 'popemobile', yet he settled into a role that some found less open and universal than defensive and particular.

How much of the welfare of any institution can or should depend on the intentions and ability of just one man? The fictional scene sketched above brings us face to face with the reality of this papacy. In his first year as pontiff, Francis has raised expectations that centre on him as an individual. In a world of more than seven billion people, and a Catholic Church of more than one billion souls, what can a single person be expected to achieve, and for whom? Would his personal annihilation extinguish hope?

Is he naive? Whisperers say that his heart is in the right place, but wonder about his head. He has made surprising comments about homosexuals, compliments to communists, encouraging words for women who wish to nurse their babies in church. Detractors may ask sarcastically if the bishop of Rome thinks that he is running some quaint parish in South America.

Already at least one cardinal has muttered publicly about the unpredictability of this papacy. Jesus may well have warned that 'you know neither the day nor the hour' (Mt 25:13) in which the Son of Man is coming, but the Curia likes to have a good idea of what is happening long term.

Predictability is not necessarily a bad thing. Revolutions do not inevitably bring happiness in their train, and faddish shifts in style or opinion may confuse as many people as they stimulate. Philosophically, if one feels that one has a coherent and rational world view then it takes quite a bit of persuading for one to change it.

And people pushing for change may have psychological or personal motivations that convince them they are correct when, in practice, they are merely self-serving. Conservative and progressive, left and right: the judgements given are the judgements received.

Any pope trying to improve the Catholic Church and to attune its teachings to contemporary knowledge or insights quickly finds himself categorised on one side or the other of various divides. It is not just cardinals and the media that like to pigeonhole people and to know where they stand. Most of us, to a greater or lesser extent, are made uncomfortable by uncertainty. A successful pope needs to be in the world but not of it; he cannot be the captive of any faction.

Already Francis has ruffled feathers. Accusations that he is a socialist are clearly wide of the mark, but he has unmistakably distanced himself from the world's dominant economic ideology. He is concerned about people's living and working conditions and about environmental sustainability.

Those who find Francis 'unpredictable' may not have been heartened by his being hailed as 'a great proponent' of breastfeeding. It was Vatican Radio's Emer McCarthy, from County Wicklow in Ireland, who thus expressed her pleasure to the *Catholic News Service* after Francis told her and other mothers visiting the Sistine Chapel that they should breastfeed their babies there.[1]

It was Cardinal Raymond Leo Burke, the Irish-American top Vatican official, who referred pointedly to 'a kind of unpredictability about life in Rome these days'.[2] According to the cardinal:

> It seems to be a question of a certain style, and every Holy Father is different. So it is quite distinct from Pope Benedict who attended very much to a certain protocol, and also to a certain discipline of schedule and so forth; so there is an element of that, that's clear.[3]

Burke proudly uses the shield of his De Burgh Norman ancestors, 'who settled in Ireland in the twelfth century', on his own coat of arms.[4] And he takes an interest in contemporary Irish politics. Asked by a weekly Catholic paper last autumn about Enda Kenny's description of himself in the Irish parliament as 'a Taoiseach [prime minister] who happens to be a Catholic, but not a Catholic Taoiseach', Burke claimed that 'the distinction made in the statement … does not make any sense'.[5] Kenny had been refusing to conform to the wishes of

1   Carol Glatz, 'Pope to Moms: It's OK to Breast-feed in Public, Even in Sistine Chapel', 13 January 2014 at http://www.catholicnews.com/data/stories/cns/1400120.htm [accessed, 20 January 2014].

2   Cardinal Raymond Leo Burke, interviewed by Raymond Arroyo on EWTN, *The World Over*, 12 December 2013, available at http://www.youtube.com/watch?v=Edq69fJLnXo [accessed, 20 January 2014].

3   *Ibid.*

4   Archdiocese of St Louis at http://archstl.org/archstl/page/raymond-leo-cardinal-burke [accessed, 20 January 2014].

5   *The Irish Catholic*, interviewed by Garry O'Sullivan, 26 September 2013.

Catholic bishops in respect to legislation regulating abortion where a mother's life is at risk.

And it is not just a prime minister's position that 'does not make any sense' to Burke. The cardinal's unease about Pope Francis was evident in the television interview that he gave to EWTN last December when he said,

> it's not altogether clear to me exactly what the result of the reforms is going to be. The Pope has had meetings; they're talking about the reorganisation of the Roman Curia. But so far, I haven't seen anything concretely of what that will be ... I cannot imagine a reform of the Roman Curia which would not somehow be continuous with *Pastor bonus*, the apostolic constitution which has governed the Roman Curia since I think 1988, when Blessed John Paul II reformed the Roman Curia, because the Church is an organic body, and the service of the Roman Curia is part of the very nature of the Church, and so that has to be respected. So I can't imagine that somehow the Roman Curia is going to take on a completely different figure. It just doesn't make sense.

Jesus Christ said that 'Foxes have holes, and birds of the air have nests; but the Son of Man has nowhere to lay his head' (Mt 8:20). Some cardinals and bishops are accustomed to levels of comfort that Pope Francis seems to be disturbing.

Francis is also exciting non-Catholics. On 14 January 2014 the *International New York Times* ran a major feature on Francis, headed 'Francis Shakes Up the Vatican'. On 11 December *Time* magazine declared Francis its Person of the Year for 2013, ahead of the whistleblower Edward Snowdon in second place. England's newspapers debate the Pope's political outlook.

He is not mouthing 'pure Marxism', despite what detractors such as one prominent US radio presenter claimed.[6] Francis recently told *La Stampa*, the Italian daily newspaper: 'The Marxist ideology is wrong. But I have met many Marxists in my life who are good people, so I don't feel offended.'[7]

---

6   *The Rush Limbaugh Show*, 27 November 2013 at http://www.rushlimbaugh.com/daily/ 2013/11/27/it_s_sad_how_wrong_pope_francis_is_unless_it_s_a_deliberate_mistransl ation_by_leftists [accessed, 21 January 2014].

7   Andrea Tornielli ('Vatican Insider'), 'Never be Afraid of Tenderness', *La Stampa*, 14 December 2013, at http://www.lastampa.it/2013/12/14/esteri/vatican-insider/en/ never-be-afraid-of-tenderness-5BqUfVs9r7W1CJIMuHqNeI/pagina.html [accessed, 20 January 2014].

Nevertheless, he is stimulating debate. Jonathan Freedland, a distinguished international journalist and frequent contributor to *The Jewish Chronicle* thinks that 'even atheists should be praying to Pope Francis'. Because 'he is now the world's clearest voice for change'.[8]

And when a writer in the British *Daily Telegraph* describes the Vatican as 'the spearhead of radical economic thinking', something remarkable is happening. However, when that person also proclaims, 'Liberation Theology is back as Pope Francis holds capitalism to account', it seems that rumours of radical change in Rome are getting ahead of reality.[9] Francis was never identified in Latin America with the philosophy of activism that became known as 'liberation theology'.

So far, Pope Francis has merely behaved in a modest and pleasant manner. He is setting a tone rather than breaking windows at the Vatican.

A key image of the Pope during Christmas saw him with a lamb draped on his shoulders. He was at the church of Sant'Alfonso Maria de' Liguori in Rome where locals were re-enacting the nativity story. This was how Christ was depicted in the early Roman church, before a crucified Jesus replaced the young shepherd as the principal visual symbol of Christianity.

The Pope is eager to project a caring and pastoral image of his Church. On a flight from Brazil on 29 July 2013, responding to questions from journalists, he distinguished between individuals who are gay and a gay lobby, asking rhetorically, 'If a person is gay and seeks God and has good will, who am I to judge him?'[10] He wishes to remind people that the fundamental message of Christ refers to a moral disposition or a way of living, rather than a precise set of rules.

At the same time, this pope expects cardinals, priests and others within his Church to give good example by living the life of the cross. I have seen Pope Francis himself driven along Roman streets in his modest Ford Focus. His vulnerability is worrying. His strictures to the hierarchy on avoiding a cushy life are unlikely to endear him to some. Most will keep their heads down and hope that he is just going through a phase. But it is his critique of greed and global ideologies that threaten powerful people outside his Church.

---

8   Freedland, *The Guardian*, 16 November 2013.
9   Ambrose Evans-Pritchard, *Daily Telegraph*, 9 January 2014.
10 See his comments with translation at http://www.bbc.co.uk/news/world-europe-23489702 [accessed, 20 January 2014].

His various comments on breastfeeding demonstrate his central concern about economic priorities. Francis also told *La Stampa* about seeing a young mother holding her crying infant behind a barrier at the Vatican. He said to her: 'Madam, I think the child's hungry … Please give it something to eat! … I wish to say the same to humanity: Give people something to eat! That woman had milk to give to her child; we have enough food in the world to feed everyone.'

Reforms that he has signalled in Rome are long overdue, and little more than what is required to sustain the credibility of Catholicism. He is diluting the influence of the disproportionate number of Italian cardinals, and placing men of a like mind to himself in key positions. He has also taken steps to reform the Vatican Bank, which has caused scandal. This scarcely makes him a socialist.

He may shift the focus of Church attention away from any fixation on issues such as abortion or homosexuality (or 'the endless parsing of sexual ethics' as *Time* magazine put it[11]), but he is highly unlikely to endorse either abortion or same-sex marriage as acceptable options.

Rumours that Francis might appoint a female and/or lay cardinal, perhaps even Ireland's own Mary McAleese, appear to be premature, if not preposterous. He told *La Stampa*, 'I don't know where this idea sprang from. Women in the Church must be valued not "clericalised". Whoever thinks of women as cardinals suffers a bit from clericalism.'

When it deemed him its Person of the Year for 2013, *Time* wrote that, 'what makes this Pope so important is the speed with which he has captured the imaginations of millions who had given up on hoping for the church at all'. Yet no one man can fulfil the vague hopes of vast numbers of people, hopes that may be contradictory and delusional. Political leaders rise and fall on the wave of such unrealistic expectations.

What a pope can do is to demonstrate that his Church is heir to teachings and traditions that may help rather than hinder anyone trying, at least occasionally, to live a compassionate and truthful life. When people are overwhelmed by the size of the world's population and by the scale of its problems, a pope may bear witness to the worth of each individual.

*****

---

[11]   *Time*, 11 December 2013.

Being in the world, but not of it, is a challenge for anyone appointed as the head of a large religious organisation. In the case of the Christian Church many of its first leaders were, by secular standards, failures. Scorned and rejected, Jesus himself was crucified after just a short public life, while his followers risked bloody martyrdoms. A deranged person, or a political ideologue, or a religious fanatic may at any time violently end the papacy of Francis. Security around his person is manifestly more relaxed than that around some world leaders.

Yet even if he lives a long life, as one hopes that he shall, his achievements will be constrained by the nature of his office and by the inertia of the organisation to which he belongs. Reforms ought not to be random, but there are no effective processes for widespread consultation with Catholics in general. Their Church is not a democracy, and many of those in its upper echelons will resist radical changes.

Moreover, some will counsel caution for the best of reasons, not wishing to risk damaging an ancient institution by changes that observers in the media and elsewhere find appealing but that are not guaranteed to result in conversions or to a return to liturgical observances by people who have abandoned the practices of what was once their religion by birth or upbringing.

Francis will be told that he is perplexing or upsetting people needlessly, both non-Catholics and the faithful alike. His advisors will say that dogma has developed slowly for good reason, in a tried and tested fashion. They will encourage him to articulate his views in a more structured manner and less frequently. They may even wear him down and curb his enthusiasm.

He is also coming under external pressure to be more circumspect when criticising theories of capitalism that assume that economic growth, encouraged by a free market alone, will succeed in bringing about greater justice in the world. It is reported that at least one wealthy American supporter of Catholic charities has been offended.[12]

Some Christians in the United States, Catholic and Protestant, have in recent years created an impression that they believe their faith to be intrinsically allied to particular political and economic perspectives. Thus, Cardinal Burke, in his interview before Christmas on EWTN,

---

[12]   Andy Soltis, 'Almighty Dollar: Pope's Rhetoric Might Scare Off Rich Donor', *New York Post*, 1 January 2014.

was openly critical of the way that 'the present administration' in Washington 'treats the Catholic Church in general'. It was just the latest manifestation of hostility towards President Barack Obama that has emanated from US Catholic bishops in recent times, based largely on mandatory provisions relating to contraception and health services. Many American lay Catholics hold a different opinion. Any pope who continues to criticise powerful interests will find that he meets growing resistance both within the Church and outside it.

*****

So what will happen when Francis is no longer pope, whether he dies suddenly or passes away peacefully in his bed two decades from now? By then will he have engineered some radical new way of electing a pope, reducing the power of cardinals and enhancing the role of others within his Church, even of lay people, when it comes to choosing future successors to St Peter?

Will he have reinterpreted teachings that he regards as outmoded, perhaps ensuring that married men may become priests and that *Humanae Vitae* is qualified so that couples who responsibly plan their families do not stand condemned by Church teachers? And will he have opened the hearts of people to the message of Jesus Christ in new ways, removing some of the stumbling blocks that certain scandals or outmoded dogmas and attitudes have constituted?

Whatever he does he ought not to allow himself to become a celebrity idol, to be safely consigned to the role of a well-meaning individual who sooner or later is doomed to failure. His narrative should not be one simply of an institutional reformer, no matter how much one believes that reform of his institution is necessary to equip it for the future or wishes him well in his efforts.

His role ultimately is that of a spiritual leader who by personal example encourages others to follow in the footsteps of the same person whom Francis follows – to be not afraid regardless of who is elected pope, or of what any pope or his cardinals say.

What Can You Expect from a Jesuit Pope?

Jim Corkery, SJ

When Jorge Mario Bergoglio from Argentina was elected pope on 13 March 2013, I feared that his hailing from Buenos Aires would be a disadvantage to his dealing with life in Rome. I remembered Jimmy Carter arriving in Washington DC from Georgia in early 1977 and how long it took the Carter people to become wise to Washington's ways, indeed to adapt to the Washington 'template'. Bergoglio had spent little time in Rome – 'I do not know Rome well,'[1] he said in an interview some months after becoming pope – and he was certainly not a curial type. 'They will chew him up,' I thought, with their quiet insistence: 'this is how we do things here, Holy Father.' But I had not yet heard those words of *Evangelii Gaudium* in which the new pope, writing about '[P]astoral ministry in a new key', would say: it seeks 'to abandon the complacent attitude that says: "We have always done it this way"' (*Evangelii Gaudium*).[2] I thought he would be out-manoeuvred, but …

I was wrong. From his first '*Buona sera*' on that balcony above St Peter's Square, this new pope seemed like an ordinary person who could think in his own way, speak in his own way, and act in his own way. He did not wear what popes usually wear (no red mozzetta trimmed with ermine fur), or say what popes usually say, or do what popes usually do. He said of himself that he was the Bishop of Rome; and the first thing he did was to ask the people to pray for him. Later we discovered that these words and actions were consistent with what

---

[1]   Pope Francis, 'The Heart of a Jesuit Pope: Interview with Pope Francis', *Studies* 102:407 (Autumn 2011), p. 256.

[2]   Pope Francis, *Evangelii Gaudium* (The Joy of the Gospel), Apostolic Exhortation on the Proclamation of the Gospel in Today's World, 2013, n. 33. All subsequent references will be denoted by *EG*, followed by the paragraph number(s).

he said and did as Archbishop of Buenos Aires; and there were others to follow. He declined to live in the apostolic palace, as he had avoided living in the official episcopal residence in Buenos Aires. He kept his clunky black shoes, rejecting the red Prada variety that his predecessors had worn. He travelled by bus with the cardinals after his election, paid his hotel bill in person, telephoned his newspaper vendor in Argentina to cancel his subscription and gave the 'thumbs up' sign several times when meeting with the crowds in St Peter's Square. Immediately, he received the cardinals, his fellow bishops, not sitting down, awaiting their homage, but standing up, shoulder to shoulder with them, greeting them as his colleagues.

Even in those first days, it quickly became clear that this man was *not* focused on how the job was done in Rome, but rather on how to do the job as himself. The first year of his papacy has not been about Papa Bergoglio 'learning' Rome, but rather about Rome learning Papa Bergoglio. Following the recent changes that he made in the composition of the Congregation of Bishops and also his replacement, in January 2014, of four of the five cardinals who oversee the Vatican Bank, one cardinal – who asked that his name remain undisclosed – responded to a reporter's question 'What is going to happen next?' with the words: '*Anything* could happen next!' This can only be true if the person who came to Rome did not come to be a Roman, but to be the only person he could authentically be: himself.

Jesuit background and influence
How is it that Pope Francis can do this? Much of it relates to his personal background and to his training as a Jesuit. This pope's sincere answer when asked point blank 'Who is Jorge Mario Bergoglio?': 'I do not know what might be the most fitting description … I am a sinner. This is the most accurate definition. It is not a figure of speech, a literary genre. I am a sinner.'[3] He expands a little on this, reflecting that he feels that what is 'most true' is that he is a sinner upon whom the Lord has looked.[4] He relates this to his episcopal motto, drawn from the homilies of St Bede for the feast of St Matthew in which the words *miserando atque eligendo* are used to convey how the Lord had mercy on Matthew and chose him. He sees himself as

---

3   'The Heart of a Jesuit Pope', p. 256.
4   *Ibid.*, p. 256.

someone to whom the Lord has shown mercy and has called to discipleship. That he should begin with his being a sinner – with the open admission that he is a sinner – is so counter-cultural in a world that is ever ready to apportion blame to others and to offer forgiveness to no one. The Pope says: I am a sinner, but God has shown me mercy and chosen me. He is able to admit the sinfulness because of the mercy (and love, he speaks also of love). He can accept the truth about himself because of God's acceptance of this truth; and from this he can move forward in response to being chosen, free to serve his Lord as a loved sinner.

No Jesuit can read these words of Bergoglio without hearing an echo (and recalling the dynamics) of the first and second weeks of the *Spiritual Exercises* of St Ignatius of Loyola. These *Exercises*, which every Jesuit undergoes fully (in a thirty-day period of intense prayer and reflection) at least twice in his life – at the beginning and at the end of his period of training – and partially every year, bring him through a process of being 'freed from' self in order to be 'free for' service of Christ's mission. At the end of the first week of these *Exercises*, the person who is engaging in them becomes aware that he/she (they are not just for Jesuits, by the way!) is a sinner, but a sinner upon whom God has bestowed boundless mercy and love. Aware of this, the loved sinner faces the questions (not paralysed by guilt but ready to be generous): 'What have I done for Christ? What am I doing for Christ? What will I do for Christ?' This places the person on the threshold of Christ's call to help in the building of his kingdom and to walk the same path that the Lord walked. In subsequent weeks of the *Exercises*, this path is then opened up before the loved sinner, who is drawn ever deeper into relationship with Christ – and, with him, out into the world – and is simultaneously drawn to radical detachment from, to genuine 'indifference' towards, those things in life that would compromise this following, in particular: riches, honour and pride.

When training (formation) by means of the *Spiritual Exercises* of St Ignatius 'works', then a person receives *life*: life to accept one's flawed, but loved self; life to love back the God who 'loved me first' and gave his Son for me; and life to go out, with this same Son, to serve the world that God loved so much that he sent his only Son into it (see Jn 3:16). There is movement and energy here, arising from the encounter with God's love in the *Exercises* and spilling out into a sharing of God's love for the world, especially for its poor and abandoned. Many of the words of Pope Francis echo, indeed embody, the life-dynamic that I describe here as being the gift of the *Spiritual Exercises*. It is a dynamic of 'going out', of being 'sent', of engaging in mission. Thus Jorge Mario Bergoglio, in 2007, warns of the danger of a self-referential Church, closed in on itself. He says that he told his priests: 'Do everything you should, you know your duties as ministers, take your responsibilities and then leave the door open.'[5] His longing is for a 'Church which goes forth' and he speaks of all of us being asked to obey the Lord's call 'to go forth from our own comfort zone in order to reach all the "peripheries" in need of the light of the Gospel' (*EG*, n. 20). The Church 'needs nearness, proximity. I see the Church as a field hospital after battle',[6] the Pope says, pointing out that what it needs most is to be able to heal wounds and warm hearts. When elaborating his vision of a missionary Church, a 'Church which goes forth', he says: 'The Church must be a place of mercy freely given, where everyone can feel welcomed, loved, forgiven and encouraged to live the good life of the Gospel' (*EG*, n. 114). In remarks such as these, especially when he speaks about reaching 'peripheries', the Pope is echoing recent Jesuit language about going to the 'frontiers'[7] and the influence of his Jesuit training and background is noticeable. The same influence is evident when one compares his utterances with what other Jesuit pastors have said.

One pastor who comes to mind is Cardinal Carlo Maria Martini, the recently deceased archbishop emeritus of Milan who served in that archdiocese from 1980 to 2002. I recall, without being able to find the text of the conversation now, that he was once asked about his diocese and he responded in the following vein: 'there are several million people in my diocese. About one million are in the Church, one million are around the Church and the remaining millions are "out there"; they do not come to us, so we must go to them.' He sounds like the former Archbishop of Buenos Aires, although their geographical contexts and intellectual backgrounds are quite different. 'Jesuits are not formed by cookie cutters and a variety of views characterizes them,' wrote American Jesuit Thomas Worcester

---

5 Sefania Falasca, 'What I Would Have Said at the Consistory: An Interview with Cardinal Jorge Mario Bergoglio, Archbishop of Buenos Aires', *30 Giorni* (November 2007), http://www.30giorni.it/articoli_id_16457_13.htm [accessed, 17 March 2013].
6 'The Heart of a Jesuit Pope', p. 265 (see pp. 265–8).
7 See The Society of Jesus, *Decrees and Documents of the 35th General Congregation of the Society of Jesus* (Oxford: Way Books, 2008).

recently.[8] And popular American Jesuit writer, James Martin, recently recalled a saying of the Italian Jesuits: *Tre gesuiti, quattro opinioni* (three Jesuits, four opinions)![9] So it is not that Pope Francis *thinks* like every other Jesuit; he certainly has his own mind. However, he does share with other Jesuits, from their common background – particularly in the *Spiritual Exercises* – an outreach towards the world that has been noticed by many and that led *Time* magazine writer, Nancy Gibbs, in her essay accompanying Pope Francis' being named *Time* magazine's Person of the Year, to end with these words: 'For pulling the papacy out of the palace and into the streets, for committing the world's largest Church to confronting its deepest needs and for balancing judgment with mercy, Pope Francis is *Time's* 2013 Person of the Year.'[10]

The theme of a Church out on the streets is forever resurfacing. An influential early Jesuit, Jeronimo Nadal (1507–80), once said: 'The world is our house.' Commenting, in 2007, on these words, the then-Superior General of the Jesuits, Fr Peter-Hans Kolvenbach, wrote:

> a stable monastery does not serve us, because we have received the entire world to tell about the good news … we do not close ourselves up in the cloister, but we remain in the world amid the multitude of men and women that the Lord loves, since they are in the world.[11]

These kinds of statements – and actions based on the thinking that they embody – speckle the (almost) five hundred years of Jesuit history; Pope Francis is familiar with them and gives expression to them today. They always combine the elements of being ever with Christ, but simultaneously at the heart of the world. In his homily to Jesuits on 3 January of this year, Pope Francis said:

> We, Jesuits, want to be designated by the name of Jesus, to serve under the banner of the Cross, and this means: having the same mind as Christ. It means thinking like him, loving like him, seeing like him, walking like him. It means doing what he did and with his same sentiments, with the sentiments of his Heart.[12]

---

8   Thomas Worcester, 'Is a Jesuit Pope an Oxymoron?' in *The Huffington Post*, 18 March 2013 at http://www.huffingtonpost.com/thomas-worcester/jesuit-pope-oxymoron_b_2900505.html [accessed, 2 February 2014].

9   James Martin, SJ, *The Jesuit Guide to (Almost) Everything* (New York: HarperCollins, 2010), p. 5.

10   Nancy Gibbs, 'The Choice' in *Time* (23 December 2013), pp. 44–5, at p. 45.

11   Peter-Hans Kolvenbach, SJ, homily, *Regimini militantis ecclesiae*, celebrating the anniversary of the approval of the Society of Jesus, 27 September 2007.

12   Accessed at http://www.vatican.va, 3 February 2014.

How close these words are to those of the 35th General Congregation of the Society of Jesus in 2008 as it sought to articulate the identity of the Society's members: 'The grace we receive as Jesuits is to be and to go with him, looking on the world with his eyes, loving it with his heart, and entering into its depths with his unlimited compassion.'[13]

Jesuit background – papal foreground

So, 'what can you expect from a Jesuit Pope?'[14] It should be clear from what has been said so far that the papacy of Jorge Mario Bergoglio will not be a stay-at-home affair! Nor will it simply do things as they have always been done. Nor will it lack creativity and boldness: 'I invite everyone to be bold and creative in this task of rethinking the goals, structures, style and methods of evangelisation in their respective communities' (*EG*, n. 33). Pope Francis' apostolic exhortation, *Evangelii Gaudium*, gives voice to his

> dream of a 'missionary option', that is, a missionary impulse capable of transforming everything, so that the Church's customs, ways of doing things, times and schedules, language and structures can be suitably channelled for the evangelisation of today's world rather than for her self-preservation (*EG*, n. 27).

If he really means these words, then his papacy will be one of reshaping, and changing, the Church's practices and procedures. Governance is a clear example; and it brings also his Jesuit background into his papal foreground.

Governance is being reshaped by Pope Francis. His appointment of eight cardinal advisors from around the world to assist him in governing the Church is a move that not only decentralises decision-making but also places the existing Roman congregations and offices in a somewhat different relationship to the Pope. When Archbishop Parolin, the new Secretary of State, was invited to meet the Pope and his eight advisors, this marked both an advance in collegial government and a distancing of any curial position – be it that of Secretary of State or of the Prefect of the Congregation for the Doctrine of the

---

13   *Decrees and Documents of the 35th General Congregation of the Society of Jesus*, decree 2, n. 15.

14   This cleverly-worded question was first put to me by Br Conor McDonough, OP, when he asked me to speak to a group of Dominicans and their friends about the new Pope; many people have been amused by it since!

Faith – from the kind of Vice-Pope status that the two offices mentioned have tended to enjoy in the recent past. Francis' clear commitment to a more collegial form of Church government and to a more consultative style reflects as much his practice as Archbishop of Buenos Aires and his ecclesiology of inclusion and outreach as it does his Jesuit history. As I have written elsewhere, his choice to have a group of cardinal-advisors reflects something of the Jesuit mode of governance also[15] – and he once governed a province of the Society of Jesus and learned from his mistakes in not consulting enough.[16] Also, the fact that he is making reforming moves in Church governance – including the making of many new appointments and the courageous replacement of long-standing senior figures – means that he is taking seriously what his cardinal colleagues asked for when they met in those pre-conclave congregations in which he also took part; indeed, his very carrying out of their wishes is reminiscent of how a newly-elected Superior General of the Jesuits pays attention to that which has been asked of him by the general congregation in which he was elected.

As a Jesuit, Pope Francis will think, judge and feel with the Church (see *Spiritual Exercises*, 352–70). There will, as many have observed, be continuity in doctrine. But he will think and judge and feel bearing the whole community of believers in mind; he does not identify the hierarchy with the Church.[17] While adhering to and promoting doctrine, he will do so with creative fidelity and will not reduce the faith to doctrinal statements alone, as if Christianity were not a matter of praying and serving also, as well as of understanding. This last, understanding, he will not short-change by simply repeating formulations that no longer make any sense in terms of people's experience today. He has little consolation to offer to 'those who long for a monolithic body of doctrine guarded by all and leaving no room for nuance' (*EG*, n. 40).

He will not speak about moral issues in a way that loses sight of their connection with the heart of the faith and with the entire nexus of its mysteries; for without connection to these, he has pointed out, no particular teaching can be appreciated in its true depth. For this

---

[15] James Corkery, SJ, *Thinking Faith: The Online Journal of the British Jesuits*, 30 September 2013 at http://www.thinkingfaith.org/articles/20130930_1.htm [accessed, 3 February 2014].

[16] 'The Heart of a Jesuit Pope', pp. 262–3.

[17] *Ibid.*, pp. 263–5.

approach, and for not talking about certain matters of individual morality all the time, he is already criticised and reproached. The kind of attitudinal, not doctrinal, shift that I am attributing to him here reflects his Jesuit, immediate post-Vatican II theological training. He is the first pope to have done his theological studies *after* the Council. He himself taught theology and he comes from a religious order that places a decided emphasis on theological reflection and, since the mid-1970s especially, on a reflection that is grounded in the issues and problems of the day. Paramount among these is the plight of the poor; and Pope Francis has called for a theology that is able to place them at the centre, thus reflecting a Jesuit emphasis, articulated robustly in 1975, on the service of faith, of which the promotion of justice is an integral part. The poor, in every way, will be more to the fore in Francis' papacy: in his gestures and lifestyle; in his chosen name; in his fidelity to the unforgettable words of his friend, Cardinal Claudio Hummes, on the day of his election: 'Don't forget the poor!'; and in those recent options of the Jesuits for a faith that does justice, including now justice for the earth, on which he is preparing a new text. In all of these emphases, Francis' Jesuit background is by no means everything, but it exerts an influence!

Concluding remarks

In his homily on 3 January 2014, at the Gesù church in Rome, Pope Francis, having in mind the life of the new Jesuit saint, Peter Faber, told his Jesuit brothers:

> An authentic faith always involves a profound desire to change the world. Here is the question we must ask ourselves: do we also have great vision and impetus? Are we also daring? Do our dreams fly high? Does zeal consume us (see Ps 68:10)? Or are we mediocre and satisfied with our 'made in the lab' apostolic programmes?[18]

These kinds of questions drive the new Pope, revealing his own restlessness and Ignatian 'zeal for souls' and expressing also another central Jesuit motif: that of the *magis*, 'the more', since Ignatius always wanted his brothers to do what is *more* for the greater glory of God (*ad maiorem Dei gloriam*).

---

[18] See http://www.vatican.va [accessed, 3 February 2014].

If Pope Francis continues in his direction of emphasising a Church which goes forth, of seeking wider counsel and fostering greater consultation in matters of doctrine and life (witness the preparations for the coming synod of bishops) and of maintaining care of the poor and the earth at the forefront of his preaching and activity, then he will have been faithful to the *magis*, the more, and have widened the Church into a space where all can feel *more* welcome including, I hope, women, young people, and others who, while they may struggle with the demands of the faith, would also love to join in the adventure.

The Francis Effect

Brian D'Arcy, CP

In the spring of 2013, Pope Benedict XVI's resignation was the equivalent of an ecclesiastical earthquake. He was the first pope in six hundred years to resign and, one would have thought, the least likely to do so. Many of us were left in a state of shock; I personally spent some days in quiet prayer repenting for the despair I had felt, whilst hoping the guidance of the Holy Spirit would be welcomed.

When the conclave for the election of a new pope was convened I was asked by a BBC current affairs presenter to put in ordinary language the kind of pope I'd like to see replacing Benedict. I first explained that Benedict was badly served by those closest to him, especially those who claimed to know his mind and who claimed to speak on his behalf. I don't remember much else of what I said but I do recall my conclusion: 'I would like the new pope to be a man who inhabits the same world as I do.'

For a decade or so beforehand I was convinced that the Jesus I had come to know in the gospels was absent from many of the pronouncements made by the then leadership of the Catholic Church. I concluded that the leadership of the Church, and most especially the leadership in Rome, did not live in the real world and therefore could never adequately communicate the saving message of Jesus to the peoples of the modern world. Neither was I convinced that a new pope would be radically different from Blessed John Paul II or Benedict XVI. The entire College of Cardinals was carefully chosen by those popes because they were compliant and safe. It would be impossible for them to choose a pope radically different from what had gone before. Once again I was wrong.

On 13 March 2013, Jorge Mario Bergoglio became the 265th successor of St Peter. He was the first ever Jesuit to be elected pope and he was the first pope to take the name Francis. From the moment he stepped onto the balcony asking for prayers it was clear that this pope was different. By taking the name Francis he was making the poor, as well as simple living, central to his mission. Almost instantly the atmosphere in the Church changed. It seemed that not only the cardinals who elected him were filled with the Holy Spirit, but many of us relived, in part at least, the excitement of the Pope John XXIII moment in the early 1960s – a light dispelling the darkness and heralding a new springtime for believers in a new world. 'And now let us begin this journey, the Bishop and the people, this journey of the Church of Rome which presides in charity over all the Churches, a journey of brotherhood in love, of mutual trust', the newly-elected Francis began.[1] Since then there is a palpable sense of hope not only within the Catholic Church, but among other religions too, not to mention those of no religion at all. Pope Francis most certainly lives in the real world.

By coincidence, there is also a new leader of the Anglican Communion, the Archbishop of Canterbury, Justin Welby – himself a follower of Jesuit spirituality – who sings from the same hymnbook as Francis. He repeatedly refers to Catholic social teaching as the basis of morality, politics and economics.

Recently Chief Rabbi Ephraim Mirvis has been appointed in Britain. During his first *Pause for Thought* on BBC Radio 2, Chris Evans asked him what he would like to achieve in his first year as Chief Rabbi. His immediate answer was that he'd like to make the same impression as Pope Francis has done in his first year.

A rising tide lifts all boats and Francis, since coming to the barque of Peter, has raised our aspirations. I count myself among those who have discovered a reason to believe and a reason to be a committed priest again. It's all due to the new atmosphere the Pope has created within the Church in the first year of his leadership.

Without wanting to labour on an often told tale, three years ago I was informed by my superior in Ireland that he had received a letter from the Superior General of the Passionist Order in Rome, who in turn had received a letter from the Congregation for the Doctrine of the Faith (CDF) in the Vatican, commanding him to inform the Irish provincial that I was not to write or broadcast any material which had not first been approved by a reputable censor. When the superior

---

[1] From the first words spoken by Pope Francis, after his election, on the balcony of St Peter's Basilica, Rome.

asked me to meet him, making me aware that there was a serious matter to discuss, the first thought that came to me was that somebody had made a false allegation of abuse against me. Obviously I knew it had to be false but, as I drove to meet my superior, I have never felt more deflated and disappointed in my entire life.

When he read the letter from the CDF to me, first there was a sense of relief that it was only the CDF who was complaining – and not a false allegation. However, I soon realised that this attempt to censor me was deadly serious; the CDF clearly warned me that failure to comply could lead to excommunication from the Church. The initial relief soon turned to anger and my initial reaction was to leave the priesthood so that I could keep on writing. That was the only choice available to me because I knew I had to continue speaking the truth. The accusation that I was causing scandal among the faithful was nonsensical. The faithful were being scandalised, not by me, but by the leadership that was now trying to 'silence' me. For almost two years I sank into a deep depression. I lost confidence in the Church to which I had given my life. Thankfully, though, I never lost faith in a merciful God.

As a human being I felt devastated. I fell apart, losing confidence in my own ability to communicate in a compassionate, merciful and hopeful manner. Underlying all this was a deep, unhealthy suspicion. I knew I had been reported to Rome by someone within the Irish Church scene because I recognised the phrases used in the letter. The fact that clerical colleagues had been responsible for persuading Rome that my writings in the *Sunday World* newspaper were causing grave scandal was not only incredible but hurt me deeply. It was done maliciously because any sensible person would realise that the opinions I expressed were in fact what about eighty per cent of the people, including many priests, were saying in private. The whole process was hypocritical in the extreme; surely Rome ought to have something better to do than try to suppress valid criticism of the way some Church leaders had hijacked the Gospel message of mercy and love and replaced it with lifeless precepts from canon law.

At this point I firmly believed that not even the Holy Spirit could save the Church; I endured many sleepless nights planning how best I could keep on communicating the central messages I believed in, from outside the priesthood. The choice was becoming clear to me: if I remained a priest I could not remain true to myself or to my vocation as a communicator of Gospel values. I tried to live with the confusion for some months but when I was the subject of an hour-long television documentary on the BBC, I realised that I could no longer co-operate with my own destruction. It was up to me to reclaim my own life and my own freedom. That's where I was when I went into hospital for an operation early in 2013.

Whilst recuperating from the operation, out of the ether news came that Pope Benedict had resigned. It's no exaggeration to say that at the beginning of 2013 the Catholic Church was a hostile place for many of us to live in. The institutional Church, as represented by Rome, had succeeded in stifling dialogue, initiative and, worst of all, hope. Personally I felt a complete stranger in the Church to which I had given my life. That's why I admire Pope Benedict's decision to resign. It was due to the power of the Spirit that he did so. Being co-operative to the promptings of God's Spirit is the mark of true holiness.

That someone like Pope Francis could be elected as his successor is another spiritual miracle of enormous proportions. Immediately it became clear that his model of Church was vastly different from Benedict's. The development of people's gifts is more important than man-made rules. He has a clear vision about the need to reform an obviously dysfunctional Church bureaucracy. He has named clericalism and careerism as parts of the problem and not parts of the solution. He has, by word and action, clarified the mandate given to him by the other cardinals during the conclave. Two sources help us to determine his clear philosophy – his interview with the Jesuit publications and his apostolic exhortation, *Evangelii Gaudium*.[2]

If anything, the shock waves created by the interview Pope Francis gave to the Jesuit magazines are growing in intensity as the months pass. Despite the protestations of the extreme right, it is clear that Pope Francis is determined to have a different style and a more compassionate Church than what went before. In the interviews, he insisted that those who drag the Church back in time are wrong and must be resisted.

Secondly, he wants a Church which *lives* the values of the Gospel of Christ. Mere words are not enough. Thirdly he contends that the

---

[2] Pope Francis, *Evangelii Gaudium* (The Joy of the Gospel), Apostolic Exhortation on the Proclamation of the Gospel in Today's World, 2013. Subsequent references will be denoted by *EG*, followed by the paragraph number(s).

members of the conservative College of Cardinals, who gathered at the conclave in March 2013, gave him a mandate to purge the Church of careerist clerics, corrupt institutions and the cynical politics which worked furiously against the Holy Spirit to undo the principles of the Second Vatican Council.

Most of all, he wishes to proclaim the primacy of the Gospel with its core message that Jesus Christ died to save everyone and not just a select few. Pope Francis began by admitting that he himself is a sinner in need of redemption. 'I am a sinner whom the Lord has looked upon',[3] he said. This has remained a constant theme of his. 'He who does not sin is not human … we need to recognise our weakness',[4] he told religious superiors recently. 'My style of government as a Jesuit at the beginning had many faults,' he admits. 'I made my decisions abruptly and by myself. My authoritarian and quick manner of making decisions led me to have serious problems and to be accused of being ultra-conservative.'

But Pope Francis learned from his failures, as all of us should. Learning from past mistakes is a necessary part of a healthy spiritual journey. So, too, is believing oneself to be a sinner embraced by God's love. As Pope, discernment will be central to his governance. He believes what Blessed John XXIII said: 'See everything; turn a blind eye to much; correct a little.'

For the Pope discernment cannot be rushed:

> Many think that changes and reforms can take place in a short time. I believe that we always need time to lay the foundation for real effective change and this is the time for discernment. Discernment is always done in the presence of the Lord, looking at the signs, listening to the things that happen, and to the feelings of the people, especially the poor.

There will be no rash judgements, no quick changes. It's a wise policy and shows that the Pope is sincere. Doubt is also part of the spiritual life:

---

[3]   From Pope Francis' interview with Antonio Spadaro, SJ, published in *America*, September 2013. The quotations following, below, are, unless otherwise indicated, taken from this interview.

[4]   Pope Francis speaking to leaders of male religious orders on 29 November 2013 in the Vatican.

> If a person says that he met God with total certainty and is not touched by a margin of uncertainty, then that is not good ... If one has answers to all the questions – that is the proof that God is not with him. It means that he is a false prophet using religion for himself.

The Pope's image of the Church is that 'of a holy, faithful People of God. The Church is the People of God on a journey through history with joys and sorrows'. He goes on to re-emphasise what was a particular theme of the Second Vatican Council, namely,

> all the faithful, considered as a whole, are infallible in matters of belief ... this infallibility in believing, through a supernatural sense of the faith of all the people walking together, is genuine and is assisted by the Holy Spirit ... we should not even think therefore that 'thinking with the Church' means only thinking with the hierarchy of the Church.

Pope Francis believes that if the Church doesn't change it will collapse like a house of cards. Perhaps he held back from stating the obvious – that it has already collapsed in the sense that it has failed the very people whose faith kept it going.

The Pope is obviously a man who believes that we can all be 'surprised by the Spirit'. The Francis factor is changing the perception of the Church. People are attracted by his openness, his simplicity and the depth of his spirituality. Explaining the central message of Christmas in a recent interview he said: 'When God meets us he tells us ... [h]ave hope. God always opens doors. He never closes them ... when Christians forget about hope and tenderness they become a cold Church.'[5]

The message of the Gospel is proclaimed in the easy-to-read apostolic exhortation *Evangelii Gaudium* (*EG*), for the most part written by the Pope himself. He was helped by Victor Manuel Fernandez, the rector of Argentina's pontifical university whose appointment, coincidentally, the Roman Curia had earlier tried to block.

One of the most helpful themes in *Evangelii Gaudium* is that of pilgrimage. 'We must never forget we are pilgrims journeying alongside one another' (*EG*, n. 244), he writes. A pilgrim, he points out, begins with inner discernment by acknowledging his/her own imperfections in resolving to follow Christ on his way of the cross,

---

5   From an interview with Pope Francis on 10 December 2013 in the Vatican.

thereby serving the world in great need of the message of resurrection through suffering.

The Pope mentions the theme of pilgrimage thirteen times in *Evangelii Gaudium*. This is a reflection of what the Second Vatican Council said in *Gaudium et Spes* that no one is excluded from the joy of the Lord. 'The dignity of the human person and the common good rank higher than the comfort of those who refuse to renounce their privileges' (*EG*, n. 218), he writes.

Pope Francis seems to align himself with Pope John XXIII when he takes on the prophets of doom within the Church. At the opening of the Second Vatican Council in 1962, Pope John experienced massive opposition from within the Roman Curia. In his opening address he didn't spare them. 'In the daily exercise of our Pastoral Office we sometimes have to listen, much to our regret, to the voices of persons who, though burning with zeal, are not endowed with too much discretion or measure',[6] Pope John said. He referred to the Curia officials as prophets of gloom always forecasting disasters instead of helping people 'to look to the future without fear'. 'Positive faith is one thing ... the way it is expressed is another',[7] he added.

The Magisterium's role is to make the faith known in a reasonable way for each new generation. More significantly this teaching must be 'predominately pastoral in care'. Pope John said that, since we are human, errors will come and go 'like the fog before the sun'. Rather than oppose error with severity, 'the Church prefers to make use of the medicine of mercy rather than severity. She meets the needs of the present day by demonstrating the validity of a teaching rather than by condemnations'.[8] These words could have come from Francis himself as he wrestles with the same destructive forces. Indeed he highlights a similar theme when he quotes the Council's documents: 'Christ summons the Church as she goes her pilgrim way ... to that continual reformation of which she always has need, in so far as she is a human institution here on earth' (*Unitatis Redintegratio*, n. 6).

Like John XXIII, this pope recognises that with each succeeding culture, eternal truth must be preached in new and understandable ways, otherwise the Church becomes an onlooker while the faith gradually stagnates. This implies that an educated laity is an essential

---

[6]   From Pope John XXIII's opening address to the Second Vatican Council, on 11 October 1962.

[7]   *Ibid.*

[8]   *Ibid.*

part of saving our Church. It also shows that Francis is not so much a revolutionary pope but one who is faithful to the infallible teaching of the Second Vatican Council.

Whilst Pope Francis is vehemently opposed to abortion, he acknowledges that we 'have done little to accompany women adequately in very difficult situations where abortion appears as a quick solution to their profound anguish, especially when the life developing within them is a result of rape or a situation of extreme poverty', as he stated in his interview in *America*.

He recognises that, if decision-making is left to clergy alone, their proposals will be largely ignored. This much at least is clear from the way the scandals of the clerical abuse of children were mishandled and which strangle the Church to this day. For too many years Church leaders uttered meaningless pious platitudes which were, in effect, an insult to concerned parents everywhere. It quickly became clear that the Church leadership was speaking with a forked tongue. No matter how sincere the platitudes and promises appeared to be, in reality the preservation of the institutional Church was considered to be a higher priority than the protection of children.

I once received a threatening letter from a senior bishop when I suggested that we clerics were incapable of coming up with a credible solution to the child sex abuse crisis. I proposed that it is absolutely necessary to involve responsible lay people in decision-making and supervision if we are to be credible. For over a decade Church leaders in Ireland arrogantly presumed that they, and they alone, had the necessary answers. This proved to be a disastrous strategy which did irreparable damage to the Catholic Church. It was only when the laity, and especially women, were allowed to design and supervise child protection policies that progress was made. This shows us how important it is to involve the laity in the Church's future. The Pope understands that risks need to be taken for the good of the Gospel message: 'I prefer a Church which is bruised, hurting and dirty because it has been out on the streets, rather than a Church which is unhealthy from being confined and from clinging to its own security' (*EG*, n. 49).

Church governance is another major area that Pope Francis will have to reform. An essential part of that reform will be engaging the laity, and especially women, at the very heart of decision-making. The Pope has told priests and bishops that they themselves must come as pilgrims on this journey of discovery. According to Francis, Ignatian spirituality holds that 'whosoever accompanies a pilgrim … should go at the pilgrim's pace, neither too far in front nor too far behind'.

At the root of reform within the Church will be collegial governance and collaborative ministry. As Mary McAleese has argued so cogently in her book *Quo Vadis? Collegiality in the Code of Canon Law*,[9] Vatican II embraced a fresh vision of the Church as the People of God and turned away from a rigid hierarchical structure. It saw the Church as a community. Unfortunately though, it left no clear structure or practical plan as to how this should be carried on. The result has been that collegiality has never been tried.

If the structures of the Roman Curia are to be adequately reformed, Pope Francis will have to outline an effective form of collegial governance which will listen to, and be guided by, the inspired voices of the laity, acknowledging that the faithful enjoy the power of the Holy Spirit in their yearnings too. Once again in *Evangelii Gaudium*, Pope Francis recalls that the People of God 'is holy, thanks to this anointing of the [Holy Spirit] which makes it infallible *in credendo*' (*EG*, n. 119). The People of God do not err in faith, even though they may not have adequate words to explain that faith.

Ultimately, the Francis affect will be judged on how radically he reforms the governance of the Church. A constant theme of reports into clerical sex abuse across the world has been that there is a systemic failure within the Church, thereby making it incapable of hearing what the people want or need.

Reform of the papacy is but one necessary step in reform of the Church's governance. As we know, civil servants are blessed with great patience. The Roman Curia knows that the Pope is an old man and that if they can wait for a few years they'll still be in place when he dies (or retires) and will ensure that the next pope will be more easily manipulated. Without proper structural reform all the good work of Pope Francis will be buried with him.

Finally, as part of that reform the Pope will need to explain more fully what the term 'Church teaching' actually means. There has been a long-simmering tension within the Church of 'creeping infallibility'. In recent years issues that have never been defined as infallible are in fact now being proposed as infallible teaching.

9   Mary McAleese, *Quo Vadis? Collegiality in the Code of Canon Law* (Dublin: The Columba Press, 2012).

The First Vatican Council (1869–70) formerly defined papal infallibility in 1870 and most experts agree that it has been clearly invoked with the proclamation of only two dogmas – both about Mary: the Immaculate Conception, in 1854, and the Assumption, in 1950. In this context, some theologians argue that, in other matters, which have never been formally proclaimed as infallible, for example, the ordination of women, *Humane Vitae* and Catholic teaching on homosexuality, continued discussion of them remains legitimate.

The debate has been going on since the 1980s when Charles Curran, an American priest and moral theologian, was fired by the Catholic University of America in Washington after being investigated by the CDF, at that time headed by Cardinal Ratzinger. Curran defended the right of dissent from what he called 'authoritative non-infallible hierarchical teaching'.

The most frequent cause of alleged theological dissent is the debate surrounding the ordination of women. Pope Francis, it appears, agrees with his predecessors Benedict XVI and John Paul II that it is infallible teaching that women cannot be ordained. Yet the Canon Law Society of Great Britain and Ireland, as well as the Catholic Theological Society of America, in the late 1990s concluded that the teaching concerning the impossibility of women priests was not infallible.

The Pope, listening to his advisors and to theologians from around the world, needs to offer clearer guidelines as to what topics are open to discussion and what topics are not. It seems to me that this is a necessary clarification to allow a healthy, free exchange of views on serious contentious matters. Showing women respect and acknowledging their enormous contribution to the life of the Church will be one of his most crucial tasks in the immediate future. Women are holding this fragile structure together – just about.

Without doubt, Pope Francis has made a huge, refreshing difference to the Catholic Church in a short time. The task ahead is difficult but he is so obviously being guided by the Holy Spirit that we must presume that God will continue to inspire him and strengthen him for the journey ahead. During these difficult times he will need our constant prayers and he himself will need to pray sincerely, as St Ignatius of Loyola – the founder of the Jesuits – did:

Teach us, Good Lord, to serve Thee as Thou deservest;
To give and not to count the cost,
To fight and not to heed the wounds,
To toil and not to seek for rest,
To labour and not to ask for any reward,
Save that of knowing that we do Thy will.

Pope Francis:
A Pastor Bearing Witness

Louise Fuller

When Pope Benedict announced his resignation in February 2013, one sensed that this was a momentous occasion in the life of the Catholic Church. He explained to the stunned cardinals in attendance that he no longer had the strength of mind or body to lead in the face of the multiple challenges facing the Church in the world today. His decision was revolutionary – a pope had not resigned since 1415. So history was being made and this was only the beginning. The conclave was convoked, bishops assembled from all over the world and the press and cognoscenti began the usual naming of cardinals who were seen as *papabile*. When the traditional *'Habemus Papam'* ('We have a Pope') was announced from the balcony of St Peter's on 13 March 2013, the name of Jorge Mario Bergoglio had hardly been mentioned, though it has emerged from many commentators since that he was second choice in 2005.

From the moment Francis emerged on the balcony overlooking St Peter's Square, there was a sense that this pope was going to be different, that a new chapter in Church history had begun. He wore the traditional white cassock, but without the red velvet mozzetta and instead of a jewel-studded gold pectoral cross, kept to the simple metal cross he had worn since he became bishop of Buenos Aires. He appeared somewhat overwhelmed and addressed the crowd informally with a simple *'Buona sera'*. Already the symbolism was in stark contrast to previous popes and this was not lost on the crowds in the Square, or the millions watching on television. He set a new tone for the papacy from the very outset and continued in this vein – dispensing with the papal limousine after the conclave, going to the hotel to pay his bill the following day, and, most notably, by his decision not to live in the papal apartments, but rather as part of the Casa Santa Marta community. Thus with his warmth and friendliness he captivated not only the Catholic faithful, but also the media, and became a celebrity overnight.

In the contemporary world obsessed with celebrity and hungry for role models, it is no surprise that his simplicity, humility and ordinariness impressed. And while one could be cynical and question whether this is just optics – the fact is that how he has acted as pope since his election is entirely in keeping with his lifestyle as bishop since 1992. And in some ways one might wonder why this way of life should be unusual at all for a bishop, or indeed a pope, who should, when all is said and done, be *the* role model for a follower of Jesus Christ, born in a stable, whose step-father was a carpenter. There has been much criticism over the centuries of the grandeur and luxury of Rome and questioning of whether this is really how Jesus would have meant the Church to witness to his life and words.

That we find his approach so uplifting says a lot about the man, and even more about ourselves because (and this is not intended to take from Pope Francis in any way) there is nothing new here. In every word, gesture and action he is simply echoing and living out the Gospel message: 'Love others as I have loved you'; 'Blessed be the poor in spirit'; 'Judge not and you shall not be judged', and one could go on. This is not rocket science, so why are we so entranced? Precisely because this is a new paradigm. Ideals will always be attractive and even more so in a world that increasingly focuses on success, status, glamour and material wealth as indicators of a person's worthwhileness. This man is preaching back-to-basics Christianity and our obligation as Christians to protect the most vulnerable in society. In the present day, witness such as this is truly countercultural, but for a pope, surely it is a case of doing his job properly? And while one does not doubt his spontaneity, it is very obvious that this pope, in terms of his manner, choice of name and lifestyle, is deliberately setting a new tone for his followers.

He is media savvy, a consummate communicator, who instinctively knows that it is first necessary to capture people's hearts. Then they just might follow the values that you 'propose', the word he repeatedly uses to describe his teaching style. He knows the importance of language. We live in a world where the medium has increasingly become the message. Appearances are (seen as) important and his approach is already gaining him a hearing. As he takes up his leadership role, he is all too aware that the Catholic Church is in crisis: religious practice in western Europe has plummeted, sex abuse scandals, banking scandals and the Vatileaks debacle have all revealed deep fault lines, if not dysfunctionality at the heart of the Vatican, and in Latin America, his own backyard, the evangelical movement has steadily been making inroads on Catholic congregations. From the outset one gets the sense that he is a man with a mission. But the challenge is enormous. Is this man of advancing years equal to the task? Does he have the mental and physical strength to set the necessary reforms in train?

It is fifty years on from the Second Vatican Council. In the face of increasing secularisation, Pope John XXIII convened the Council so that the Church could update its teaching and structures to respond to the many social and cultural changes which had taken place since the turn of the nineteenth century. In his opening speech to the Council Fathers, John XXIII signalled his rejection of the siege mentality which had characterised the Church since the Council of Trent and stressed the importance of the Church's engaging with the modern secular world. He made a distinction between 'the substance of the ancient doctrine of the deposit of faith', which could not be changed, and its presentation, which had to be updated to make it more responsive to the changing times. While these were the goals, they have never been delivered. The collegial horizontal model of Church proposed by the Council was hijacked from the outset by conservative elements in the Curia, who stymied the implementation of the Council decrees, and the Church has become more and more centralised in Rome to the detriment of the local church and the office of bishop. The vision of Church as the 'People of God' has scarcely been realised.

The general verdict of many committed Church people, clerical and lay, is that the Vatican Council provided a blueprint for change which, if it had been implemented, would have saved the Church from the sorry state it finds itself in today. It was a missed opportunity and disillusionment has increasingly set in. In 1960s Ireland, the Catholic Church was embedded in the culture;[1] for many Catholics now it has become, at best, irrelevant to their lives. At the time of the

---

[1]   Louise Fuller, *Irish Catholicism since 1950: The Undoing of a Culture* (Dublin: Gill and Macmillan, 2002).

Council, weekly Mass attendance was practically universal; a recent survey recorded it at about thirty-five per cent.[2] While eighty-four per cent of Irish people still profess to be Catholic,[3] surveys have shown that when it comes to their private lives, they increasingly ignore the moral teachings of the Church. So how does the Church deal with a situation whereby many of its members find much of its teaching irrelevant? Pope Francis has injected much needed hope, but is it humanly possible to fulfil the multiple expectations that he has raised?

The fact that Francis in his style, utterances and approach echoes John XXIII represents a very hopeful sign for many. What comes across forcefully is his spontaneity, humility, warmth of personality and humanity. Perhaps his greatest asset in terms of leadership is, in fact, his humanity. The clerical sex abuse scandals have cast a dark shadow over the pontificates of his predecessors John Paul II and Benedict XVI. The Church was never in more need of humility and atonement for its sins, and for not practising what it preaches, to restore its moral credibility. The days are long gone when the Church can preach down to anyone. Pope Francis repeatedly attests to his own sinfulness, to having made mistakes, to being in need of mercy and forgiveness. In an interview with two Argentinian journalists three years before he became pope, he told them: 'I don't want to mislead anyone – the truth is that I'm a sinner ... I had to learn from my errors along the way ... I made hundreds of errors ... Today I ask forgiveness ...'[4] He has the common touch, comes across as someone who has had his own inner struggles and who has learned from his experiences. So who is this man and what has helped define him?

He was Provincial of the Jesuits in Argentina from 1973 to 1979. In the 1970s theologians in Latin America were developing their own indigenous theology of liberation, focusing on the fact that poverty was not God-given, but caused by unjust economic and political policies. This had a profound impact on religious working among the poor and oppressed, not least Jesuits. The Church establishment was wary of liberation theology, seeing in it elements of Marxist revolutionary theory. Bergoglio shared this wariness, pointing out in

---

2   *Contemporary Catholic Perspectives*, survey carried out by Amárach, commissioned by the Association of Catholic Priests, February 2012, p. 7.
3   *Census of Population of Ireland*, 2011.
4   Sergio Rubin and Francesca Ambrogetti, *Pope Francis: Conversations with Jorge Bergoglio* (London: Hodder and Stoughton, 2013), pp. 46–7.

his conversations with Skorka that during the 1970s 'social engage-ment flourished' and that priests in some cases 'fell into the trap of becoming ideological'.[5]

His caution was understandable. 1976 to 1983 was a period of military dictatorship in Argentina and citizens could be simply rounded up and 'disappeared', if they were seen as a threat to the regime. In this political climate, priests helping the poor to analyse their situation could be deemed to be subversives. During his tenure of office, two of his priests working in the slums were kidnapped and held for five months and he had to answer allegations as to whether his disciplining of them had facilitated their abduction and incarceration. This tragic event against the background of a volatile political situation and divisions among the Jesuits and in the broader Church on the best approach to tackling poverty and injustice, gave rise to a highly-charged and polarised atmosphere, making Bergoglio's position increasingly difficult. In 1986 he was posted to Córdoba, where it would appear he underwent his own dark night of the soul.

Referring to that troubled period in an interview with Antonio Spadaro, SJ, he confessed that his 'authoritarian way of making decisions … created problems',[6] and revealed that he 'lived a time of great interior crisis when [he] was in Córdoba'.[7] When he returned to Buenos Aires as auxiliary bishop in 1992, he had undergone a transformation.[8] He had always been committed to the poor; he now renewed this commitment, increasingly focusing attention on the slums. When in the very first days of his papacy, he called a media press conference, another unprecedented move, and announced that the theme for his papacy would be 'a poor Church, for the poor', this was entirely in keeping with his priorities and lifestyle as bishop. And while he may have been wary of aspects of liberation theology in the past, there is no doubt now that he sees poverty and inequality as built into the very structures of society. In his first apostolic exhortation, *Evangelii Gaudium*, he points to 'the need to resolve the structural

---

5   Jorge Mario Bergoglio and Abraham Skorka, *On Heaven and Earth: Pope Francis on Faith, Family and the Church in the Twenty-First Century* (London: Bloomsbury, 2013), p. 206.

6   Antonio Spadaro, SJ, 'The Heart of a Jesuit Pope: Interview with Pope Francis', in *Studies*, 102:407 (Autumn 2013), p. 262.

7   *Ibid.*

8   Paul Vallely, *Pope Francis: Untying the Knots* (London: Bloomsbury, 2013), pp. 192–5.

causes of poverty',[9] that we can no longer trust 'the invisible hand of the market' (*EG*, n. 204). He seeks to help those 'in thrall to an individualistic, indifferent and self-centred mentality' (*EG*, n. 208). 'The current model', he points out, 'does not appear to favour an investment in efforts to help the slow, the weak or the less talented to find opportunities in life' (*EG*, n. 209). His election has meant that the Church's centre of gravity has shifted and it is entirely understandable that his first priority should be the immediate and more pressing problems of poverty, inequality and injustice, which are endemic in the Third World, but of course by no means confined to it.

He is very aware, however, that he is Pope for the whole of humanity and in the more affluent west perhaps the single greatest problem Francis faces is that the Church's moral teachings, particularly in the area of sexuality, have become problematic for increasing numbers of the faithful, and many simply ignore them. The question as to whether the Church can, or should, adapt its teachings to keep pace with modern developments is far more urgent now than fifty years ago, and is not easily resolved. The new Pope's interviews and his off-the-cuff remarks and homilies have raised expectations at many levels of Catholic life that the Church may rethink its approach to certain matters of conscience.

On some of the burning issues facing the Church at the present time, his position is clear, but nuanced. On divorce he points out that the Church always condemns divorce, but today while divorced persons who remarry live 'on the margin of what indissolubility of marriage and the sacrament of marriage require of them … they are asked to integrate into the parish life'.[10] On the issue of priestly celibacy it is a matter of 'discipline, not of faith', so 'it can be changed', but 'for the time being', he is 'in favour of maintaining celibacy'.[11] On same-sex marriage, his opinion is that giving it the same status as marriage between man and woman would be 'an anti-value and an anthropological regression'.[12] On the issue of women and ordination, he explains: 'in the theologically grounded tradition the priesthood

---

[9] Pope Francis, *Evangelii Gaudium* (The Joy of the Gospel), Apostolic Exhortation on the Proclamation of the Gospel in Today's World, 2013, n. 202. Subsequent references will be denoted by *EG*, followed by the paragraph number.

[10] Bergoglio and Skorka, *On Heaven and Earth*, p. 110.

[11] *Ibid.*, pp. 48–9.

[12] *Ibid.*, pp. 116–17.

passes through man'.[13] Of all the areas that he has ventured into yet, his reflections on women have been seen to be weakest and given that half the human race is female, as Cardinal Suenens observed at Vatican II,[14] this is probably the most dangerous banana skin of all for the new pope. He is known to be conservative on these issues, declares himself to be 'a son of the Church', but points out at the same time that the Church's whole attention cannot be on such matters. He is more than aware of the perennial dilemma for the Church: it must keep up with modern developments, keep relevant to people's lives, while at the same time remaining true to the 'received inheritance', which he has emphasised is 'not negotiable'.[15] It is a delicate balancing act, but he knows what is at stake if the Church cannot get it right; in his own words, 'the moral edifice of the Church is likely to fall like a house of cards'.[16]

So the question arises to what extent can the Church revise what it has hitherto regarded as fundamental teachings? The answer is that it probably cannot, but what it can do is to rethink the presentation. This was proposed at Vatican II, but for the most part never realised, or perhaps never preached. From what he has said and written so far, it appears that he is, in his own way, taking up this challenge and the words he uses are pertinent. Firstly, he makes it clear that he wishes to 'propose' a way of life and values, but he does not impose. At the beginning of *Evangelii Gaudium*, he states that he does not believe 'that the papal magisterium should be expected to offer a definitive or complete word on every question which affects the Church and the world' (*EG*, n. 16). When the Church sets out its teaching it is the responsibility of local ministers to guide the faithful. Elsewhere, he is very clear on where this role begins and ends. He explains:

> The religious minister, at times, draws attention to certain points of private or public life because he is the parishioners' guide. However, he does not have the right to force anything on anyone's private life. If God, in creation, ran the risk of making us free, who am I to get involved? ... God left the freedom to sin in our hands. One has to speak very clearly about values, limits, commandments, but spiritual and pastoral harassment is not allowed.[17]

---

13 *Ibid.*, p. 102.
14 John W. O'Malley, *What happened at Vatican II* (Cambridge: Harvard University Press, 2008), p. 187.
15 Bergoglio and Skorka, *On Heaven and Earth*, p. 25.
16 Spadaro, *Studies*, pp. 266–8.
17 Bergoglio and Skorka, *On Heaven and Earth*, p. 114.

Essentially he is saying that ultimately people have responsibility for their own lives and salvation. There is nothing new here of course, but it is a different approach. The fact that there are grey areas in moral theology was not impressed enough in the past. When Spadaro probes him about 'the way human beings are reinterpreting themselves', he allows that 'the thinking of the Church must … better understand how human beings understand themselves today, in order to develop and deepen the church's teaching',[18] but during the interview he is quite happy to admit that he does not have all the answers, and makes it clear also that he can live with doubt.[19] He often points to the importance of 'discernment'; at times he appears to be thinking out loud. He is critical of 'those who today always look for disciplinarian solutions, those who long for an exaggerated doctrinal "security", those who stubbornly try to recover a past that no longer exists …'[20]

What comes across clearly in the course of the interview is his conviction that 'God is in every person's life',[21] that he is always merciful, that people have to be dealt with in the context of their own lives and that nobody, not even the pope himself, has the right to judge anybody. In *Evangelii Gaudium*, he points out that 'there is a place for everyone' in the Church 'with all their problems' (*EG*, n. 47). Indeed he could not be plainer. And perhaps that is as far as he can, or will go. In a sense he is steering Catholics away from the dogmatism and legalism of the past and the old-time religion and proposing a more nuanced approach to morality. It is a long way from the penny catechism black-and-white answers. We are entirely free to discern our path and ultimately God – and God alone – will be the judge. Perhaps this is *aggiornamento*, the updating of presentation that John XXIII spoke about at Vatican II?

Pope Francis is challenging Catholics to adopt a more independent, responsible attitude towards morality and religion, but it goes without saying that he cannot do it all. Structural and organisational changes which would bring about a more democratic, participative Church at every level are needed to realise his vision. The pastoral role of bishop is obviously crucial. Concern has been voiced over a long number of years that the centralisation of power in Rome has undermined the autonomy of the bishop in his local area and furthermore that

---

18   Spadaro, *Studies*, pp. 276–8.
19   *Ibid.*, pp. 271–2.
20   *Ibid.*, p. 272.
21   *Ibid.*, p. 273.

overemphasis on loyalty to Rome and orthodoxy of views has prevented the appointment of bishops who can provide the kind of prophetic leadership needed at a time when the Church is facing many challenges.[22]

In all of his discourses, Francis has shown himself to be in favour of a more dialogical, collegial Church. From the outset he has presented himself as Bishop of Rome, and addressed his fellow cardinals as 'brothers'. He does not see power as concentrated in the centre. He has stated clearly that 'it is not advisable for the Pope to take the place of local bishops in the discernment of every issue which arises in their territory' (*EG*, n. 16). In his interview with Spadaro, he recalls the Vatican II vision of Church as the 'People of God', in which all members – pope, bishops, laity and theologians – play their respective roles in discerning the signs of the times. Indeed he conceptualises infallibility along these lines,[23] which if it were to be implemented has revolutionary implications, because he emphasises that he does not mean 'token consultations', but rather a role for the broader Church in decision-making. His early appointment of a representative group of eight cardinals to advise him on the running of the Church shows that he means business. Cardinal Maradiaga, the co-ordinator of this group has announced plans for reform of the Curia and the Synod of Bishops and also favours a new Congregation for the Laity. These are among a number of significant changes that hold out hope of a more democratic style of governance for the Church.

But organisational reforms, Francis has pointed out, are 'secondary'; he is aiming for a more fundamental reform of 'attitude'.[24] He has challenged bishops and clergy to move outside their comfort zone to draw in the poor, the marginalised and the alienated, and he is leading by example. He is not afraid of the modern world. He is happy to meet the press and answer questions – a risky strategy which many churchmen avoid, but he is undaunted by fears of misinterpretation. Echoing John XXIII's opening speech at the Council, when he dismissed 'the prophets of doom', Francis writes that every period is marked by human weakness and urges his readers: 'let us not say … that things are harder today; they are simply different' (*EG*, n. 263).

---

22   See Fuller, *Irish Catholicism since 1950*, pp. 261–2.
23   Spadaro, *Studies*, pp. 262–4.
24   *Ibid.*, p. 266.

That said, he realises that the challenges facing the Church have become ever more complex since the early 1960s and he obviously shares many of the reservations of his predecessors in relation to developments in modern life. But he is meeting challenges head-on. Of course, he would like to change the world, but he is a realist – and again has identified with John XXIII's approach and motto: 'See everything; turn a blind eye to much; correct a little.'[25] There is a wealth of homely wisdom here about striking the right balance. The Church has not always managed this in the past. And perhaps we too need to temper our expectations. Can Pope Francis steer the People of God in new directions? Clearly, just one year on, it is far too soon to say. We shall have to wait and see, but there are many hopeful signs.

---

[25] Spadaro, *Studies*, p. 258.

Finally Comes the Mystic

Daniel O'Leary

'When I saw him walk out through those prison gates on Robben Island', a young man with shining eyes declared on television after Nelson Mandela's funeral, 'the deepest experience of a personal freedom surged through my heart.' Listening to the young man speak, you just knew that his life had radically changed. Something precious had been unlocked in the core of his being and he would never forget.

We notice the same kind of phenomenon with regard to the presence of Pope Francis among us. Seemingly effortlessly, he has reached into countless hearts and unlocked their blocked capacity for dreaming the possible, for seeing imaginatively. And once the first blindfold is removed, the rest follows. This chapter celebrates the recovery of their mystical essence for the human heart and for the Church.

Beyond anything the Pope may or may not achieve by way of structural reforms and rebuilding, this breath of inner freedom has already happened for innumerable seekers in the most profound regions of their souls. The veil has been lifted, the hunches of their hearts have been validated, their prophetic and mystical voices restored.

Every day that passes, Pope Francis is shifting the focus from the outside to the inside, from the abstract general principle to the living breathing human being. People feel trusted now, a divine gift that enables them to trust themselves. It is difficult to describe that surge, that lurch of the heart, that liberation of the soul when such a realisation happens. In 'The Opening of Eyes', poet David Whyte writes:

> It is the opening of eyes long closed.
> It is the vision of far off things
> seen for the silence they hold.

> It is the heart after years
> of secret conversing
> speaking out loud in the clear air.[1]

It may be once in a decade, or once in a lifetime that eyes are ready to open for this fragile recognition, this unrepeatable moment when something blurred comes into focus, when something vaguely known comes into sharp relief. An irreversible transformation takes place. And only transformed people transform others. Pope Francis talks like a man who, after much personal fear and anxiety, much personal distress and guilt, has found love, a wondrous love, a confident love, and wants nothing more than to share it.

Most of us, too, endure a hard apprenticeship for the giving and receiving of such revelatory moments – a painful darkness, the distress of being wrong, a lot of sins, maybe a winter of despair. The situation may seem hopeless, and then, one day, someone walks through our world and our souls come alive again, courage flows back into fearful hearts, eyes are opened and blink in the new light. Enter the mystic! A personal sense of something innately true emerges and people begin to see in a way they never saw before – but somehow suspected. It is something they have long waited for, something they were born for. Writer Maya Angelou has these lines in her 'On the Pulse of the Morning':

> You, created only a little lower than
> The angels, have crouched too long in
> The bruising darkness
> Have lain too long
> Face down in ignorance.[2]

The human spirit is diminished by constant constraint. There is a straitjacket that prevents creativity, self-expression and becoming. Fearful religion, with its brainwashing, its threats, and its self-obsession, isolates people from their own inner wisdom and authority. And then there is a moment in people's lives when, in this cellar of the sleeping soul, an awakening happens. At the most precious part of human nature a voice is heard, a finger beckons, a long-awaited dawn is breaking.

---

[1] David Whyte, *Songs for Coming Home* (Washington: Many Rivers Press, 1984), p. 22.

[2] Maya Angelou, *The Complete Collected Poems of Maya Angelou* (New York: Random House, 1993), p. 269.

From the rubble of clericalism and narcissism, from the confusion and frustrations of decades, new and liberating paradigms of possibility, like a long-awaited summer, begin to bless the people, the Church, the world. Whyte ends his poem with a description of people's astonishment at recognising the transcendent mystery in the solid realities of their lives.

> It is Moses in the desert
> fallen to his knees before the lit bush.
> It is the man throwing away his shoes
> as if to enter heaven
> and finding himself astonished,
> opened at last,
> fallen in love with solid ground.[3]

A whole other attractive space opens up for us, a way of seeing, of choosing, of being – an invitation to a radically renewed way of living the mystery. This is the work of the mystic. A compelling True North is calling us towards another horizon. Something within us, from the very beginning, is coded for this calling. There is a blueprint within us for recognising the inner truth of things, an imagination for finding the loving meaning at the heart of everything. Pope Francis describes this readiness as 'a deep yearning, an unconscious kind of heart-knowing about the truth of God, the truth about humanity' (*Evangelii Gaudium*).[4]

The new Pope's liberating vision, 'my one dogmatic certainty', is that every single person is the home of God, that all created reality is the place of revelation. He is teaching us to sense a holy presence in everyone and in everything. This aching awareness was surely visible, etched into the lines of his face as he tenderly wrapped his arms around the head of the man disfigured by neurofibromatosis, when he kissed the feet of a Muslim woman who had committed a crime. There was something beautiful, uncontrived, and deeply sacramental in these instinctive gestures.

Here was a man who believed in the sacred power of the senses, those human conduits of divine love. On the spur of the moment he trusted the truth of the Incarnational now. Mystics like Pope Francis

---

[3]   Whyte, p. 22.

[4]   Pope Francis, *Evangelii Gaudium* (The Joy of the Gospel), Apostolic Exhortation on the Proclamation of the Gospel in Today's World, 2013, n. 265. Subsequent references will be denoted by *EG*, followed by the paragraph number(s).

are great champions of raw, real human happening. In poetic expression, writers know that nothing can match the magic of authentic experience. In his 'Leaves of Grass' Walt Whitman believes that by writing 'in the gush, the throb, the flood of the moment, without deliberation or framing, the very heartbeat of life is caught'.

Poets and artists have kept alive the old and orthodox 'catholic imagination' that Pope Francis is making his own. It is this sacramental vision that distinguishes Catholic Christianity at its core – but it is a vision long forgotten, neglected and even denied. It is the water of life for people, the melody they were born to hear. In the light of Incarnation, the Pope perceives the mystical disclosure in everything, feels the human pulse of God's heart, adores the Real Presence in all that is really present. He looks, he sees, he recognises, he loves, he reaches out.

He knows that our spirit longs for the gift of seeing things truly, of recognising St Bonaventure's *vestigia Dei*, the traces, the signature, the finger- and footprints of God everywhere. Priest and scientist Teilhard de Chardin wrote that, 'by virtue of Creation, and still more of Incarnation, nothing here below is profane for those who know how to see'. This flash of recognition, the Pope explains, is not the fruit of doctrines, creeds, external rites. It is a contemplative gaze, the pure gift of the Holy Spirit. It cannot be merited, 'only freely experienced'. And usually in the most unexpected places – in his visits to the slum dwellers, in the sacrament of their conversations, in the Eucharist of their honest presence around a table sipping *mate* tea.

In *The Snow Geese*, Mary Oliver tells of the day she was captivated by the sight of a flock of geese, whose white wings, in the turning, caught, for an eternal instant, the reflected gold from the sinking sun:

> The geese flew on,
> I have never seen them again.
> Maybe I will, someday, somewhere.
> Maybe I won't.
> It doesn't matter.
> What matters
> is that, when I saw them,
> I saw them,
> as through the veil, secretly, joyfully, clearly.[5]

---

[5]   Mary Oliver, *Why I Wake Early* (Boston: Beacon Press, 2005), p. 34.

We must dig deep to understand that grace of how to see. Pope Francis had many a hard hour during which he acknowledged his sins, and painfully purified his motives. How did he cope with the accusations made against him of cowardice, of collusion with military atrocities, of supporting traditionalist clericalism, of being anti-Vatican II and the enemy of liberation theology? Or is it this very endurance of that winter of painful conversion, the crucifying embracing of those ambiguous episodes of his life, that are currently infusing the divine power into his human presence? He surely believes now, more than ever, that Incarnation is an invitation to find God in the midst, the mess and the mystery of his life; that there is no other way to learn humility than to experience the depth of things in the furnace of his soul.

A constant theme in all of Franciscan Richard Rohr's teachings is the gold to be found in the rubble of our lives. What makes a thing sacred or profane is precisely whether we live on the surface of things or not. This is what theologian Karl Rahner called 'the mysticism of ordinary life'. The divine is hidden but accessible in every authentic experience of despair, beauty and love. 'Whenever we encounter another person in love, we learn something new about God,' the Pope writes, 'it opens up spiritual horizons within us' (*EG*, n. 272). Holiness, he repeats, is not to be found in a religion of rituals and regulations but in the flesh and feelings of the world, in senses and experiences, in excitement and disappointment, in real well-being and real tragedy, in moments of paralysing fear and of blessed courage, in living more passionately, more respectfully, more mystically. It is experienced, the Pope writes, 'in a mystical community, a contemplative one' (*EG*, n. 92), where we 'remove our sandals before the sacred ground of the other' (*EG*, n. 169).

That is the vision that drives our Pope. He has absorbed that whole revelation. He believes it and he has become it. 'This way is not an extra add-on to my life,' he said, 'it is something I cannot uproot from my being without destroying my very self' (*EG*, n. 273). He has identified with the mind of Christ, trying to see with the eyes of God. It is against this spiritual imagination of incarnate divinity that he will continue to approach the huge and challenging issues awaiting him – the needs of the poor, the reform of the Curia, the pain of divorced people, the plight of jobless young people, the neglected elderly, the inclusion of women at every level, debates around homosexuality, abortion, euthanasia, same-sex marriage, financial and other scandals in the Vatican, ecumenical issues at many fragile levels. In all of the extremely daunting complexities that await him, including the vexed questions of authority, collegiality and subsidiarity, his guiding star will always be the one that once hovered in the sky over Bethlehem – the redeeming revelation of Incarnation.

Pope Francis' contemplative vision and action spring from that understanding – the mystery of the fullness of God in the poverty, contrariness and sinfulness of humanity. Everything he says and does, whether he refers to it or not, is infused with that revelation. For instance, when asked 'What is holiness?', his immediate reply shows his desire to 'touch human misery, touch the suffering flesh of others, entering into the reality of other people's lives through the power of tenderness' (*EG*, n. 271). He did not dwell on the usual 'marks' of a Catholic or of 'the one true Church'. He spoke of the patience of people, the woman struggling to raise children, the man working to bring home bread for the family, those with many wounds who can still smile, those who hide their sacrificial service of others, those who strive to stay open-minded, and the holiness of his Dad and Mom and his Grandma Rosa 'who loved me very much'.[6]

There is a word that helps us express a key dimension of the 'Francis factor'. Even though labelled a 'conservative' he talks of 'magnanimity' quite often in his interviews and homilies. This is an uplifting, liberating and life-giving word. It is the mystical core of inner health. 'Let ours be great souls,' he preached, 'cherish what is most beautiful, most grand, most appealing and most necessary' (*EG*, n. 35). Big-heartedness! St Thomas Aquinas saw magnanimity as the major attribute of God. Live out of your *anima magna*, he preached, your big heart. Be expansive, let go of many things, let love dominate your life.

In almost all his recent written and spoken words, and certainly since his astonishing 'conversion' of mind and heart, Pope Francis emphasises the mystical, the creative and the imaginative. He sees all human encounters – with sinners, devotees of other faiths, agnostics, atheists – as potential moments, not for preaching, poaching or proselytising, but for developing some new synthesis, 'a creative apologetics' (*EG*, n. 132),

---

6   Pope Francis' interview with Antonio Spadaro, SJ, http://www.vatican.va/holyfather/francesco/speeches/2013/september/documents/papa-francesco20130921intervista-spadaroen.html [accessed, 10 November 2013].

another small incarnation, a graced foundation for future generations to build on. 'The People of God', he wrote, 'are incarnate in the peoples of the earth' (*EG*, n. 115). 'We love this magnificent planet on which God put us and we love the human family which dwells there with all its tragedies and aspirations' (*EG*, n. 183).

As we reflect on what makes our new Pope significantly different from his predecessors, setting people free at their most human and divine depths, a tentative word about the kind of theology that colours and nourishes his sacramental vision, that underpins his discernment, decisions and priorities, may enrich our understanding of him. Of all the current Christian theologies that can be identified in the Church today is there one that takes the hard, judgemental edge off the Fall/Redemption doctrine that still dominates Church teaching, that offers a renewed mystical story of original grace and beauty rather than of original sinfulness?

Obscured by an overemphasis on reparation, sacrifice and moral perfection, there is a prior theology of nature and grace. Creation, our earth, our human condition, our death – all that we mean by our existence, by what is natural – all are already graced, created and fashioned in the divine image. That is one reason why Pope Francis, in his interview with Eugenio Scalfari, the founder of *La Repubblica*, in October 2013,[7] so easily refers to the power of the artistic experiences of his life – the literature, the music, the films, the paintings, evolution itself – knowing that such 'secular' creations and becomings are all pathways along his 'Way of Beauty' (*EG*, n. 167), all small sacraments of the divinity at their core.

The Pope's theology of nature and grace, of creation, of liberation, of the poor (and they are all inter-related), is both mystical and incarnational. It is intrinsic to his deeply-interiorised understanding of the reasons for creation in the first place, and for the later fleshing of the Word. It is his way of being in a world created by love and sustained by love. He quotes Thomas Aquinas' assertion that God, right from the beginning, desired to become human simply because divine love needed to express itself outside of itself – first in creation, and then, finally, in Incarnation. 'God is sheer joy', Aquinas wrote, 'and sheer joy demands company.' And then, by virtue of solidarity and derivation, this love is embodied to a greater or lesser degree in

---

[7]   Pope Francis' interview with Eugenio Scalfari, http://www.news.va/en/news/interview-with-pope-francis-by-eugenio-scalfari-ed [accessed, 8 December 2013].

all of us, and in the evolving world itself, most especially in all that we mean by the *anawim*, the truly poor.

Our Pope knows that being human does not mean (as we were mostly taught) being banished, fallen, cursed – a *massa damnata*, as St Augustine put it – as if God's original dream for us was, at some stage, radically destroyed. Instead, God's seed, the divine image and dream were intrinsically a part of the eternal plan from the very beginning of creation, and the very beginning of every human life. That is why Francis is so slow to generalise, to condemn – he is always finding traces of God in everyone, no matter what way they have lived their lives, or how they might appear to others, especially those we misguidedly judge to be unworthy of sitting at the table of the Lord.

Across the world God's people are watching this unfolding scenario, and the mystical image in their own hearts is unfolding too. In our deepest selves, too long repressed and fear-bound, there is an expansion happening, a damaged beauty is finding its original design again, and the frustration within us is healing as an original wholeness returns. And that graced process is released in us, as it was in Pope Francis, only in the costly surrender to the hidden light when the darkness is too heavy. There is no other way.

It is not good for the soul to sleep too long in the shadows. Many theologians of creation today speak of an awakening in human perception and awareness. They claim that evolving human beings are transcending the rationality of dualistic thinking and are opening themselves to a mystical consciousness that leads to the unity of all beings. 'Human consciousness', the Jesuit William Johnston wrote, 'is evolving towards mysticism … [there is] a universal vocation to mysticism.'[8]

The recovery of a mystical theology, based on the radical revelation of Incarnation, will have profound implications for many Christian teachings and pastoral emphases, for our understanding of sacrament, for community ministry, for the religion/science debate, and for a new evangelising of young and old. But before that, it will transform our self-image as originally sinful failures, complicit somehow in the death of Jesus, into a vibrant awareness of our role as very imperfect, but vital co-creators with a patient God, of a steadily harmonising humanity, of a mystical Church, and of an ever-evolving universe of love.

---

8   William Johnston, 'We need a revolution', *The Tablet*, 1 June 2002, p. 12.

Pope Francis and the Poor

Peter McVerry, SJ

Bread for myself is a material question;
bread for my neighbour is a spiritual one.
(Nicholai Berdyaev)

There is an excitement abroad; a new energy has been released. A new religious teacher has appeared who talks about God in a way that enthuses people, even excites them. Everywhere he goes, crowds of people turn out to see him and to listen to him. He is criticised by good-living religious people for not affirming traditional teaching. Is this Jesus of Nazareth or Francis of Rome?

Everywhere Jesus went, crowds followed him. Five thousand people, not counting women and children, listened to him all day long, even forgetting that they were hungry (Lk 9:10–11). Every town he went into, the whole town, we are told, turned out to hear him (Mk 2:2). The poor man who was paralysed and wanted Jesus to cure him couldn't get near Jesus because of the crowds (Lk 5:17–26). 'And great crowds followed him from Galilee, the Decapolis, Jerusalem, Judaea, and from beyond the Jordan' (Mt 4:25), the gospel writer tells us.

On the Copacabana Beach at Rio de Janeiro, three million young people turned out to see and listen to Pope Francis. 6.6 million came to see and listen to him in St Peter's Square during 2013. Everywhere he goes, crowds of people turn out to listen to him.

The crowds didn't come to listen to Jesus laying down new laws or reinforcing existing laws. They had had their fill of laws, laid down by their own religious leaders. No, they came to listen to Jesus talking, not about a God of the Law, but about a God of compassion, a God who cares. And not just talking about a God of compassion: in their encounters with Jesus, the sick, those with disabilities, the prostitutes, the tax collectors, the sinners, *experienced* the God of compassion, as he healed them, dined with them, defended them against the condemnation of the righteous.

The crowds are not coming to hear Pope Francis laying down new laws or reinforcing existing laws. They, too, are hearing him talk about a God of compassion. And not just talking about a God of compassion. In their encounters with Pope Francis, the migrants, those with disabilities, the homeless, the children, those in gay relationships, those who have had an abortion, those in second relationships, they too are *experiencing* the God of compassion, the God who cares, as he visits them, reaches out to embrace them, kisses them, and defends them against the condemnation of the righteous.

Some have said that Pope Francis is not offering fundamental change in the Church, but simply putting old wine in new wineskins, making the Church seem more appealing and more appetising, like a good cook serving up the same old meal but dressing it up in a different way. I disagree. While Pope Francis is careful to affirm his continuity with the tradition of the Church – by quoting frequently from his predecessors, from John XXIII onwards, and most frequently Benedict XVI – what he is saying and doing offers perhaps something much deeper: he offers a different understanding of our relationship with God, a God that people have been searching for but often not finding within the Church. At the time of Jesus, as now, people have been thirsting for a God who cares, but were being fed a God who judges and condemns. Pope Francis' emphasis on a God who cares has profound implications for the way we live our lives – and for our spiritual lives.

The God of the law

The dominant image of God which the Church has proclaimed for many decades or even centuries has been that of God as Judge. Jesus, the Son of God, came to tell us how to live our lives according to the laws which God has laid down. It is the role of the Church to interpret those laws and explain them to the faithful. Our relationship with God is determined by our observance of the laws: if we obey them, God will be pleased with us and reward us with a place in heaven; if we disobey them, God will be displeased with us and we risk God's anger and condemnation. Obedience to the laws of God, then, is the proof of our fidelity to God.

This was also the dominant spirituality at the time of Jesus, a spirituality which is inward-looking and self-centred, focused on *me*, on what *I* want – namely getting to heaven – and on what *I* must do to achieve my goal. But it was a spirituality which Jesus rejected. In its place, Jesus presents a spirituality in which the focus is on others and not myself, on their needs and not my wants – not even my spiritual wants. Francis brings that spirituality back to centre stage.

A God of compassion
The gospels associate Jesus with the poor. He is regularly to be found among the poor, the sick, the blind, the lame, the deaf, the dumb, and tax collectors and sinners. Indeed, his constant association with such people was a cause of scandal to the more respectable people in his society. 'Why does your teacher eat with tax collectors and sinners?' (Mt 9:11), his disciples were often asked. For Francis, this too is where the Church must be:

> If the whole Church takes up this missionary impulse, she has to go forth to everyone without exception. But to whom should she go first? When we read the Gospel we find a clear indication: not so much our friends and wealthy neighbours, but above all the poor and the sick, those who are usually despised and overlooked … There can be no room for doubt or for explanations which weaken so clear a message. Today and always, 'the poor are the privileged recipients of the Gospel' (*EG*, n. 48).[1]

So what *was* Jesus saying to the poor that had them following him in droves to listen to him? Jesus addressed the real, concrete issues that affected poor people's lives. He spoke about the rich man (Lk 16:19–31) 'who was dressed in purple and fine linen and who feasted sumptuously every day' and who couldn't even be bothered to gather up the crumbs that fell from his table to give them to the poor man at his gate. The people Jesus was talking to knew exactly what he was talking about. If they went to the cities to look for work, or up to Jerusalem for one of the festivals, they could see the homeless people sitting outside the mansions of the poor, hoping for some alms. Pope

---

[1]   Pope Francis, *Evangelii Gaudium* (The Joy of the Gospel), Apostolic Exhortation on the Proclamation of the Gospel in Today's World, 2013. Further references will be denoted by *EG*, followed by the paragraph number(s).

Francis also protests at the inequality that exists in today's world and the physical hunger of so many: 'Can we continue to stand by when food is thrown away while people are starving?' (*EG*, n. 53).

Jesus talked about the rich landowner (Lk 12:13–21) who had a massive harvest and said to himself: 'What should I do, for I have no place to store my crops? Then he said, "I will do this: I will pull down my barns and build larger ones"' – without the slightest consideration for those around him who were hungry. The people Jesus was talking to knew exactly to whom he was referring. Pope Francis too talks about the indifference of many towards the poor:

> To sustain a lifestyle which excludes others, or to sustain enthusiasm for that selfish ideal, a globalisation of indifference has developed. Almost without being aware of it, we end up being incapable of feeling compassion at the outcry of the poor, weeping for other people's pain, and feeling a need to help them, as though all this were someone else's responsibility and not our own. The culture of prosperity deadens us (*EG*, n. 54).

Jesus talked about the labourers who waited in the market square all day long, hoping to get a few hours work so that they could earn enough to feed their families (Mt 20:1–16). The people Jesus was talking to knew exactly what he was talking about: some of them, perhaps, had themselves 'been there, done that'. Pope Francis too criticises a system that leaves people trapped in unemployment:

> Today everything comes under the laws of competition and the survival of the fittest, where the powerful feed upon the powerless. As a consequence, masses of people find themselves excluded and marginalised: without work, without possibilities, without any means of escape (*EG*, n. 53).

The stories Jesus told were not made-up stories: he was talking about real life in the kingdom of Caesar, a kingdom characterised by greed, by the accumulation of wealth, and by enormous inequality which left many people struggling to survive and bereft of dignity. Pope Francis also talks about real life in the world today, a world characterised by greed, growing inequality, and abuse of power:

> While the earnings of a minority are growing exponentially, so too is the gap separating the majority from the prosperity enjoyed by those

happy few … The thirst for power and possessions knows no limits. In this system, which tends to devour everything which stands in the way of increased profits, whatever is fragile, like the environment, is defenceless before the interests of a deified market (*EG*, n. 56).

And Jesus announced the coming of a new kingdom. This new kingdom would be ruled, not by a ruthless Herod who cared nothing about the plight of his subjects, but by One who was compassion, One who cared about the suffering of the poor and homeless. In this new kingdom, the kingdom of God, it was the poor man, Lazarus, who would receive a welcome, not the selfish, rich man. In this new kingdom of God, the large landowner would not be allowed to enjoy his new wealth while others starved. In this new kingdom of God, all the labourers would receive a wage sufficient to feed their families for the day, even if they had not earned it. Likewise, Francis talks of a new era and its characteristics: 'I beg the Lord to grant us politicians who are genuinely disturbed by the state of society, the people, the lives of the poor!' (*EG*, n. 205); 'the dignity of the human person and the common good rank higher than the comfort of those who refuse to renounce their privileges' (*EG*, n. 218); resolving 'the structural causes of poverty' (*EG*, n. 202); and 'we can no longer trust in the unseen forces and the invisible hand of the market' (*EG*, n. 204).

But Jesus didn't just *talk* about this wonderful kingdom that was coming. In their encounter with Jesus, the poor *experienced* the God of compassion. When Jesus ate with tax collectors and sinners, they *experienced*, in their table fellowship with him, the unconditional forgiveness of the God of compassion. This caused enormous offence to the religious authorities who had rejected them in the name of the God of the Law.

Pope Francis was chosen as 'the single, most influential person of 2013 on the lives of LGBT [Lesbian, Gay, Bisexual, Transsexual] people'[2] by *The Advocate*, America's oldest gay rights magazine, representing people who had only experienced condemnation and exclusion from the God of the Law, and from those that worshipped the God of the Law. And Francis reaches his hand out in friendship to those divorced and remarried, who were excluded from the Eucharist by the God of the Law:

---

[2]   *The Irish Times*, 30 December 2013.

The Eucharist, although it is the fullness of sacramental life, is not a prize for the perfect but a powerful medicine and nourishment for the weak. *These convictions have pastoral consequences that we are called to consider with prudence and boldness* (my italics) ... The Church is the house of the Father, where there is a place for everyone, with all their problems (*EG*, n. 47).

And when Jesus reached out, in friendship, to the unwanted and marginalised, they *experienced* God's acceptance of them. The Vatican had to repeatedly deny the rumour that Pope Francis slipped out of the Vatican at night to bring soup and food to the homeless. Many do not believe this denial, as Pope Francis was known to do this when Archbishop in Buenos Aires.

And when Jesus cured the blind and the lame and the lepers, who were told by their own religious leaders that they were cursed by God, they actually *experienced*, in the very act of being healed, the God of compassion that Jesus revealed. 'The Church is a field hospital', says Francis. 'Our first duty is to tend to the wounded.'

Jesus proclaimed a kingdom in which the God of compassion would ensure that the needs of all, and especially the poor, would be met. How were their needs going to be met? By the caring and sharing of the followers of Jesus in the Christian community. In this community, people were to live together in a totally different way. Instead of accumulating wealth to enjoy for themselves, as in the kingdom of Caesar, people in the community of God were to share their wealth with those in need. The rich young man was a good-living, righteous young man and 'Jesus, looking at him, loved him'. But Jesus would not allow him to follow him because he was unable to share his wealth with the poor (Mk 10:17–22). Francis also refers to a world in which wealth is shared with the poor: 'Not to share one's wealth with the poor is to steal from them and take away their livelihood. It is not our own goods which we hold but theirs' (*EG*, n. 57).

Jesus talks about the community of God where, instead of rejecting some, as in the kingdom of Caesar, everyone would be equally valued and respected, regardless of their role or status. So, too, Francis talks about a world where all will be respected and valued: 'The Pope loves everyone, rich and poor alike, but he is obliged in the name of Christ to remind all that the rich must help, respect and promote the poor' (*EG*, n. 58).

Just as Jesus proclaimed, in the name of God, that life, as it was lived in the kingdom of Herod was an affront to God, who is Father of all, so Francis is proclaiming, also in the name of God, that life, as it is lived in our world today, is an affront to the God we worship.

Jesus was not put to death because his moral laws were at variance with those of the Jewish faith of his time: 'Love your neighbour' is at the heart of both the Christian and Jewish moral law. Jesus was crucified because the God of compassion whom he revealed required from his followers a love that was so radical, and so challenging to the way we live together, that those who felt threatened by such a change wanted to get rid of him. What Pope Francis is pointing to is also a challenge to the securities which many may wish to hold on to:

> I prefer a Church which is bruised, hurting and dirty because it has been out on the streets … More than by fear of going astray, my hope is that we will be moved by the fear of remaining shut up within structures which give us a false sense of security, within rules which make us harsh judges, within habits which make us feel safe, while at our door people are starving and Jesus does not tire of saying to us: 'Give them something to eat' (*EG*, n. 49).

A backlash from some who are wealthy is already evident.[3] Francis is challenging well-established systems of power, wealth and privilege and questioning the morality of ever-widening inequality and the way systems develop to shield some people's wealth at the expense of opportunity for others. It is a God-filled message that some of his critics are unwilling to hear.

Of course, poverty and injustice have always been concerns for the Church, as evidenced by many social encyclicals. What Pope Francis has done is to put the poor, the problems of inequality and structural injustice at the heart of the Church's mission, and therefore at the heart of Christian spirituality and living.

---

[3]   http://www.ajc.com [accessed, 7 January 2014].

Discerning and Evangelising from 'the Ends of the Earth'

Brendan Leahy

On the night of his election, Pope Francis noted how the cardinals had gone 'to the ends of the earth' to find a Bishop of Rome. Since then he has repeatedly invited all of us to go to the peripheries in our discerning and evangelising. We need, as it were, to look at life from within ourselves, and from there go out in the joy of evangelisation. In many ways, it is Francis' clarion call for personal and ministerial conversion to 'going outwards' in missionary zeal that is most striking in this first year since his election as Bishop of Rome (see *EG*, nn. 20 and 24).

There are so many inspiring words and gestures emerging from Francis that it is difficult to know where to begin commenting on his impact to date. Taking up his invitation to go to the peripheries, I thought I might concentrate in this chapter on his words to the bishops of Brazil that he met during the World Youth Day last July.[1] 'From the ends of the earth', they speak to us too in Ireland. After all, in his conversation with the Union of Superiors General of Religious Men in November 2013,[2] Francis commented that great changes have come about in the course of the Church's history when reality has been viewed from the periphery. Here and there I will also make some references to *Evangelii Gaudium*.

---

[1] Meeting with the bishops of Brazil, Archbishop's House, Rio de Janeiro, Saturday, 28 July 2013. All the quotes in this chapter, unless otherwise referenced, are taken from that speech.

[2] For the original text of the meeting of Pope Francis and the Union of Superiors General of Religious Men, see *La Civiltà Cattolica*, I (2014), pp. 3–17.

The Aparecida story

The Brazilian National Shrine of Aparecida contains a small statue of Our Lady of the Immaculate Conception that tradition has it was found in 1717 by three fishermen in the waters of the Parnaíba River. During the 2005 Assembly of the Latin American Episcopal Conference (CELAM), the bishops started their day with a Mass concelebrated in the huge basilica. Great crowds of people were there early in the morning. The future Pope (who was to be a major contributor to the final Aparecida document) was very struck by that experience. He obviously reflected much on the simple Aparecida account of the fishermen finding the statue. Speaking last year to the Brazilian bishops, he surprised them with his reading of the story. In typical style, he let the image teach his listeners. We can hear him lead us in the spiritual exercise of discernment.

Francis notes, firstly, that the fishermen were poor. They were looking for food. Today too, he comments, people always start with their needs. The fishermen had a dilapidated, ill-fitted boat; their nets were old, perhaps torn and insufficient. The results of their toil in fishing were negligible. But then God entered the scene out of the blue: 'The waters are deep and yet they always conceal the possibility of a revelation of God.' The fishermen found a broken clay statue: 'And God arrived in a novel fashion, since God is wonder: as a fragile clay statue, darkened by the waters of the river and aged by the passage of time. God always enters clothed in poverty, littleness.'

Noting how first the body of the statue was found, and after that the head that was then joined to the body, Francis directs us to the theme of unity: 'Walls, chasms, differences which still exist today are destined to disappear. The Church cannot neglect this lesson: she is called to be a means of reconciliation.'

Francis also observes that the fishermen who first found the body of the statue took their time. They waited until they found the head. Again, there's a lesson here for us: 'There are pieces of the mystery, like the stones of a mosaic, which we encounter. We are impatient, anxious to see the whole picture, but God lets us see things slowly, quietly. The Church also has to learn how to wait.'

Then a favourite theme of Francis comes to the fore. He notes that the fishermen brought the statue home and comments: 'Ordinary people always have room to take in the mystery. Perhaps we have reduced our way of speaking about mystery to rational explanations;

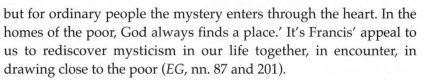

but for ordinary people the mystery enters through the heart. In the homes of the poor, God always finds a place.' It's Francis' appeal to us to rediscover mysticism in our life together, in encounter, in drawing close to the poor (*EG*, nn. 87 and 201).

Francis summarises what he has learned from the simple story of the Aparecida fishermen who called their neighbours to tell them of their discovery:

> Without the simplicity of their [fishermen's] approach, our mission is doomed to failure. Dear brothers, the results of our pastoral work do not depend on a wealth of resources, but on the creativity of love … Another lesson which the Church must constantly recall is that she cannot leave simplicity behind … At times we lose people because they don't understand what we are saying, because we have forgotten the language of simplicity and import an intellectualism foreign to our people. Without the grammar of simplicity, the Church loses the very conditions which make it possible 'to fish' for God in the deep waters of his Mystery.

It is clear that Francis himself exhibits this simplicity, love and way of the heart. The Jewish Rabbi Abraam Skorka, who co-authored a book with Bergoglio, has described the Pope as very close to the religious existentialists such as Søren Kierkegaard, Martin Buber and Karl Barth.[3] The revolution of tenderness that he proposes was very much in evidence a few months ago in the Pope's embrace of Vincio Riva, a severely disfigured man suffering from a rare disease that causes painful tumours to grow throughout the body. Afterwards, Mr Riva commented: 'the thing that struck me most is that he didn't think twice about whether or not to hug me … I'm not contagious, but he didn't know that. He just did it: he caressed me all over my face, and as he did I felt only love.' Images of that moment went all over the world.

The icon of Emmaus

Pope Francis is realistic. He knows that in our time it might be easy to yield to disillusionment, discouragement and complaint. He knows the truth of what John Henry Newman once wrote that 'the Christian

---

[3]   See Jorge Bergoglio and Abraham Skorka, *Sobre el cielo y la tierra* (Buenos Aires: Sudamericana, 2010).

world is becoming sterile, and it is depleting itself like an over-exploited ground, which transforms into a desert'.[4] Many in the Church today can feel they have worked much and gained little. 'We feel like those who must tally up a losing season as we consider those who have left us or no longer consider us credible or relevant.' Yet, Francis holds up the icon of the disciples on the road to Emmaus (see Lk 24:13–15) and encourages us not to lose heart and to discern the way forward.

The disciples had left Jerusalem, disappointed and disillusioned. There are many today, Francis comments, who now think that the Church – their Jerusalem – can no longer offer them anything mean-ingful and important. So they set off on the road alone, with their disappointment. Somehow the Church can appear too distant, too caught up with itself, perhaps a prisoner of its own rigid formulas. It finds it hard to speak to people 'come of age' who have new questions. Faced with this situation, what are we to do? Pope Francis offers a powerful word of encouragement to relive the Emmaus story:

> We need a Church unafraid of going forth into their night. We need a Church capable of meeting them on their way. We need a Church capable of entering into their conversation. We need a Church able to dialogue with those disciples who, having left Jerusalem behind, are wandering aimlessly, alone, with their own disappointment, disillusioned by a Christianity now considered barren, fruitless soil, incapable of generating meaning.

In a simple point that cuts to the chase, Francis reminds us that the reasons why people leave also contain reasons why they can eventually return. That's why he invites his brother bishops in Brazil: 'let us recover the calm to be able to walk at the same pace as our pilgrims, keeping alongside them, remaining close to them, enabling them to speak of the disappointments present in their hearts and to let us address them.'

Francis has been doing this in all kinds of ways. For instance, we see it in his response to a letter from Eugenio Scalfari, a non-believer and former editor of the Italian newspaper, *La Repubblica*. In the course of his response, the Pope commented:

---

4   J. H. Newman, Letter of 26 January 1833, in *The Letters and Diaries of John Henry Newman*, vol. III (Oxford, 1979), p. 204.

First of all, you ask if the God of the Christians forgives those who do not believe and do not seek faith. Given that – and this is fundamental – God's mercy has no limits if the person who asks for mercy does so in contrition and with a sincere heart, then the issue for those who do not believe in God is in obeying their own conscience. In fact, listening and obeying it, means deciding about what is perceived to be good or to be evil. The goodness or the wickedness of our behaviour depends on this decision.

Scalfari described the deep emotion he experienced in receiving the Pope's letter:

An openness so broad to modern and secular culture, such a profound vision of conscience and its autonomy has never been experienced up to now from the chair of St Peter … The Pope does me the honour of wishing to make a journey along with me. I would be delighted to do this. So I wish a long life and affectionate brotherhood with Francis, Bishop of Rome and head of a Church that also is involved in the struggle between good and evil.

Today's agenda

The theme of incarnation is important for Francis (*EG*, nn. 231 and 233). He moves from story and icon to action. Discerning priorities is important for him.

A first priority is *formation*. He invites us to have courage and undertake a thorough review of the structures in place for the formation and preparation of the clergy and the laity of the Church. We need 'ministers capable of warming people's hearts, of walking with them in the night, of dialoguing with their hopes and disappointments, of mending their brokenness'. That can't remain a vague aspiration. What is needed is the practical wisdom to set up lasting educational structures of quality formation on the local, regional and national levels calls. It is something fundamental for the journey of your Churches.

A second priority is *collegiality and solidarity*. It is not enough to have a notional communion. It must involve the sharing of our experience of God just as the disciples on the road to Emmaus recounted their meeting with the risen Christ. Here Francis is expressing the 'theology of the people' that he was close to over many years in South America. There's no doubting his 'spiritual taste for being close to people's lives' (*EG*, n. 268).

A third priority is a *permanent state of mission and pastoral conversion*. Mission is a very personal reality. Francis compares it to a relay race and the handing on of a legacy: 'In order to transmit a legacy, one needs to hand it over personally, to touch the one to whom one wants to give, to relay, this inheritance.' In terms of pastoral conversion, there's a need to recognise how pastoral life is an expression of the Church's maternal profile. It requires a new focus on mercy: 'So we need a Church capable of rediscovering the maternal womb of mercy. Without mercy we have little chance nowadays of becoming part of a world of "wounded" persons in need of understanding, forgiveness, love.'

A fourth priority is the *Church in society*. The Church need not be afraid to offer its contribution to society. It has something to say about education, health and social harmony, areas that call for more than merely technical solutions. Francis points to the Amazon Basin as a litmus test for Church and society in Brazil. For all of us it's vital that we don't close in on ourselves, that we go out and, in prophetic spirit, be able to 'wake up the world', as he said to the superiors general at the meeting mentioned above.

Conclusion

The words spoken to us from Brazil clearly resonate in the Irish ecclesial experience. The Aparecida story, the Emmaus icon and the agenda that Francis discerns invite us to let ourselves hear Jesus Christ knocking on the door, prompting us to enter into a new phase in the history of Irish Christianity. All of us need to be open to God's intervention while also respecting God's time. Archbishop Diarmuid Martin has alerted us to the risk of admiring Francis or thinking his message is for others and so perhaps failing to hear the real call that is coming to us through him:

> we have not just to admire the measure of Pope Francis but to find the true measure that fits us for our mission. We could easily admire Pope Francis and keep going on as we were. Change is painful … We find it hard to move outside our own comfort zone, even when intellectually we can see that we ought to.[5]

---

5   Homily at the Opening Liturgy of the Enniscorthy Eucharistic Gathering in St Aidan's Cathedral, Enniscorthy, County Wexford, 31 May 2013.

Francis clearly encourages us to renew our belief that the Risen Jesus can do for us what he did for the two lost and disillusioned disciples of Emmaus – warm our hearts and give us new and certain hope. He entrusts us to Mary that she may be the star that illumines our task and our journey of bringing Christ to all.

Models of Episcopal Leadership: Reflections on Pope Francis' Approach to Leadership in the Light of Gregory the Great's *Pastoral Care*

Louise Nelstrop

> Our people need priests [...] who venture out and yet remain close to the tabernacle, who return to it to fill their lamps with oil before going out again.[1]
> (Cardinal Jorge Bergoglio)

Introduction

The image of 'venturing out' but 'remaining close' can be read in a number of ways. It can, for example, be understood as representative of a relatively conservative agenda, in which innovation is always to be tempered with tradition. It can be read as a reference to the importance of educational preparedness in those who will act as guides – especially when linked to the image of lamps filled with oil. It can equally be read as pertaining to a rich spiritual life; a prerequisite for one engaged in pastoral care. It is this latter reading that I am particularly interested in, and the sense in which this reflects an important agenda in the nascent papacy of Francis.

The role of the papacy has developed over the centuries. A number of significant shifts have occurred, which in the medieval period saw the papacy becoming a pivotal political as well as an ecclesiastical power. As Kathleen G. Cushing notes, in the mid-fifth century 'the pope was effectively the first among equals'.[2] It was only later, with the

---

[1] Pope Francis, *Encountering Christ: Homilies, Letters, and Addresses of Cardinal Jorge Bergoglio* (New York: Scepter, 2013), p. 95.

[2] K.G. Cushing, *Papacy and Law in the Gregorian Revolution*, Oxford Historical Monographs (New York: Oxford University Press, 1998), p. 57.

development in the eleventh and twelfth centuries of what historians have called the 'papal monarchy', that justifications were made concerning the 'absolute' primacy of pope in both jurisdictional as well as spiritual matters.[3] One marker of this shift lies in the way in which the pope was addressed. Cushing notes that in the early period 'the pope as Peter's successor was known chiefly as the Bishop of Rome; in fact, the title *papa* was seldom used before the late eleventh century'.[4] In expressing a preference for the title 'Bishop of Rome', the former Archbishop of Buenos Aires, Cardinal Jorge Bergoglio, now Pope Francis, is making an important statement about how he sees the power he holds and the elements of his role which he wishes to emphasise.

This, alongside his adoption of the name Francis – after Francis of Assisi – can be read as a signal that he places pastoral responsibilities at the heart of Christian leadership, and that, whilst not necessarily wishing to undermine the historical fabric of the papacy, he sees a need to re-emphasise pastoral care, as well as humility over absolute authority. In this relation I want to offer some reflections on how pastoral care within Christian leadership, particularly papal leadership, has traditionally been understood by referring to what is undoubtedly the most influential account of this, Gregory the Great's *Regulae Pastoralis*, commonly translated into English as the *Pastoral Care*. In the light of this, I will explore some of the ways in which Francis is endorsing a pastoral approach to Christian leadership, and the sense in which this is bound up with the legacy of Vatican II.

1. Gregory the Great on pastoral care

Gregory I (*c.*540–604), also known as Gregory the Great, was arguably the first real medieval pope. He was appointed pope in 590, and was passionate about Christian leadership, writing on it most systematically in his *Pastoral Care*. This work came to shape Christian thought on leadership and Christian lifestyle throughout the medieval period. Indeed in the early Middle Ages it was used and translated in such far-flung corners of the Roman Empire as England.[5]

---

[3]   This, even though under the pontificate of Gregory I an emphasis on jurisdiction can be found alongside spiritual and pastoral concerns: Cushing, *Papacy*, p. 58.

[4]   Cushing, *Papacy*, p. 57.

[5]   N. G. Discensza, 'Alfred's Verse Preface to the *Pastoral Care* and the Chain of Authority', *Neophilologus* 85 (2001), pp. 625–33; F. Leneghan, 'Teaching the Teachers: The Vercelli Book and the Mixed Life', *English Studies*, 94/6 (2013), pp. 627–58.

In his late nineteenth-century modern English translation, H.R. Bramley stresses that the work has lost none of its relevance and vigour, even though it is now some 1400 years old: 'What modern work could supply the place of Chrysostom's *De Sacerdotio*, or Gregory the Great's "Pastoral?"'[6]

Gregory wrote his *Pastoral Care* in the first year of his pontificate – although the key ideas it contains are anticipated in various letters and talks that he composed around the same period.[7] A central feature of the *Pastoral Care* is what later came to be known as the 'mixed life'. The 'mixed life' or the 'medled lyf',[8] as it was termed in Middle English, was the idea that a truly Christian life involved both contemplation and action – that is both prayer and engagement with the world. Although in Christian tradition we often find a distinction made between the role of lay people, who are said to be the actors, and that of professional religious people, who are said to devote themselves to contemplation and prayer, albeit on behalf of others as well as themselves, Gregory I believed passionately that Christian leadership demanded both. For Gregory, contemplation was the well-spring out of which right action flowed. Without a right heart there could be no right action. Yet equally right action both signalled and underpinned a heart of prayer. Indeed, a Christian leader must excel both outwardly and inwardly:

> He must be pure in thought, chief in action, discreet in silence, profitable in speech, a neighbour to everyone by sympathy, absorbed in contemplation above all men, a companion to well-doers by lowliness, prompt in the zeal of righteousness against the vices of transgressors, abating not his cares for things within through his employment or things without, nor abandoning the management of outward matters in his anxiety of things within.[9]

The need for both prayer and action in leadership was re-emphasised by the mendicant orders that arose in the thirteenth century, with the Franciscans assuming a special responsibility for the

---

6   H.R. Bramley (ed. and trans.), *S. Gregorii Magni Regulae Pastoralis Liber/S. Gregory on The Pastoral Charge: The Benedictine Text with an English Translation* (Oxford: J. Parker, 1874), p. vii: quoting A. Möhler, *Pastologie* i, p. 3.

7   See, for example, his talks on Job, which he compiled into the *Moralia* around this time.

8   N. Watson, *Richard Rolle and the Invention of Authority* (Cambridge: Cambridge University Press, 1991), p. 14.

9   Bramley, *Pastoral*, Part II, ch. 1, p. 49.

care of the poor.[10] When, on the eve of the Reformation, the Jesuits were founded, they too stressed that both must be held together – indeed they are famed for fostering 'contemplation in action' as an ideal.[11] As one formed within the Jesuit order, but also expressing a clear admiration for the action-based approach of the Franciscans, Francis lays claim to a tradition within the Catholic Church in which Christian leadership is closely wedded to service. The seeds of this theology of Christian leadership are to be found in Gregory I's *Pastoral Care*.

One of the qualities which give Gregory's work its contemporary feel is its psychological astuteness. He argues that people tend to fall into two main character types. There are those who are naturally outward in their orientation, and so are keen to serve others with good works. Equally there are those who are naturally inward in orientation, keen to serve God in prayer. Today we might call them introverts and extroverts. For Gregory these two personality types are epitomised in the lives of two Old Testament prophets: Isaiah and Jeremiah. Isaiah was the extrovert. When God wanted a messenger, he instantly responded: 'send me'. Jeremiah, on the other hand, had little desire to take up a preaching vocation. Gregory does not suggest that one of these types is better than the other. Rather he indicates that together they demonstrate the qualities of a good leader – both prayerful and active – practices that will always be in tension in any person, albeit it differently so. What is important, whatever our personality type, is that we constantly need to strive to attain our inverse if we are to lead well:

> For there are two commands of charity, the love of God, that is, and of our neighbour. Isaiah, therefore, desiring by the life of action to do good to his neighbours, seeketh the office of preaching. Jeremiah, wishing by the life of contemplation to cleave diligently to the love of his Maker, speaketh against his being bound in the duty to be sent to preach. What, therefore, the one laudably sought, that the other laudably dreaded. The latter, lest he should squander the gain of silent contemplation by speaking; the former, lest by keeping silence he should have experience of the loss of diligent labour.[12]

---

10 M. D. Lambert, *Franciscan Poverty* (New York: Franciscan Institute Publications, 1998).
11 J. A. Munitiz and P. Endean (eds and trans), *Saint Ignatius of Loyola: Personal Writings* (London: Penguin Books, 1996), *Letter* 23: p. 53.
12 Bramley, *Pastoral*, part I, ch. 7, p. 27. Spelling slightly modernised.

This mixed life, of both action and contemplation, is more than a simple Aristotelian median. It is recognition of the need to be caught between two right but opposing demands. Neither action nor contemplation is wrong. The challenge for the Christian leader is that both are demanded; he is called to exist in a constant and exacting tension.

This sense of living a life in constant motion between necessary but diverging poles is clarified by Gregory when he discusses in more detail how a Christian leader should live. It is clear that he should preach. And in doing so he should not neglect his duty to admonish those who do wrong. Gregory goes so far as to claim that he is called to stand surety for those entrusted to him, which means that he assumes their guilt by proxy. Working to correct faults is therefore imperative! Yet preaching should never been considered simply a matter of words. It is no use, Gregory states, just preaching with words to those who are hungry. A true preacher also needs to meet their physical needs: 'Let pastors, therefore be in such wise zealous about the inner pursuits of those that are under them, as not to abandon provision of their outward life […].'[13] Leadership is also a question of example. Anyone who fails to live a blameless life risks leading those entrusted to them into wrong-doing – for which, Gregory states, he will be doubly punished: 'Rulers ought to know that if ever they do perverse things, they are worthy of so many deaths as they set examples of perdition to their subjects.'[14] There is every reason to be like Jeremiah – hesitant before assuming leadership.

As such, Gregory argues a key skill for those who do take up the mantel of leadership is an ability to be psychologically-sensitive at a deep level. To be a truly effective Christian leader one needs to be alert to the oppositional dynamics that operate at the core of human nature. This involves more than a simple awareness that some are extroverts whilst others are introverts. It is no use, for example, working in the same way with those who are naturally good-natured and those who have a propensity to envy. The envious are to be encouraged to love the good in others so that they too might make their own that good which they cannot otherwise attain (rather than pinning away with regret for what they do not have). The good-natured, on the other hand (who might appear more spiritual), are to be reprimanded

---

13 Bramley, *Pastoral*, part II, ch. 7, p. 99.
14 Pope Francis, *Encountering Christ*, p. 143.

where their support for others prevents them from realising the potential of which they themselves are capable. Neither a naturally good-natured personality nor a naturally envious one represents the ideal: rather, the preferred option lies in the dynamic exchange between the two.

The same is true of the silent and the talkative. The talkative must be chastened to be less obsessed with each minute thing, lest in discussing every aspect of life they fail to find space to quietly reflect on higher things. The silent, on the other hand (who perhaps seem more spiritual), should be admonished against storing up in their hearts what they are truly thinking, and so simmering with resentment. There is nothing spiritual, he assures us, about not speaking when it arises from a fear of criticism. Such measured, socially-aware and psychologically-nuanced advice is typical of Gregory's *Pastoral Care*, which extends to discussions on how one best corrects those who are either proud or timid, for example, or those who are either arrogant or naturally self-effacing.

Yet, while he discusses at length how a leader should relate to others, at its root the focus is on the Christian leader himself; how the life of one who is called to such leadership needs to be 'perfect'. He must mirror Christ, who privileged both action and contemplation, thus reflecting the inseparability of humanity and divinity within the Incarnation. No wonder Francis professes to shudder each time he reads Gregory the Great's advice on pastoral care! Indeed I doubt he would much like the title of this chapter. Not because Gregory's advice is bad, but because it is so exacting; a constant reminder of the standards demanded of those who lead, which are impossibly high and therefore incredibly humbling.

2. Pope Francis on Christian leadership

Francis has been pope for less than a year. Yet he has already been named *Time* magazine's Person of the Year. The media are captivated by a pope who appears to place such great emphasis on social justice and humility. We cannot of course say anything definitive as to how history will view this approach to leadership, nor do we know the directions in which he will move in future years. What we can see is that in sermons, homilies and presentations written in the years just prior to his appointment, there are clear indications that the then

Cardinal Jorge Bergoglio had come to believe that a Christian leader must be a man of action. As he stated, 'When someone puts Jesus' approach into action, sharing the bread of mercy and solidarity, people sense this and offer their collaboration to those who work to help others.'[15] This, Bergoglio suggests, is the most audible message in an age marked by scepticism and unfamiliarity with Church tradition and culture. Yet we find in his homilies and addresses that such activity is always counterbalanced by prayer and reflection. As he stated in an address to priests: 'Every proclamation of the gospel is always translated into some concrete act of teaching, mercy, and justice – but only as an obligatory action following reflection.'[16]

Inner vitality and a spirit-filled anointing are, in his mind, essential to social justice. Thus in these communications we do not find him advocating a liberal theology of pure immanence. There must be social justice, but not at the expense of a belief in a transcendent God: 'We anoint others when we allow ourselves to be anointed by the Spirit of Christ, meek and humble of heart [...].'[17] As he states just prior to this in the same homily, 'The fount of living water never runs dry, the fire of his love is never extinguished, and neither is the breath of his inspirations, which enlighten our minds and set our hands and feet in evangelical motion.'[18] Likewise there is no radical departure from the heritage of the Catholic Church. Rather there is a sense that one must always draw one's resources out of this wellspring, even as one cleanses it.

We find this, for example, in his opening homily to the Ninety-Eighth Plenary Assembly of the Argentinian Episcopal Conference in 2009, where he spoke on Jesus cleansing the Temple. He calls on his bishops to be those who are part of the Temple on the one hand, but also open to the movement of God's spirit: 'The blessings call upon the man who is open to God, who plants himself firmly in the life-giving streams that flow from the temple, accepting the law and guarding it in his heart.'[19] Caught in this tension, they are now best able to lead: 'men of prayer and penance so that our faithful can encounter God: men aware of their call, with attitudes of humility and service'.[20]

---

15   *Ibid.*, p. 79.
16   *Ibid.*, p. 104.
17   *Ibid.*, p. 101.
18   *Ibid.*, p. 101.
19   *Ibid.*, p. 119.
20   *Ibid.*, p. 121.

It is in this regard that we see what we might call Bergoglio's 'soft' liberation theology emerging. He does not want a Marxist overthrow of the powers that be. But he does want social justice and a Church that is not afraid to engage with the structural causes of injustice. What he wants is co-operation and partnership between parties that cannot easily coincide: 'The economic sector is not ethically neutral, nor is it inhuman or antisocial by nature. It is an activity of man and, precisely because it is human, it should be articulated and institutionalized ethically.'[21] Here, he suggests not naive idealism, but dialogue and dialectic engagement. Thus he believes that this uncomfortable movement, that is willing to wrestle with its opposite, presents the only real possibility for eradicating the social debt that he so despises because of the ways in which it cripples the poor, denying them basic human dignity and rights. Such a position, it seems to me, is far more than cutting a middle path or the discomfort generated by sitting on the fence. It is a call for dynamic dialogue and the risk that this involves when we really speak with and listen to another.

We might, I suggest, see this as bound up with the legacy of Vatican II which Francis endorses. The idea of dialogue, admittedly a complicated term within Vatican II theology:[22] nonetheless, at its heart it arguably gestures towards inculturation. The term 'inculturation' was first used and popularised by members of the Society of Jesus shortly before Vatican II, and is an idea central to Vatican II's sense of mission as 'evangelisation'.[23] Aylward Shorter helpfully distinguishes it from two related terms, sometimes treated as synonyms: 'acculturation' and 'inculturation', but which are not, in fact, identical. The latter, 'inculturation', derives its origin from sociology, where it is largely

---

[21] *Ibid.*, p. 147. It is interesting in this regard that he has requested some of the writings of Leonardo Boff.

[22] This is further complicated by the range of understandings given to conversion within Vatican II and related literature. Post-Vatican II encyclicals, such as *Redemptoris Missio*, and instructions from the Pontifical Council for Interreligious Dialogue (established post-Vatican II), such as *Dialogue and Proclamation*, contain multiple definitions of 'conversion'. These are further complicated by the Pontifical Council for Interreligious Dialogue, which holds dialogue and the proclamation of the Gospel to be 'interrelated components': C. Zene, *The Rishi of Bangladesh: A History of Christian Dialogue* (2002), p. 9.

[23] A. Shorter, *Towards a Theology of Inculturation* (New York: Orbis Books, 1994), p. 10. It was not until 1979 that the term 'inculturation' appeared in a papal document. It appears in *Catechesis Tradendae*: Shorter, p. 10, n. 12. On the importance of evangelisation for Pope Francis see his apostolic exhortation, *Evangelii Gaudium* (The Joy of the Gospel), 2013.

taken to mean the learning process by which one becomes a part of one's own culture. 'Acculturation' is contact between cultures. Ideas from both terms lie behind the theological idea of 'inculturation'; but on their own, individually, they are much less dynamic. Inculturation is both a coming together of cultures and at the same time an entry into a culture, not of a person, but of a faith.[24] As such, inculturation is transformational, even as it grapples with that which it encounters as it seeks to engage in dialogue. It is a transformation that is not only one way, but which is never willing to lose sight of its values – both inner and outer. Shorter offers the following insightful definition, writing that as envisaged in Vatican II, inculturation is:

> The Incarnation of Christian life and of the Christian message in a particular cultural context, in such a way that this experience not only finds expression through elements proper to the culture in question (this alone would be no more than a superficial adaptation) but becomes a principle that animates, directs and unifies the culture, transforming it and remaking it so as to bring about a 'new creation'.[25]

Such risky dialogue, liable not to please radicals on either end of the spectrum, in many ways mirrors Gregory the Great's vision of the vocation to which a Christian leader is called, namely to renegotiate the union between valuable opposites.

In this respect, it is interesting to note that in his recent biography of Francis, Paul Vallely, the acclaimed international journalist and Visiting Professor in Public Ethics and Media at the University of Chester, suggests that Bergoglio is a man marked by paradox. Nowhere does he find this more apparent than in the manner in which Bergoglio lays claim to humility. More than any value, Vallely believes that Francis is marked by humility – it is this which so fascinates the media, who recount how he has washed the feet of prisoners and sneaks out of the Vatican at night to work with the homeless in Rome. Yet he does not see this as a virtue which comes easily to Francis, it is rather an orientation that is crafted and deliberate, and not to be confused with a subservient meekness. In Bergoglio, he suggests that, '[h]umility is a consciousness which wrestles against the unconsciousness of the

---

[24] Shorter, pp. 3–16.
[25] Pedro Arrupe, SJ, 'Letter to the Whole Society on Inculturation' in *Aixala* (ed.) vol. 3 (1978), pp.172–81 at 172 in A. Shorter, *Towards a Theology of Inculturation* (New York: Orbis Books, 1994), p. 11.

human ego.'[26] He sees it as a hard-won characteristic, always in danger of losing out to the naturally authoritarian propensity of Bergoglio's personality:

> It is a mode of behaviour which Bergoglio chose to adopt, after prayerful reflection that this was what God required of him. It was calculated. This is not to suggest that it was fake but it was thought-through [...] In Pope Francis humility is an intellectual stance and a religious decision. It is virtue which his will must seek to impose on a personality which has its share of pride and a propensity to dogmatic and domineering behaviour.[27]

It is interesting that in reading him in this way, Vallely is unknowingly vocalising Gregory the Great's model of Christian leadership, which so clearly calls on leaders to counter their natural tendencies as they strive to live out their calling. It is this which for Gregory underlines the need to hold both action and contemplation in creative tension. Every desire for action throws the leader back to contemplation – for only this can provide the resources out of which right action can arise.

It is, Bergoglio stressed, only in realising the impossibility of the task to which priests are called that the task can in any way be achieved; for only then does the leader realise that need to be fuelled by prayer and the Holy Spirit.[28] As he writes:

> We are poor priests of the Great Priest, little shepherds of the Great Shepherd. The grace which passes through our lips and hands is infinitely greater than we can imagine, and the oil of the anointing is what makes us good leaders – leaders who are led.[29]

It is this sense of being 'leaders who are led' that he sees enabling the 'pastoral gentleness'[30] that underpins the role of Christian leadership – an ability to joyfully engage with whatever is required, humbly serving but at the same time bringing the needed grace.

---

[26] Paul Vallely, *Pope Francis: Untying the Knots* (London: Bloomsbury, 2013), p. 196.

[27] Vallely, *Pope Francis*, p. 196.

[28] Vallely reports that Francis gets up at around 5.00 a.m. to pray each day.

[29] Pope Francis, *Encountering Christ*, p. 102.

[30] The topic of his opening homily in 2010 to the same gathering: Pope Francis, *Encountering Christ*, pp. 123–6.

Conclusion

There is perhaps a certain arrogance in even suggesting this is possible. Yet it is the kind of daring which arguably has historically led to rejuvenation in the Church, and for both the Franciscans and, later, the Jesuits it was so as they held action and contemplation in creative tension. Vallely sees this also as Francis' vision:

> Bergoglio knew that calling himself Francis was a gesture of some audacity. What he wanted, he proclaimed, was a Church which practices what it preaches. It is a philosophy encapsulated in the words attributed to St Francis of Assisi – the inspiration for Bergoglio's papal name: You must preach the gospel at all times, and if necessary use words.[31]

It is a vision which I have been arguing also finds its roots in Gregory the Great's *Pastoral Care*. As such, it is important to note that Gregory realises that in setting out on the impossible path of perfection that he was advocating, there was a strong possibility of failures, both large and small. And whilst he calls for nothing less than perfection from his leaders, at the same time he reminds those whom they serve that it is to miss the point if they are only too eager to rubbish all the positive elements of their leaders at the slightest hint of a slip or of them falling short of the mark.[32] To hold action and contemplation in an endless dynamic movement, one necessitated by the myriad of circumstances and people with which any leader is confronted, means that there are no simple answers to complicated questions. All the leader can do is to live within this tension, constantly relying on prayer to help him discern right action. This at least is Gregory's vision and, through the model of leadership that Francis appears to be advocating, we are, to my mind, seeing that, despite being inaugurated in the sixth century, it has lost none of its relevance or vigour.

---

31 Pope Francis, *Encountering Christ*, pp. 195–6.
32 Bramley, *Pastoral*, part III, ch. 3, p. 147ff.

Pope Francis' Journey:
A Journey for All of Us

Len Kofler, MHM

Millions and millions of people from all kinds of backgrounds and cultures admire Pope Francis to such an extent that *Time* magazine declared him the Person of the Year after only nine months of his pontificate.

People ask themselves what it is in Pope Francis that attracts such regard. After all, he was elected to perform the most difficult task in the world – to renew one of the oldest institutions, and that at the age of seventy-six, when most people retire. What qualities in this man have charmed the minds and hearts of so many people? How did he acquire these admirable characteristics? Are these excellences in the reach of every person? What do we need to do to acquire such attributes?

What are some of the features of this pope that made him so popular in such a short time working with the arduous tasks the cardinals set before him during the conclave?

- His simplicity appeals to many people. When I gave a talk on 'New Joy for the Church', I asked the question: 'What do you think about Pope Francis?' An elderly lady put her hand up and said: 'I like him, because I understand everything he says.' The simple language he uses is an essential element to get across his messages and touch people's hearts. It flows out of the person he is. Not only is his language simple, but his whole uncomplicated way of living makes him an authentic witness for Christ.

- Together with his simplicity goes his humility and desire to serve others. Everybody knows by now the many ways his humility comes across, from choosing the name of St Francis, to travelling on public transport, washing the feet of criminals, to making a cup of tea for a Swiss Guard.

- His love for the poor is shown not only in his frequent appeals to deal with the hunger of the many people who suffer from starvation, but also in his frequent actions. He wants a Church of the poor, the outcast, the marginalised, the persecuted and the rejected.

- Bergoglio was always a person with great determination. Without this the Jesuits would not have appointed him provincial at such a young age, under such difficult and delicate circumstances in Argentina. They knew that he would achieve what they wanted him to achieve just as the cardinals, when they elected him pope, knew that he would work to achieve what they want him to achieve – the renewal of the Church. Once he sees what he has to do, he does it regardless of the effects his decisions have on him. We can see this from the many efforts he has made to change and renew the Church in the last year. As a young Jesuit he may have been much more rule-oriented. As he became more experienced in his pastoral ministry, he has become much more person-oriented. It is clear that now, as pope, every person is important to him and he seeks to mediate God's mercy to all people.

- Pope Francis is a man of God. He is prayerful. He spends much time with God in private prayer. He is with God when he is alone just as he is with God when he is with people. He makes his decisions when he is with God in prayer. He puts himself in the presence of God dwelling on God's word, finding out what God wants him to do, and then he does it.

- Pope Francis is an outstanding leader, not with a huge army, money or might behind him, but the power of humble service. He has inspired many leaders in the wider world who have changed their leadership style. Some have sold their expensive cars and bought a simpler one. Some have acknowledged that they feel challenged by the Pope's simple lifestyle.

- Wisdom has become part of his personality. He does not get involved in arguments about statements he makes, in spite of the pressure put on him to do so, but rather stresses the essentials of the Good News.

- He is a man of action, and not just of long and arduous discussions and beautiful documents. When he sees that something needs to be done, he does it.

- Pope Francis is a warm person, full of love, who wants to make Christ known wherever he goes.

- He is an extraordinary missionary with followers all over the world and from all kinds of backgrounds. He is always keen to bring the Good News of the mercy and love of God to people. He stresses that the Church is not a refuge for sad people, but a house of joy.

- He is a forgiving person. If he gets hurt, he will forgive. He will not harbour resentment and revenge. He has learned that as leader he has to forgive those who hurt him if he is to be able to unite and not to divide.

- Pope Francis is authoritative, but not authoritarian. Authoritative people help others to grow. Authoritarian people often block the growth in themselves and others.

These twelve pillars are some of the characteristics of this great man. For us the question arises: Did he inherit these qualities or did he learn them in the course of his personal history? This is a question psychologists have argued about for many years; is it nature or nurture? Has he inherited these features or learned them? Or are they an interplay of both? What I would like to look at is this: How did he grow into the person he is now? He may have built upon inherited dispositions, but he definitely reflected on his life as he grew up.

Deep faith and trust are two important elements of Bergoglio's present personality which he acquired already in his family as a little boy. These permeate his whole life and activities. The way he perceives God comes very much from his experiences with his mother, father and other pivotal people in his life, like his grandmother Rosa. As the oldest child he acquired some traits of leadership. His most important training for leadership came from the Jesuits. He learned from early childhood that authentic power is service.

Also life events such as his illness contributed their share in moulding his personality. He made the decision to become a priest rather than to get married after his lung operation as a late teenager.

His Jesuit training deepened some of his characteristics and helped to develop others. He learned discipline and determination as a Jesuit. He acquired theological and psychological knowledge and insights in his training and teaching career. Ignatius wanted Jesuits to be humble, because Jesus, their model, was humble. Pope Francis is a true son of his spiritual father Ignatius. His Jesuit spirituality is a key to understanding some of the underlying convictions that are driving his pastoral activities and missionary zeal. His leadership experiences as Jesuit provincial and his years in charge of formation provided him with much material to reflect on later as he went to Germany and Córdoba. The picture of *Our Lady of Untying Knots* gave him insights into the knots in his psyche which he needed to untie. How can he reconcile love, which was deeply part of him, with discipline and obedience? How can he marry radical humility with dogmatic and authoritarian streaks?

His stay in Germany gave him the opportunity to get in touch with his deeper feelings of homesickness. His stay in Córdoba away from his native Buenos Aires was a further opportunity to reflect upon his experiences as teacher and provincial. After his stay in Córdoba in 1992, his style of leadership became more consultative and merciful as he grew in security and humility. Humility became a living reality in his life, not just a spiritual concept in his head. To be a good shepherd, one needs to be humble. He developed humility more and more through the spiritual exercises and their practical application in his daily ministry. His humility and simplicity became an expression of his convictions as a Christian and as a priest. We may ask: is his radical humility a reaction formation to dogmatic and authoritarian streaks or part of a process of integration? It seems to me that both psychological processes may have been involved together with God's grace.

Through his frequent visits to the slums as archbishop and cardinal, he deepened his simplicity, humility, and love of the poor. Bergoglio did not allow his doctrinal orthodoxy to overrule the priority of pastoral concerns as bishop or cardinal. The deep love for people became a force for good, no longer enslaved by rules and regulations, but animated by the love of Christ. From all these personal psycho-spiritual growth experiences he has acquired an abundance of resources for renewing the Church – a process he started from his first appearance on the balcony of St Peter's until now. He has many ideas of the various steps which are necessary for the deep, ongoing renewal of the Church.

In his address to the apostolic nuncios on 21 June 2013, Pope Francis made it very clear what type of person they should recommend as future bishops. In Brazil when he addressed bishops, religious and priests, he pointed out the importance of a holistic formation and training of future priests and religious. He models many essential aspects of our Christian faith in his personal lifestyle. This is the most influential educational tool for all the faithful and, indeed, for everyone. He has a warm heart and unconditional love for all people. Future leaders need to model themselves on Pope Francis who models himself on Christ. Thus, he is going back to the foundations of Christ's Church and presents that Church to the people of our time who are searching for meaning in their lives.

It is a great tribute to our society that we appreciate the values of the Pope which inspire his work and lifestyle. We are searching for deeper values. Our economic system needs these as a secure basis. Some fundamental attitudes which he acquired in his training as a Jesuit are very much part of his present ministry as Pope Francis.

He has learned to know himself deeply over the years through constant reflection. He knows his desires, feelings, motives and aspirations. He has learned to conquer his anger, fears and feelings of revenge and retaliation. He had many opportunities as a young provincial of the Argentinian province of Jesuits to learn to forgive when other members acted out their authority problems. In his many years as a Jesuit he has become aware of his likes and dislikes, wants and needs, drives, motivations and passions and how to use them to build up God's kingdom in himself and others. He is aware that his decisions need to be made not under the influence of retaliation, envy, hatred, lack of forgiveness or stubbornness, but out of mercifulness and love.

Simultaneously he has brought this self-knowledge into his pastoral service. He lives to serve others. He loves his people and wants to be with them. His desire to mediate God's love and mercy to them has grown so strong that he needs to watch his zeal and allow prudence to take over. It is obvious that he has great trust in God. He has to weigh up the need for self-care with his extraordinary desire to help the poor, the outcast and the marginalised, and also with his commitments as Bishop of Rome and Pope.

As a true follower of St Ignatius of Loyola, he is steeped in the spiritual exercises. He is used to meditation and contemplation. He has learned to immerse himself in the world, but also to withdraw from the world daily. This is a central principle for pastoral workers in our time. Only in this way can we remain the leaven in the world. In these frequent times with God, he struggles with his own drives, desires, wishes, likings in his pastoral setting and dwells on what kind of person God wants him to become. The world encourages us to live in luxury and comfort but God wants us to live a simple life as modelled by Pope Francis, like Jesus born in a stable.

The frequently quoted interviews with Rubin and Ambrogetti show us part of his struggles: 'It would be wrong for me to say that these days I ask forgiveness for the sins and offences that I might have committed. Today I ask forgiveness for the sins and offences that I did indeed commit.'

His changes of behaviour were not achieved simply or quickly. He needed to keep up his efforts and persevere in his internal struggles. He kept on making small steps and persevered despite inevitable setbacks. In this way he became more and more aware of God's mercy. Therefore, he keeps on repeating this theme of mercy. Mercy is the most powerful message which Our Lord taught us in the parables of the prodigal son and the woman caught in adultery: 'Neither do I condemn you.'

Francis has also learned to live in the present and revere the tradition, but at the same time to shape the future as he does in a massive way. He is now motivated by an ingrained passion to serve, not by an uncontrolled craving for status, power or money. This has initiated a massive cultural change across the Church and the world. His leadership style is a model for every leader – parents, teachers, company directors, bishops. His leadership style inspires and encourages cardinals, bishops, priests and lay pastoral workers.

What we admire in Pope Francis, we, too, can imitate. We can model our lives on Francis, who models his on Christ's. Our first step is that we become aware of ourselves, our behaviours, our emotions, our inspirations, our values and our motivations. Then we need to ask ourselves: What do we want to change in ourselves? We need to put this question to ourselves in the presence of our merciful God who will give us the courage and strength to look honestly at ourselves and to change the areas of our lives which are not in harmony with his will.

Change does not come quickly; we have to persevere. We may need to change thought patterns which generate anger, fear, resentment, bitterness and hatred. We may need to stop gossiping which is always destructive. It will take time to change habits, but it is well worthwhile as we can see in Pope Francis. We have to be satisfied with small steps in the right direction and celebrate these. This will encourage us to persevere.

As it is important to be among people serving them, so is it equally important to withdraw daily and spend time with Our Lord in meditation and reflection on our pastoral work, our family life, our interpersonal relationships, our handling of emotions, our conflicts. Whatever experiences we have during the day are worth reflecting on and learning from. The most painful experiences in our daily life can become means for personal spiritual growth and enrichment.

As we change our inner world of thoughts from destructive to constructive, we will slowly experience more positive emotions of joy and peace. These will affect our relationships with other people. We are better equipped to go out in love to people rather than in annoyance, with warmth rather than coolness. We bring ourselves to any pastoral situation and that is the reason why it is so important to work on our own psycho-spiritual journey. How Christlike are we? How much do we grow into the maturity of Christ in our pastoral work?

If parishioners or other people do not respond with love, but rather negatively, we can use such occasions as external graces to grow more spiritually. We can learn to be patient with them. We can learn to understand them. We can learn to love those who hate us. We can become more Christlike. Infinite opportunities open up for us as we realise that everything that happens to us is God's external grace. Our calling is to work together with that grace so that we keep on growing into the person that God, who is Love and Mercy, wants us to become. The more we grow in love the more we can warm people's hearts.

We may find it difficult to trust God's mercy. We may find it difficult to trust other people and ourselves. To grow in true trust, we have to learn to practice trust prudently after discerning whom we can trust. We have to learn to do it, because without practising it we cannot grow in trust. Jesus speaks words of love and mercy. These invite us to conversion in any area of our lives. Just as Bergoglio changed and learned to trust the mercy of God, we can learn to trust and surrender ourselves to God completely.

All structural changes initiated by the Pope, whilst very important, won't achieve the envisaged renewal of the Church unless our training of priests, religious and lay people changes. Pope Francis would not have been able to introduce these changes, if he himself had not undergone psycho-spiritual growth towards wholeness and holiness through suffering and personal struggles.

If we want the renewal in the Church and the world to continue, we need to change ourselves, our formation and our education. Pupils, students, candidates for priesthood and religious life all need to learn the values which the Pope puts before us and how to live them. Most people want to improve themselves but they do not know how to go about it. Society would change for the better, if people learned that authentic power consists in serving, that simplicity and humility are not signs of weakness but strength, and that warmth and love are central to human relationships. All these need to become part of education and formation. We need to teach students and people *how* to achieve this integration by facilitating them in their growth journey in seminaries and educational centres. We need to use the insights and skills of the human sciences, particularly of psychology and sociology, and integrate them with spirituality. Formation personnel have to undergo the same kind of transformation as the Pope if they are to be able to model and facilitate it to their students, who will then be able to 'heal wounds and warm the hearts of the faithful'.

Pope Francis asked Brazilian bishops bluntly: 'Are we still a Church capable of warming hearts?' On 18 May 2013 he gave the answer to this question in his address from St Peter's Square: 'Today's world stands in great need of witnesses, not so much of teachers but rather of witnesses. It is not so much about speaking, but rather speaking with our whole lives.'

A New Pope:
An Outside Appraisal

Richard Clarke

The name Bergoglio did ring the faintest of bells in my memory bank – albeit barely audible – as it was sonorously announced across St Peter's Square and across the world on that Wednesday evening last March. Googling was the only obvious response.

This quickly revealed an Argentinian cardinal archbishop of Italian descent, a Jesuit, who perhaps – and it could only have been a 'perhaps' – had been the runner-up in the last papal election, but relatively little else emerged. The unprecedented choice of the name Francis also seemed to raise enticing questions. Given that the new Pope was a Jesuit, might it not most probably be Francis Xavier, although just possibly Francis of Assisi, who lay behind the choice of name? But as the new Pope, dressed simply in a white cassock, began speaking to his new flock, it looked certain – without disrespect to Francis Xavier – that it could only be Francis of Assisi.

For those of us old enough to remember the arrival of John XXIII as pope, and more recently John Paul I, the impact was similar, instant and instinctive. The open smile, subtle self-deprecation and gentle humour could never have been something rehearsed or contrived. Here was someone who may have been in awe of the office he now held, but was not in the slightest awe of himself. The initial impression was confirmed in the snippets of news over the next few days. A pope who paid his hotel bill in person rather than through a flunkey, who seemed totally uninterested in papal attire, and who did not wish to live in a large and splendid apartment was certainly setting a new style of papacy. To the outsider, it appeared that although the new Pope was undoubtedly someone who was very streetwise and who understood fully the strength and impact of the symbolic gesture, it was equally clear that this was perfectly normal behaviour for him.

In his previous manifestation as a cardinal archbishop in Argentina, he had used public transport, lived a frugal lifestyle and had been an unstinting advocate for the poor and dispossessed. This was therefore – it had to be believed – not clever grandstanding by a new celebrity Pope, although those in the grandstands certainly appreciated what they were seeing.

In a cynical world that will seek instantly for any available Achilles' heel in the hope of dragging down a potential hero, it was inevitable that stories would begin to emerge of his alleged inaction and silence, while Superior of the Jesuits in Argentina thirty years earlier, when fellow Jesuits were kidnapped by government forces during the Dirty War in Argentina. There was never any serious suggestion that Fr Bergoglio – as he then was – had ever supported the Argentinian military regime of that time, but the tale of an apparent lack of personal courage was given the fullest of airings. Refreshingly, there was no major attempt at whitewashing or public relations 'explanation' on the part of the Vatican. The new Pope had made it clear from the outset that he fully believed himself to be – in company with the rest of humankind – a sinner in need of grace and mercy, and it is very difficult to land metaphorical punches on someone who is not concerned with projecting an image of moral beauty.

As time has gone on, deeper reflection has been demanded of all thinking Christians (and in more general terms) than simply on the immediate impact of a particular pope. As an outsider to the Roman Catholic tradition, I have found myself increasingly convinced that the papacy, post-Benedict, could only ever have been radically different, in every way, and for us all. Pope Benedict's resignation from the office of pope has changed forever our understanding of the papacy. It cannot now be seen by anyone – inside or outside the Roman Catholic Church – as an office which is *ontologically* distinct from other episcopates within the Church of God. It is now clearly and visibly an office which may be held by an individual for a period of time and then vacated, and this locates the papal office very firmly *inside* the life of the Church. It has been said frequently that in the modern world only a theologian-pope of the calibre of Joseph Ratzinger could have created what is in effect a new and radical break with accepted tradition, even if there had been historical precedent for a voluntary resignation from the papacy (albeit none for almost six hundred years).

Modern Roman Catholic canon law had, however, provided for such a possibility, and we therefore have to regard the action of Pope Benedict XVI not so much as a stepping outside of the tradition as of giving visible effect to that which was possible even if seemingly implausible. The ecclesiology *per se* of what the papacy is may therefore not have changed, but the *vernacular understanding* of it most certainly has. This does not mean that a pope should – or will – be treated with any less dignity or respect by any within the Church, and nor should the office he holds. Ecumenically, however, it has considerable implications. It allows those of us outside the Roman Catholic tradition to look on the papacy far more in terms of *patriarchate* and hence, dare one say, far more calmly and creatively.

Returning now to the particularity of this new pope, I find myself rather bemused by what appears, to a respectful outsider's eye, to be the apparent sidelining of the former pope from the ongoing narrative. This is not the intention of Pope Francis, and it seems clear that there is a continuing and cordial relationship between 'the two popes'. However, we should never forget that – as outlined above – it was Papa Ratzinger who graciously, unselfishly and generously paved the way for this exciting and invigorating new style and understanding of the papacy. He deserves better than constant (and generally unfavourable) contrasts with his successor. Joseph Ratzinger's apparent human enjoyment of some of the accoutrements of his office should not be a matter for sneering and sniping. Although he was far less adventurous theologically than I might personally have wished, I believe him to be not only a very fine theologian, but also an individual of huge spirituality and pastoral depth. On the only occasion on which I met Pope Benedict (and it was a brief and formal encounter) I was struck by his deeply personal touch coupled with a genuine and absolute focus on the person with whom he was holding the conversation. Entranced as we should be with Pope Francis, let it not be accompanied by any disparagement of his predecessor.

As the months have come and gone, we have all found ourselves admiring the new mood music that has been created by the ministry of Pope Francis, and it is certainly a music that has had echoes in the wider Church. Christians everywhere, and particularly in the western world, undoubtedly now feel a greater confidence in themselves, that they are not the remnant of a species that is so endangered as likely to become almost extinct in this part of the globe. This is in no small measure due to an upbeat yet humble papacy that has self-assurance without the semblance of arrogance.

On evangelism, we are hearing things from Pope Francis that we all need to hear and to propagate. We are not to get so obsessed with minutiae, structures and, in particular, with fashionable although possibly unfixable issues (certainly in the short term) that we forget Christ's primary command to make disciples. And at least part of the call to make disciples, the Pope suggests, must include the determination not to be so utterly repulsive in our self-righteousness that potential disciples of Jesus Christ will be understandably alienated from his Church. Above all, there has been Pope Francis' insistence that the poor of the world are Christ's deepest concern, and must therefore be our constant care as Christian disciples. And with this call to compassion comes the concomitant demand that there will be justice for all. Over many years the best of Roman Catholic social theology and the declarations of succeeding popes make it clear that this is all indeed at the heart of the Church's message of salvation. This is therefore no new teaching, but the simplicity of lifestyle that so characterises Pope Francis has undoubtedly conveyed a new impetus and purpose for all Christians.

One turns ineluctably from here to the fundamental question: Is the new Pope saying anything breathtakingly new or radically different, or is he simply saying things in a better way? Has the substance changed, as distinct from the style? It is of course hard to be totally certain at this point. There is no indication that Pope Francis will make dramatic pronouncements on any of the issues that seem to monopolise outside interest in the Church. From all that we have seen and heard thus far from the Pope, it would be surprising if there were to be any spectacular institutional *volte-face* on clerical celibacy, on the ordination of women to priesthood or episcopate, or on issues of human sexuality. On the other hand, the Pope has not only changed the tone of all public ecclesiastical discourse but, with particular regard to homosexuality, took a starting point (in the course of his famous airborne media interview) that was as unexpected as it was refreshing – the judgement of God on individuals is for God to make, not for us to presume. This is not to suggest, the Pope has been quick to underline, that there are no Church teachings or rules on personal morality, but his comments indicate that utter humility before God

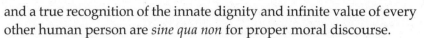

and a true recognition of the innate dignity and infinite value of every other human person are *sine qua non* for proper moral discourse.

Inevitably, I have a particular interest in how our new Pope views the ecumenical scene. As a member of the international Anglican-Orthodox dialogue, I am delighted that Pope Francis places a considerable importance on rapprochement between the Western and Eastern traditions of the Church. The path to unity between Western Christians may – counter-intuitively – pass through 'Constantinople'. In other words, if we within the Western traditions are to grow together it may well be through individual closer relationships with the Orthodox traditions of the Church. In addition, there appears to be a genuine 'chemistry' between Pope Francis and the equally new Archbishop of Canterbury, Justin Welby. This should be seen as of great significance and encouragement for members of both traditions. Whereas it is incontestable that Popes John XXIII and Paul VI understood and valued Anglicanism hugely, there is – to be candid – little indication that Pope John Paul II had any deep understanding of Anglican Christianity. Although Pope Benedict XVI and Archbishop Rowan Williams had an unaffected admiration for one another both spiritually and as fine theologians, there is much to be done if we are to return to the easy and companionable relationship that pertained in particular during the pontificate of Pope Paul VI. My hopes and prayers are that Pope Francis and the current Archbishop of Canterbury may enable us to return to that good time for the Western Church.

It has also been of great interest to observe the Pope's relationship with those of no religious faith. From the outset of his pontificate, he has demonstrated both adroitness and self-effacement in his dealings with the media, including those who would never have claimed any religious attachment. Within a few months of his arrival in Rome, Pope Francis had embarked on some thought-provoking public interaction with Eugenio Scalfari, the founder the Italian newspaper, *La Repubblica*. Scalfari, an atheist, posed a number of questions to the Pope. The responses of Pope Francis were both respectful and also what might only be described as modest. Although happy to speak of his own faith he made it clear that he was not intent on converting Scalfari to religious faith, a strange comment indeed! Entirely coincidentally I was able, a few days later, to hear (in the course of an inter-faith gathering in Rome) Eugenio Scalfari's own 'take' on his dialogue with Pope Francis. It was in fact rather disappointing, as Scalfari's understanding of Christian belief appears to be as rudimentary and fatuous as that of Richard Dawkins. If – as an aside – I might presume to advise the Pope as to a neighbour in Rome with whom he might hold extremely useful dialogue on non-religious humanism, it would rather be with Giuliano Amato, the former Prime Minister of Italy. He is not a religious believer, but he is both knowledgeable and insightful (and I have heard him speak on a couple of occasions) on the truly constructive relationship that should exist between the religious believer and the non-believer. Regardless of this, the deeply humane and immensely warm open-heartedness displayed by Pope Francis to those of no religious faith is a sign of real hope in a culture which too often chooses to believe that there can be no common ground between faith and non-faith.

It is of course far too early in his pontificate to make categorical pronouncements on the lasting influence and future legacy of this fascinating Pope. We may be certain, however, that he has made the task of being a Christian in our world feel more joyful and more purposeful for many disciples, not only within his own tradition but also for very many of us who are of other Christian traditions.

The Times They Are A-Changin'

Fáinche Ryan

Recently, while patiently manning a stall for the Loyola Institute, Dublin at the University Open Day, a young man came over and pointed to a picture of Pope Francis which someone had put at our stall, and with confidence proclaimed: 'That man is the reason that I am proud to be a Catholic.' A young Irish man, not afraid to proclaim that he is 'proud to be a Catholic', now that is remarkable. It does indeed say something of the person of Jorge Mario Bergoglio, Bishop of Rome and Pontiff of the Roman Catholic Church. It seems the journalists are correct in saying this pope has 'captured the imaginations of millions who had given up on hoping for the Church at all'.[1] Indeed the decision of *Rolling Stone*, the iconic rock music magazine, to make him the first pontiff to grace its cover speaks volumes. It is a typical picture of this pope, smiling and waving, accompanied by the words: 'The times they are a-changin'.[2]

There is however an attendant danger to all this popularity, and one could easily create a 'pop pope' and think this is just a pope with no goal to his pontificate except to make people feel good.

Joy

We – and by 'we' I mean not only Catholic Christians but all who find in Pope Francis things to be admired – need to look beyond the popular press and seek to discover what this man is seeking to communicate to us. This quite simply is *Evangelii Gaudium* (*EG*), the joy of the Gospel, the title of his first apostolic exhortation. I think this

---

1   'Pope Francis, The People's Pope', http://poy.time.com/2013/12/11/person-of-the-year-pope-francis-the-peoples-pope [accessed, 8 February 2014].

2   'Pope Francis graces the cover of Rolling Stone magazine', http://www.theguardian.com/media/greenslade/2014/jan/28/pope-francis-magazines [accessed, 8 February 2014].

is a good place to look to if we wish to discover something of how Francis perceives his mission as pontiff, his vocation as a baptised Christian.[3] He is not changing the Gospel message, it has always been Good News, but perhaps the difference lies in the simple yet at once profound understanding of the Gospel message. The fact is this person proclaiming the message is not afraid to let us know that he himself has experienced life, has suffered and made mistakes, and he has learned from his mistakes. He invites us all to be open to an encounter with Jesus for 'no one is excluded from the joy brought by the Lord'.[4] This is a constant message, extended evenly to all – 'God never tires of forgiving us; we are the ones who tire of seeking his mercy' (*EG*, n. 3). This man is real. He knows our frailty, for it is his frailty, but he also recognises the unfailing love of a God who

> time and time bears us on his shoulders. No one can strip us of the dignity bestowed upon us by this boundless and unfailing love. With a tenderness which never disappoints, but is always capable of restoring our joy, he makes it possible for us to lift up our heads and to start anew (*EG*, n. 3).

Dignity

The really striking message here is that of dignity, the 'dignity bestowed upon us by this boundless and unfailing love'. This message of our goodness, our inherent dignity, is one which most of humankind has a deep need to hear. Pope Francis tells us he thrills to read in the prophet Zephaniah about a God who rejoices over us with gladness, who renews us in love, and exults over us (Zeph 3:17).

Pope Francis continually reinforces this message of human dignity which he preaches. He embraced Vinicio Rina, a man severely disfigured as a result of a rare genetic disease, neurofibromatosis. Of greater significance from a Catholic ecclesiological perspective, on Holy Thursday he washed and kissed the feet of two young women as well as ten young men at the celebration of the Mass of the Lord's Supper at a youth prison (Casal del Marmo) on Rome's outskirts. For the first time a pontiff included females in the rite. Two of the twelve

---

3 Pope Francis, *Evangelii Gaudium* (The Joy of the Gospel), Apostolic Exhortation on the Proclamation of the Gospel in Today's World, 2013. Subsequent references will be denoted by *EG*, followed by the paragraph number(s).

4 Paul VI, Apostolic Exhortation *Gaudete in Domino* (1975), n. 297. Cited in *EG*, n. 3.

whose feet were washed were Muslim inmates. This was a radical action of a man who believes in our dignity, human dignity, a dignity bestowed upon us by the boundless and unfailing love of God. If we seek to call ourselves Christians, then we must live recognising the dignity with which God has gifted us, and we must seek to proclaim this message to others.

This is what Pope Francis asks of us. One man alone cannot carry out the message of Christ. We are all invited to respond to the invitation to share the joy of the Gospel, to invite all people to rejoice in their own humanity, and in the humanity of the other, in particular the 'strange' other. In Francis' preaching and teaching we find an inherent challenge to a clericalised Church structure: his vision of a Church is of a people who share the responsibility of proclaiming the Good News of a people loved by God. This is the duty of all Christians, indeed it is an obligation, as all peoples have a 'right to receive the Gospel' (*EG*, n. 14).

Ecclesiology

The ecclesiology, the vision of Church, which inspires this Bishop of Rome, is a source of joy to many. His remarks, 'I have sought advice from a number of people' and his consciousness of the need to promote a sound 'decentralisation' (*EG*, n. 16) all give hope to a people who oft-times have felt removed from a Church structure which seemed not to listen, or seek their advice. The Church that is now being proclaimed is one which includes not only those who faithfully seek nourishment in the word and the bread of eternal life but also those who 'preserve a deep and sincere faith ... [while] seldom taking part in worship' (*EG*, n. 15). It is a Church seeking relationship with the baptised whose lives no longer 'reflect the demands of Baptism',[5] in the hope of restoring 'the joy of faith to their hearts' and inspiring a commitment to the Gospel (*EG*, n. 15). Then there are the many who do not know God, or have rejected Jesus Christ, all of these people have a right to receive the Gospel. To ensure the joy of the Gospel can be shared, ecclesial structures, he notes, may need renewal.

---

[5] Benedict XVI, Homily at Mass for the Conclusion of the Synod of Bishops (28 October 2012): AAS 104 (2102), p. 890. Cited in *EG*, n. 15.

Herein lies a challenge, for change is always difficult, and people tend to think that the way things have been for their lifetime, is the way things always have been. We see courage in this man's decision to live in Casa Santa Marta, a Vatican residence for visiting clergy and lay people, and not in the papal apartments. By his actions, and his words, Pope Francis is not only challenging the structures of the Roman Curia, he is also calling each one of us out of our comfort zone. 'God's word', he writes, 'is unpredictable in its power … The Church has to accept this unruly freedom of the word, which accomplishes what it wills in ways that surpass our calculations and ways of thinking' (*EG*, n. 22).

The Unruly freedom of the word

This is where I would like to turn our attention to now – to the unruly freedom of the word. Pope Francis calls the Church to a 'renewal of preaching … to a reform of the Church and her preaching which would enable it to reach everyone' (*EG*, n. 43). Christian preaching must proclaim the 'beauty of the saving love of God made manifest in Jesus Christ who died and rose from the dead' (*EG*, n. 36). In this world of instant communication, the message being communicated can too easily be reduced to secondary aspects, and this is the message which many can begin to confuse with the foundational truth of God's love, and the gift of human dignity. This clarity with which Pope Francis seeks to communicate the central message of the Gospel, is one of joy for, as St Thomas Aquinas points out: 'the precepts which Christ and the apostles gave to the people of God "are very few".'[6] Care must be taken not to deform the integrity of the Gospel message. This, Francis implies, we are prone to do. Perhaps we too easily forget the dignity of our sister and brother.

In *Evangelii Gaudium*, particular attention is paid to the issue of 'preaching within the liturgy', and here we again encounter a pastor in touch with his people: 'We know that the faithful attach great importance to it, and that both they and their ordained ministers suffer because of homilies: the laity from having to listen to them and the clergy from having to preach them!' (*EG*, n. 135). This is a man who knows his people – all of them. He has a sense of humour, and yet notes that this reality 'is sad'. God, in the homily, displays God's

---

[6] S. Th., I–II, q. 107, a. 4. Cited in *EG*, n. 43.

power through human words. God seeks to reach out to others through the homily. Catholic preaching must be renewed if the joy of the Gospel is to reach its audience, to be heard by them, and thus form and inform them so that the world and the Church, *semper reformanda* – always in need of reformation – may slowly be transformed.

Smell the sheep

Here we reach the heart of the matter for Francis. Preaching, in particular the homily with its Eucharistic context, is part of the ongoing dialogue between God and the people. The preacher must know the community, and its needs for the Gospel joy. The homily 'cannot be a form of entertainment like those presented in the media', it should be brief and measured, and the Eucharistic context 'demands that preaching should guide the assembly, and the preacher, to a life-changing communion with Christ in the Eucharist' (*EG*, n. 137). It is the Lord who should be the centre of attention. This is the clear message of Francis – in liturgy and in life, for a Christian, Christ must be both the guiding compass and the one to whom we are directed.

Paul VI agreed with Francis' awareness that the 'faithful … expect much from preaching'.[7] If the preaching is to meet their rightful expectations, Francis is clear – good preaching demands good preparation, prolonged study and the use of the necessary tools provided by literary analysis to discover the central message of the readings in order to communicate it intelligibly. Good preaching is to be about God, and thus about joy and hope. God is allowed to speak, and God speaks Good News. The Holy Spirit and prayer are all to be called upon in the preparation of the homily. A good homily should communicate truth, beauty and goodness, the 'beauty of the images used by the Lord to encourage the practise of good'. 'To encourage the practice of the good', the very phrasing here gives an insight into how Francis understands God, and the reality of human living. We have a phrase in Irish, '*Mol an óige, agus tiocfaidh si,*' which means: 'Praise the young and they will flourish.' This seems to be how Francis has chosen to minister – to encourage and praise so that the practice of the good is encouraged. The homily breaks open the readings, providing the gathered community with a memory of the wondrous things done by God, an encouraging memory, for each word of

---

[7]   Paul VI, Apostolic Exhortation *Evangelii Nuntiandi* (1975), n. 33. Cited in *EG*, n. 158.

scripture is a gift before it is a demand. The focus is positive, suggesting what we can do, and not pointing out what shouldn't be done. 'We become fully human when we become more than human' (*EG*, n. 8). This, Francis is clear, shall be God's work.

The dignity of the human is the ever present message of this papal exhortation. Human reason is identified as an important participant in the journey towards human flourishing. In response to the process of secularisation which reduces faith and the Church to the sphere of the private and the personal, Francis notes that 'we need to provide an education which teaches critical thinking and encourages the development of mature moral values' (*EG*, n. 64). Critical thinking, theology, a theology in dialogue with other sciences and human experiences, and trust in a God who always takes the initiative, are all identified as crucial to authentic evangelisation, and indeed critical to good preaching.

Locked doors

Words and theology must be realised in our actions and practices. Can we preach a loving God and restrict access to the sacraments? We must give very careful and prayerful thought to the matter. Francis seems doubtful. In response to the tendency to all too often close the doors of access to the sacraments, he reminds us that the Eucharist 'is not a prize for the perfect but a powerful medicine and nourishment for the weak' (*EG*, n. 47). In this, he is restating a traditional teaching. Words are not minced by this smiling pope. He admonishes: 'Frequently, we act as arbiters of grace rather than its facilitators. But the Church is not a tollhouse; it is the house of the Father, where there is a place for everyone, with all their problems' (*EG*, n. 47). Yet we cannot be naive. We need to remember how St Paul addressed the problem of Eucharistic participation in a letter to the Corinthians:

> Whoever, therefore, eats the bread or drinks the cup of the Lord in an unworthy manner will be answerable for the body and blood of the Lord. Examine yourselves, and only then eat of the bread and drink of the cup. For all who eat and drink without discerning the body, eat and drink judgement against themselves (1 Cor 11:27–9).

In this admonishment there is great joy and great hope to be found for the many who have become alienated from the house of the Father.

Francis writes that 'one concrete sign of such openness is that our church doors should always be open, so that if someone, moved by the Spirit, comes there looking for God, he or she will not find a closed door' (*EG*, n. 47). This is a challenge for those who wish to keep their church buildings safe and secure, with reduced hours of public access. It is as if Jesus is kept locked up safely in his tabernacle, safe but alone. Increasingly, churches are locked when not being used for liturgy. It makes it more difficult for a chance visit, such as the visit undertaken by Edith Stein to a church where she was able to observe a woman with a shopping bag enter and pray:

> For me, it was a completely new experience. People went to the synagogues or Protestant churches I had visited only for divine service. Here, however, people came to an empty church during their workaday activities as if for an intimate talk. I have never forgotten it.[8]

The smiling pope chastises those of us who lock our doors to safeguard our treasures, and might advocate, that just as a missionary heart must allow 'its shoes to get soiled by the mud of the street' (*EG*, n. 45) so too must our churches get soiled by the mud of the street. Exclusion from our society, for economic reasons, or from our Church for moral reasons, or from our churches for security reasons are all to be questioned, challenged. They are all, in their own ways, processes of dehumanisation.

'Leave this earth somewhat better than we found it'
This pope is undoubtedly one to be listened to, and to learn from, both in his writings and in his actions. He advocates that we 'leave this earth somewhat better than we found it' (*EG*, n. 183). He communicates a joy that is for our time. He is a disciple who leads by example and one who seeks to see the dignity in every human being – to recognise that dignity in how he relates to people. There is much we can learn from him. Perhaps that which inspires most confidence, is his realistic approach. While constantly inviting us to rejoice in the glory of Christ's cross, Francis at the same time recognises that for many Christians life can all too often seem like Lent without Easter. Even then, he speaks of a joy 'which adapts and changes', but 'always

---

8   Edith Stein, http://www.catholicireland.net/edith-stein [accessed, 8 February 2014].

endures' because of the personal certainty that, despite all, we are 'infinitely loved'. He is aware that he, with us, is part of a long story, and that

> becoming a people demands something more. It is an ongoing process in which every new generation must take part: a slow and arduous effort calling for a desire for integration and a willingness to achieve this through the growth of a peaceful and multifaceted culture of encounter (*EG*, n. 220).

We are a people on pilgrimage. 'The important thing is not to walk alone' (*EG*, n. 33). We have reason for hope and to be joyful.

'Beautiful Morality':
A One-Man Vatican III

Richard Rohr, OFM

From the moment he took the right name, we knew something was different and even good about this new pope. But little could we have imagined! Maybe we *did* have to go to the 'ends of the earth', as he himself said, to find such an extraordinary and compelling man as Jorge Bergoglio. Even one popular American television host said: 'He is threatening my time slot!' And another said: 'This man seems to do something newsworthy every day. We have never had anyone like this!'

Apart from his astute, pastoral and honest statements on so many important issues, his admirable Gospel lifestyle, his engaging personality, Pope Francis has become for many of us a living example of the healthy fruit that comes from the true 'discernment of spirits' that Paul speaks of (1 Cor 12:10) and that the Society of Jesus has so skilfully unpackaged for the larger Church. In this man, we are seeing discernment in action, and what I would then describe as 'performative Christianity' (practice over theory).

The result for the rest of us is an emotional subtlety which action often allows and words often do not. I am afraid we have not come to expect this emphasis on practice from the hierarchy, along with an intelligence that is non-dualistic, an amazing courage that could only be sustained by very real prayer 'contact', and a compassion that is both a challenge and inspiration to much of the world. Pope Francis is not dismissing the old; like all true prophets he is revealing what the tradition was really trying to say all along. In looking at much of our Catholic past, I can only think of Jesus' words to Jerusalem in his time: 'How often I have longed to gather your children together as a hen gathers her brood under her wings, *and you were not willing!*'

[emphasis added] (Mt 23:38). Now we cannot get enough of it! We actually have a pope who gathers instead of scatters (Lk 11:23).

As a teacher of contemplative prayer and the contemplative mind, I have come to believe that the Western Church has put far too much effort and fight into metaphysical questions ('What certainly is') and not nearly enough energy into practical epistemology ('How do you know what you think you know with such certainty – about what is?'). This lack of honest self-knowledge and self critique (prayer?) has made most of us victims of our own temperament, prejudices, culture, small history, and already-in-place agendas, while presuming we are speaking for that which is 'truly catholic'. Thus I have always felt that 'too Roman' and 'truly catholic' were oxymorons. Far too often, it has been our small mind's understanding and some very recent traditions that have had to pass for 'what eternally is', even from many popes. The bias is revealed when we see how many of the emphasised 'eternal truths' seem to be concerned with keeping us co-dependent on the clergy, their authority, and their ministrations. Soon a self-serving understanding of obedience became more the Gospel ideal than love. Any contemplative knows that is not anywhere close to true.

In Pope Francis' ability to critique and balance out his own mind and feelings ('discernment'), he is ironically able to *trust his own experience*, use it in a contemplative way, while still beautifully illustrating it from both Scripture and Tradition. This is a very solid methodology that we have not taught most Catholics, and has allowed us to use both Scripture and Tradition in very wooden and mechanical – and small – ways. I am not sure, however, which comes first. Does the contemplative mind naturally discern instead of just 'decide'? Or does the discerning person naturally develop a broad contemplative mind? It does not really matter. All I know is that we see both of them highly developed in Pope Francis.

After a year as pope, I would describe him as a one-man Vatican Council and, if you listen and read closely, he has made astute and compelling comments on almost every one of the major themes and documents of Vatican II and – even more – from use of Scripture, to the Church in the modern world, to seminary formation, interfaith dialogue, science and faith, religious life, Gospel spirituality, mission, ethics, and issues of peace and justice. Fifty years after the Council, after surely seeing the sad state of both Church and culture, he courageously shows no temptation to backtrack, to move towards cynicism, to blame others or to negativity of any sort; but all we hear is a profound sense of 'What are we waiting for?', as he writes in *Evangelii Gaudium (EG)*.[1]

Pope Francis is proudly reclaiming words that we were formally taught in the 1960s by the bishops gathered in official assembly: *subsidiarity, collegiality, dialogue* and *solidarity*. These are words that were not just forgotten in the intervening years, but often outrightly opposed and even denied as Gospel. Quite sad! He fully reinvigorates biblical concepts that further developed after the Council, like 'preferential option for the poor', which had been dismissed by some cardinals and bishops as 'class warfare'. So much post-Vatican II retrenchment made many of us wonder if the Roman Church was basically irreformable. One man, his preferences and devotions, could seemingly undo an entire Council of the Church. With popes and his 'court' dressing the part, people said as they abandoned the Church: 'It really is a monarchy after all.' Although most did not fully exit, they just lost interest in what should have been, and could have been, pearls of great price for the whole world, ecclesiastical and political.

This pope also has singular authority, yet it proceeds precisely because he builds on the Council and even more because he builds on the Gospel. In a short time, he has moved the conversation from continuous verbal clarification to a *lifestyle* understanding of the teaching of Jesus ('performative'),[2] just as his namesake Francis of Assisi did. He reasserts 'a hierarchy of truths', and clearly places *mercy* at the very top of that hierarchy. Further, he brilliantly encourages a fitting sense of proportion (*EG*, nn. 34, 38, 40–1) in regard to emphasis and frequency of various Gospel themes. Without this proportionality he says that the whole message 'will run the risk of losing its freshness and will cease to have "the fragrance of the Gospel"' (*EG*, n. 39). And he even dares to speak of a needed 'conversion of the papacy' (*EG*, n. 32) itself, which maybe only a pope can fittingly assert without sounding rebellious.

After challenging his own office, he moves through every major group in the Church, calling each of us to reform, and he is not afraid

---

[1] Pope Francis, *Evangelii Gaudium* (The Joy of the Gospel), Apostolic Exhortation on the Proclamation of the Gospel in Today's World, 2013, n. 1. Subsequent references will be denoted by *EG*, followed by the paragraph number(s).

[2] See Second Vatican Council, *Unitatis Redintegratio*, n. 11.

to describe a precise shape to the 'conversion' of each group, sometimes in embarrassing detail, but always based on Gospel values and the love of God, and not just moralistic housecleaning. 'Sourpusses', 'spiritual consumers', 'mummies in a museum', 'young monster priests creating young monster people', and 'antiquarians' all come in for a scolding in his interviews. We need no more 'diagnostic overload' as a substitute for actual faith, he says. None of us could get away with this honesty, but now it comes from 'Daddy' himself! I am told he is the first pope to use exclamation points and colloquialisms that we all understand; we also do not doubt his sincerity. (Admittedly, the last two popes said some of these same things, but why is it that we did not believe they really believed them? Was it their appointees, their actual lifestyle or their grandiosity? Or something else?)

Pope Francis is also wise enough to avoid the ecclesiastical overreach that has characterised so much of Catholic history, saying that 'neither the Pope nor the Church have a monopoly on the interpretation of social realities or the proposal of solutions to contemporary problems' (*EG*, n. 184). He is eager to give autonomy and authority to other sciences and disciplines because he can trust that truth – if it is the truth – is one and will necessarily show itself through all disciplines (*EG*, nn. 242–3). In other words, he has a strong belief in the abiding presence and power of the Holy Spirit working in the world and in the Church. Surely that is the basis for his obvious joy. The best we can do, he hints, is to turn the world's clean water into the intoxicating wine of the full Gospel. But the water is already there waiting to be served.

As a preacher and teacher, I find his direct and pastoral advice on preaching quite extensive and very practical (*EG*, nn. 135–75). He tells us, for example, quoting Augustine, that people only love that which is 'beautiful', and we should make our homilies short, to the point and with the attraction of beauty, appealing to both good scholarship and the 'spiritual sensitivity' that only comes from prayer, love of God and actual love of the people right in front of you.

All in all, I believe we have the rarest of combinations in one man. He is both a prophet and a priest, both a reformer and one who 'knows how to pope' at the same time. Tell me how often that has happened in Catholic history. Has it ever happened? I will have to ask the historians. Pope Francis is on the offensive in the best sense of that term, and wasting no time circling the wagons, presiding over a funeral or defending the Church from heretics and sinners, but is calling us all to our very best selves. He often uses the phrase: 'Do not allow yourself to be robbed of the Gospel!' (or 'joy', or 'mission', or 'community'), as if he is guarding and promoting a great treasure which he knows we surely have. This is one reason the world trusts and likes him. One survey said he enjoys a ninety-two per cent approval rating, which is almost unknown of for public figures.

Perhaps it is idle imagining, but I cannot help but wonder how many of the historical divisions and endless acrimony in Christian history could have been avoided, or at least seriously softened, if the Vicar of Peter had simply lived the Gospel the way we see Pope Francis live it. Why would you want to fight him or separate from him? I am afraid many, if not most, of the Vicars of Peter, created their own backlash by holding themselves so much higher than the rest of the Body of Christ. 'Every action creates an equal and opposite reaction.'

Once the Pope took the entire Christ image to himself and had to think of himself as the very 'Vicar of Christ' (which, biblically, is clearly the whole Body of Christ and never one person), he just set himself up for centuries of resentment and rebellion when he could never possibly live up to such an exalted title. I think the Australians call it the 'tall poppy syndrome'. (I observe the stiff and utterly inhuman pictures of Pope Pius XII with a real sympathy for his entrapment, especially after reading his biographies.) Of course, we cannot just blame him, because it was we Catholics, just like the Israelites, who wanted a 'king' (1 Sam 12), and then he only tried to play this impossible role. Many appear to want and love this pomp and circumstance down to our own time, whether it has anything to do with Jesus or not. Maybe we never knew the opposite was possible until Pope Francis?

One would have thought that such obvious teaching as Jesus' statement that 'all who exalt themselves will be humbled, and all who humble themselves will be exalted' (Mt 23:12) would have been more commonly heeded among the hierarchy. But at last we now have a pope who rightly begins his first formal interview by saying 'I am a sinner'.[3] Now the world and the news media have no need to pull

---

[3]   From Pope Francis' interview with Antonio Spadaro, SJ, published in *America*,
    September 2013.

him down, nor do they even want to. A largely fatherless world instead longs for a good 'daddy' that they can admire and trust. He is creating a lovely party at the so-called bottom, where no one is competing to go, but everybody really is. Pope Francis, just like Jesus, is quite ready to go 'down', and just as the cross itself promised us he pulls us *up* from that free and honest position.

Pope Francis is helping a lot of us to see that 'style', when it is grounded, authentic and heartfelt ends up being much more than style, and is actually *substance*. He is helping us to see that 'the fragrance of the Gospel' (*EG*, n. 39), as he calls it, comes mostly from attitude, intention, and the energy that an action is done with, much more than the bare action itself. I have come to call formal moral responses without the right energy 'ugly morality', and the world has rightly grown tired and mistrustful of it, just as Jesus did with the Pharisees. Whereas almost all people of good will still see a moral response that is formally imperfect (aren't they all?) but energetically right (for example, other-centred, generous, trusting, sincere and humble) as 'beautiful morality'. Pope Francis is not just teaching but also exemplifying – and shocking the whole world – with such *beautiful morality*. Style is, in fact, very real substance, and might just be at the heart of the Gospel's subversive message.

Many of us are waiting 'with eager longing for the revealing of the children of God' (Rom 8:19), and pray every day that God will give Pope Francis the protection and the years to complete his mission. I sense that he is going to pick his battles in his 'hierarchy of truths'. Hopefully, as his credibility and authority increase, he will take on even more contentious issues that we all know are not essential to the Gospel (for example, priestly celibacy, contraception and forms of female leadership), and some that we know are clear distortions of the Gospel (such as our exclusionary and punitive policies on almost anything). With his obvious Christian imagination, I suspect he will make very clear some Gospel messages that we have come to believe were merely impossible ideals (for example, love of enemies, non-violence, option for the poor, acceptance of the probably eight to ten per cent of humanity that has always been LGBT [Lesbian, Gay, Bisexual, Transgender], critique of money and money systems).

I think a brilliant contribution he has already made – subtle but substantive – is his ability to distinguish text from context, and pointing out quite early that the Gospel cannot be a list of separated doctrines and moral positions that try to stand on their own apart from any underlying world view or Gospel conversion. It seems to me this is where a rather large percentage of teachers and teachings have come from in recent centuries, and from both progressive and conservative sides. One is given the impression that 'if I do this, or if I agree with this, then I am saved, go to heaven, or God will love me', but there is no evidence of a foundational transformation, conversion or encounter with grace that changed everything in one's heart and mind. He is telling us that we have too much morality and doctrine and leadership that operate outside of our own personal transformation. Hear him speak in this regard:

> The message we preach runs a great risk of being distorted or reduced to some of its secondary aspects. In this way certain issues which are part of the Church's moral teaching are taken out of the context which gives them their meaning. The biggest problem is when the message we preach then seems identified with those secondary aspects which, important as they are, do not in and of themselves convey the heart of Christ's message (*EG*, n. 34).

He also states that we must not be 'obsessed with the disjointed transmission of a multitude of doctrines to be insistently imposed ... the message has to concentrate on the essentials, on what is most beautiful, most grand, most appealing and at the same time most necessary' (*EG*, n. 35).

As someone who has been on the road for over forty years, in many countries, cultures and so many different church situations, this quote alone could have cast 'bread upon the waters' (Eccl 11:1), and brought needed discernment and a lovely common sense to over half of the issues and controversies that I was asked to address. The transformative message of the Gospel too often got lost as everyone from seminarians to cardinals seemingly tried to establish an identity through identification with this issue or that, when often the underlying 'fragrance of Christ' was not at all apparent, yet its counterfeit was. The creating of image and persona is one of the common ways we all avoid transformation, and the one that Jesus spots and condemns so consistently. Liturgical minutiae, vestments, titles (only the ordained can properly be called 'ministers') and 'proper translations' (of often bad theology), became the obsessive talking points instead of conversion itself for much of the last twenty-five years. But the sanctuary was our only remaining, if shrinking, field of influence and control.

Following the momentous reforms of Vatican II, we were allowed to regress into small culture wars, identity politics, temperamental conservatism and temperamental progressives – both groups claiming the mantle of the full Gospel. Another fine Jesuit, the Canadian Bernard Lonergan, said that 'conversion is the experience by which one becomes an authentic human being'. This is almost too simple, it seems, and also too demanding – so we became liberals or conservatives instead. No wonder our wonderful Jesus simply became 'an authentic human being' or, as he most commonly said of himself, 'a son of man'. He seemed to know that that is what we would most avoid, deny and run from – in the name of being spiritual and religious.

But we now have a pope who is offering both the world and the Church 'third force wisdom' beyond the dualistic world of either fight or flight. He points out the idols on both sides with words that can only be called honest, obvious common sense once you hear it, and a humanly attractive personality that makes the world think he really lives his own message. He makes the truth believable and even loveable.

The Revolution of Tenderness: The Theology of Pope Francis

Tina Beattie

Pope Francis has begun a transformation in the Church, which many interpret as bringing to fruition the reforms that started with Vatican II and stalled under Pope Benedict XVI. Although most of the changes so far have been in style rather than substance, Francis has effected a paradigm shift in the way the papacy functions and in the way the Catholic Church is perceived. We should not however forget that this radical change began with Benedict XVI's retirement – a courageous personal decision with vast ramifications for the papacy.

If Francis proves faithful to his word, and if he is graced with the courage, health and stamina to continue what he has started, then the possibilities as well as the challenges are immense. Apart from the institutional changes he has already set in motion with regard to the workings of the Curia and the management of Vatican finances, we can expect to see a shift to greater collegiality, which was a key reform endorsed by the Council but never implemented, a more influential role for the laity, including women, and a renewed emphasis on the parish as the living heart of the Church. Fundamental to these changes will be his repeatedly stated desire to promote 'a poor Church for the poor'. He has shown himself to be opposed to all forms of clericalism, and to be far less concerned with discipline and rules than his predecessor. His attitude might be summarised in his observation that 'the Son of God, by becoming flesh, summoned us to the revolution of tenderness'.[1]

In this chapter, I focus on Francis' theology and on what effect some of these changes might have on the life and teachings of the

---

[1] Pope Francis, *Evangelii Gaudium* (The Joy of the Gospel), Apostolic Exhortation on the Proclamation of the Gospel in Today's World, 2013, n. 88. All subsequent references will be denoted by *EG*, followed by the paragraph number(s).

Church. I explore some of the main themes in his apostolic exhortation *Evangelii Gaudium* (*EG*), and I also refer to the interview which he gave in September 2013 to Antonio Spadaro, SJ, editor-in-chief of the Italian Jesuit journal, *La Civiltà Cattolica*.[2] This deeply personal interview offers important insights into the man and his vision for the Church. However, I begin by giving a brief overview of the changing situation of Catholic theology since the Council as the context in which we must approach Francis' emergent theological vision.

The Second Vatican Council was a revolutionary event which affected every aspect of Catholic life, but perhaps one of its most controversial and far-reaching effects was not just on Catholic theology but on what it means to be a Catholic theologian. The idea that a Catholic theologian was an ordained man with a licentiate to do theology in accordance with the teachings of the Church became diluted by the emergence of large numbers of lay theologians from the late 1960s, including many women, working beyond the direct control of the Congregation for the Doctrine of the Faith (CDF). Encouraged by the dialogical spirit of the Council, many were inspired by the various liberation movements sweeping through society in the 1960s. Catholic universities became host to contextual, feminist and liberationist theologies, while theology degrees in secular universities gradually began to incorporate Catholic sources and ideas into their curricula.

While Catholicism has always been able to accommodate a wide range of traditions, the rapid processes of inculturation and liberation which followed the Council led to considerable magisterial anxiety. By the end of the 1980s, John Paul II had overseen a purge which had eliminated many of the liberationist influences from the Latin American hierarchy and seminaries, where it had gained its strongest foothold. By the time of Benedict XVI's election, issues of sexual rights, including women's reproductive rights and homosexual rights, had overtaken liberation theology to become the most neuralgic challenge confronting the Magisterium. The *sine qua non* of being Catholic came to be focused not on faithful discipleship of Jesus Christ within the sacramental unity of the Church, but on unquestioning adherence to a growing list of prohibitions to do with contraception,

---

[2]   See Antonio Spadaro, SJ, 'A Big Heart Open to God' in *America*, 30 September, 2013, http://www.americamagazine.org/pope-interview [accessed, 20 January 2014]. All subsequent quotations are from this online translation of the interview.

abortion, homosexuality and women's ordination, while conservative Catholics used the blogosphere to launch a concerted campaign against theologians accused of 'dissent'.

This was the situation when Francis became Pope, but from the outset he made it clear that he intended to change the agenda. In his interview with Spadaro, he explained that, although he is 'a son of the Church', he wanted to avoid insisting 'only on issues related to abortion, gay marriage and the use of contraceptive methods', because it is important to avoid becoming 'obsessed with the transmission of a disjointed multitude of doctrines to be imposed insistently'. Rather, the moral teachings of the Church must flow from the 'simple, profound, radiant' proposal of the Gospel, because 'the proclamation of the saving love of God comes before moral and religious impera-tives'. In *Evangelii Gaudium* he makes clear his impatience with 'querulous and disillusioned pessimists, "sourpusses"' (*EG*, n. 85), and with those whose preoccupation with rules and institutions produces a 'tomb psychology' which obliterates the joy of evangel-isation (*EG*, n. 83).

In keeping with its title, *Evangelii Gaudium* is first and foremost an evangelical celebration of the joy of the Gospel. Francis wants a joyful, courageous and daring Church that is not afraid to take risks, a Church which accepts the 'unruly freedom of the word' (*EG*, n. 22). This must be a community of evangelisation which is willing to 'stand at the crossroads and welcome the outcast', and to take on 'the smell of the sheep' (*EG*, n. 24). In the Spadaro interview he describes the Church as 'a field hospital', and in *Evangelii Gaudium* he repeats a message we have heard in one form or another many times: 'I prefer a Church which is bruised, hurting and dirty because it has been out on the streets, rather than a Church which is unhealthy from being confined and from clinging to its own security' (*EG*, n. 49). These themes are the prism through which all his reflections and obser-vations on the nature of evangelisation are refracted, with an emphasis on beauty, newness and joy because 'it is not by proselyt-ising that the Church grows, but "by attraction"' (*EG*, n. 14).

With all this in mind, let me attempt to situate Francis as a theologian. In the years since Vatican II, the Church's teachings have been shaped by two very different theological influences – first Karl Rahner, and more recently, Hans Urs von Balthasar. These two great theologians, one German and one Swiss, represent polar opposites in terms of the issues that have divided the Church since the Council. Rahner was more open than von Balthasar to the salvific significance of other traditions and cultures and more willing to engage with contemporary issues of society and politics, but his theology remained essentially western European in outlook. Von Balthasar was a major source for the development of John Paul II's 'theology of the body', which for all its celebration of married sexuality is a conservative theological movement targeted at the suppression of campaigns for sexual and reproductive rights. Von Balthasar's vast theological output was haunted by nostalgia for the pre-conciliar Church and informed as much by the romanticism of nineteenth-century European culture as by the Catholic theological tradition.

Francis is introducing a different theological perspective, nurtured by Ignatian spirituality and rooted in the theology of the Latin American Church – although not necessarily liberation theology. In *Evangelii Gaudium*, he repeatedly cites documents from the Latin American Bishops' Conference, particularly the Aparecida document which, as Cardinal Bergoglio, he helped to draft. It is significant that this document takes its name from the Marian shrine in Brazil at which the 2007 general assembly of Latin American and Caribbean bishops took place, because this associates it with the devotions of the millions of pilgrims who visit the shrine. This emphasis on popular piety is a crucial key to understanding Francis' theology.

Theologians in Argentina never embraced liberation theology in the way that theologians in countries such as Brazil, Peru, Nicaragua and El Salvador did.[3] Argentinian theologians promoted what is sometimes referred to as 'the theology of the people', also sometimes associated with Peronism, which was more populist and less political than liberation theology. While liberation theologians tended to distance themselves from popular piety and devotions in favour of politicised programmes of conscientisation and awareness-raising, Argentinian theologians celebrated popular piety as an expression of the religion of the people, and in that way they sought to align themselves with the poor. This includes the work of Argentina's slum priests, who live and work among the slum dwellers and whose work was enthusiastically supported by Bergoglio when he was Archbishop of Buenos Aires – although controversy still surrounds what some see

---

[3]   I am grateful to Argentinian theologians Emilce Cuda and Augusto Zampini for helping me to understand Francis' theological context.

as his failure to offer such priests sufficient protection from the military during Argentina's Dirty War.

The theological influences of Francis' Argentinian background are clear in *Evangelii Gaudium*. He observes that '[g]enuine forms of popular religiosity are incarnate, since they are born of the Incarnation of Christian faith in popular culture', inspired not by the 'vague spiritual energies or powers' promoted by some spiritual quests, but by 'fleshy' devotions arising out of personal relationships with God, Christ, Mary and the saints. He praises the Aparecida document for its affirmation of 'the people's mysticism' and 'a spirituality incarnated in the culture of the lowly', whose content is, says Francis, discovered and expressed 'more by way of symbols than by discursive reasoning' (*EG*, n. 124).[4]

Yet it would be a mistake to see Francis as a theological ingénu because he has this popular touch. He is not a holy fool bumbling benignly into controversial issues where only the angels dare to tread. He is a pragmatist whose past performance suggests a shrewd capacity for compromise and negotiation – skills that will undoubtedly serve him well in his dealings with the Curia.[5] He is also a learned and cultured man. In his interview with Spadaro, he speaks of his love for great musicians, writers and artists such as Dostoevsky, Hölderin, Mozart, Caravaggio and Chagall, and it is clear that he knows their work with the kind of appreciation that comes from deep attentiveness and contemplative immersion.

The sense of contemplative and mystical awareness which suffuses Francis' theological vision can be traced back to his Ignatian formation. In conversation with Spadaro, he refers repeatedly to the need for discernment, including what he calls 'the mystical dimension of discernment' as a form of wisdom which 'redeems the ambiguity of life'. He observes that Jesuit life becomes distorted when it inhabits 'an environment of closed and rigid thought, more instructive-ascetic than mystical'.

Yet Francis is no solitary contemplative. He explained to Spadaro that he joined the Jesuits partly because of his need for a community.

---

4   Quoting the Fifth General Conference of the Latin American and Caribbean Bishops, *Aparecida Document*, 29 June 2007, n. 262–3. This concluding document of the conference with an introductory letter by Pope Benedict XVI can be found at http://www.celam.org/aparecida/Ingles.pdf [accessed, 20 January 2014].

5   For more on Francis' life and personality, see Paul Vallely, *Pope Francis: Untying the Knots* (London: Bloomsbury, 2013).

This also accounts for his decision to live in the communal house of Santa Marta, rather than in the cavernous solitude of the apostolic palace.

In *Evangelii Gaudium*, Francis beautifully expresses how all this comes together by way of 'a mystical fraternity, a contemplative fraternity' (*EG*, n. 92). To be an evangelical community means rising to 'the challenge of finding and sharing a "mystique" of living together, of mingling and encounter, of embracing and supporting one another, of stepping into this flood tide which, while chaotic, can become a genuine experience of fraternity, a caravan of solidarity, a sacred pilgrimage' (*EG*, n. 87).

We might describe Francis as a mystical communitarian, a narrative theologian who finds meaning not in abstract ideas and arguments but in the communal living out of the mystery of faith unfolding in time through the shared memories and devotions of the People of God. Yet I want to go back to the question of where liberation theology might fit in to all this.

Although he has in the past distanced himself from liberation theology, the language Francis uses in *Evangelii Gaudium* to describe the current economic system is resonant with that of some of the most radical liberation theologians of the 1970s. For example, he invokes the commandment 'Thou shalt not kill' to indict 'an economy of exclusion and inequality' on the basis that 'such an economy kills'. He condemns the free market ideology as 'tyranny' and uses the language of idolatry when referring to 'a deified market', in a system 'which tends to devour everything which stands in the way of increased profits' (*EG*, n. 56). Such language goes far beyond a populist theology of the poor. It is radically political and indeed liberationist in its naming and shaming of the modern economic system and the inequalities, ethical degradation and violence which it produces. Yet it is a mistake to suggest, as some have, that this makes him a Marxist. Francis belongs within the tradition of Catholic social teaching and indeed of a more ancient tradition of Christian concern for the poor, illuminated by a vivid appreciation of the mystery of faith and the newness of life that flows from the Holy Spirit. His theology draws nourishment from many sources and he refuses to be trapped by any set of rules or prescriptive moral teachings which would stifle the freedom and beauty of a living faith in the incarnate Christ. He says that theologians should avoid 'a

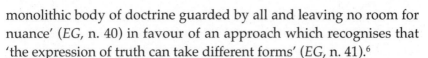

monolithic body of doctrine guarded by all and leaving no room for nuance' (*EG*, n. 40) in favour of an approach which recognises that 'the expression of truth can take different forms' (*EG*, n. 41).[6]

For those of us who have been struggling to do theology that is critically faithful, academically rigorous and searching in the questions it asks, while finding ourselves increasingly targeted as dissenters by the self-appointed custodians of doctrine, all this is balm to the spirit. There is a sense of freedom, even of exhilaration, as a spirit of anti-intellectualism and dogmatic authoritarianism yields to a more open and creative approach to theological issues. Yet much of this remains at the level of a visionary agenda which has yet to be tested and put into practice within the messy realities and power struggles of the institutional Church. Questions remain as to how far Francis might be willing to challenge established teachings and practices.

Conservatives seek reassurance in the claim that, although his style might be different from his recent predecessors, Church teaching cannot be changed. This would mean that controversial teachings such as the prohibition by *Humanae Vitae* of artificial birth control, and the Church's opposition to same-sex marriage and to women's ordination must remain, even if they might be presented in a more pastorally sensitive way than has sometimes been the case. Francis himself has insisted that the question of women's ordination is not open for discussion, and he has also reiterated the Church's teaching on abortion – although he acknowledges that the Church has not always done enough to understand the dilemmas of women facing such decisions (*EG*, n. 214). Worryingly for those at the liberal end of the spectrum, he has reappointed the doctrinaire Archbishop Gerhard Müller as head of the CDF. The recent excommunication of Australian priest Fr Gregory Reynolds seems to be a complex situation which goes beyond the claim that it was because he supported women priests, but it certainly indicates that the Church under Francis will not be one in which anything goes.

At the same time, it seems possible that the Church's teaching on the admission of divorced and remarried Catholics to the sacraments might change, and there might be some greater accommodation of same-sex relationships which I suspect will stop short of marriage. To

---

6   This is a quotation from John Paul II, *Ut Unum Sint*, Encyclical Letter, 1995, n. 19.

say that the Church's teaching cannot change on any of these issues is to subscribe to the spirit of creeping infallibility which has had such a distorting effect on moral theology in recent decades. We can trace back to St Thomas Aquinas the distinction between the revealed mysteries of faith which are not open to debate, and the outworking of these mysteries in the social and ethical practices which express the life of faith and which entail the use of our rational and cognitive capacities. From this perspective, the Church's social and moral teachings can and should change in response to changing social contexts and to advances in scientific knowledge. These issues are too large to explore here, but questions of sexual and reproductive ethics must be guided by science and responsive to changing cultural norms, while always upholding the fundamental dignity and relationality of the human made in the image of God.

One of the most urgent questions facing Francis is that of the role of women. He has spoken repeatedly of the need for women to play a greater role in all aspects of the Church's life, yet it remains to be seen how determined he is to challenge the hostility to women's participation and leadership which remains the entrenched mindset of some sections of the hierarchy. The issue is not only how far Francis will go in opening up debate, but to what extent he will insist upon women being fully represented in that debate with authority equal to that of their male counterparts. If that is not a condition of the conversation, then little will have changed.

The question of women also has a profound bearing on Francis' vision for a Church of the poor, because women and children are the poorest of the poor. Poverty impacts on women's lives with the most acute and tragic consequences around issues of reproductive health, pregnancy, childbirth and motherhood. An estimated eight hundred of the world's poorest women die through pregnancy-related causes every day, but official Church documents offer little if any acknowledgement of the extent to which maternal mortality constitutes one of the most serious threats to family life in poor societies, corroding the dignity of women and impacting with terrible consequences upon the lives of children. There is something profoundly wrong with a teaching tradition which claims expert knowledge on issues of contraception, abortion, marriage and the family, and yet which is virtually silent with regard to maternal mortality.

So there are momentous possibilities, and there is also scope for inevitable disappointment on the path ahead. While it is a shame that once again we have a pope who has become the centre of a personality cult – a phenomenon which is not healthy for the life of the Church – Francis' popularity shows that he has awakened a profound hunger in human hearts. He stands for an entirely different set of values from the economics of greed, alienation and exploitation which drive our modern political systems, and he seems able to reach beyond the hardened cynicism of our age to a tender yearning in the human spirit. This is a rare opportunity – a *kairos* moment for the Church – but for it to bear fruit we must all be willing to rise to the challenge. He for his part must ensure that we are not beaten back into submission, by those 'querulous and disillusioned pessimists' who have in recent years sought to define and defend Catholicism as the most authoritarian and restrictive of cults.

Pope Francis:
Architect of Reform?

Michael Collins

By the time you read this chapter, it will in all likelihood be out of date. Such is the pace of Francis' pontificate that changes are regularly overtaken with evermore noteworthy events.

The first year of the pontificate gives the opportunity to compare and contrast Francis with his predecessors. It is axiomatic that popes follow in the tradition of the Church, but often pontificates are in marked contrast from each other.

Following Benedict XVI's announcement of his intention to retire, there was much speculation on the reasons for the sudden abdication. A series of global scandals certainly played a considerable part in his decision to resign the papacy. The fact that private documents had been purloined from his desk by his chamberlain and subsequently published by a journalist caused enormous embarrassment. Benedict made up his mind to retire following a gruelling trip to Mexico and Cuba in March 2012, although he did not decide the date until early the following year. The uproar following the publication of the book *Your Holiness* by journalist Gianni Nuzzi in May 2012 may have well precipitated his decision.

The cardinals who were obliged to elect his successor also wondered about the Pope's true motives. During formal and informal discussions following the announcement of his abdication on 11 February 2013, several cardinals discussed the effectiveness of the Roman Curia.

The Curia is the administrative system used by the Bishop of Rome to govern the universal Church. All dioceses have a series of offices through which bishops oversee the needs of the people and clergy of their district. Naturally, given its global dimension, the

Roman Curia is pre-eminent. The Pope governs the universal Church through the offices of the Roman Curia while the diocese of Rome is entrusted to the Cardinal Vicar. The Vicar administers the diocese of Rome through a Vicariate at the Lateran Cathedral. In terms of workforce and resources the Roman Curia is smaller than a number of dioceses throughout the world.

The Roman Curia derives from the administrative organs devised by the kings and emperors of ancient Rome. The very term *curia* dates to the sixth century BC when the legendary King Tullus Hostillius established an administrative body of ten men from each of the three tribes to govern the city. These were called the *curiae Hostillia*. A meeting house, the *comitia curata*, was built in the public meeting space of the *forum Romanum*. The early civil laws of Rome were enshrined in the Twelve Tables.

In order to assist the king, and later dictators and emperors, the senators established a number of sub-committees. As the monarchy was replaced by a republic and then grew into an empire the offices expanded. It was the responsibility of the elected representatives, the lictors, to confirm the ruler's *imperium*, conferring on him power and authority to rule. They granted such authority on praetors, consuls and dictators. The authority conferred, the *imperium* was transferred to the elected officials and remained with them.

For a Roman entering politics, the administration of the city or the provinces a course of honours was laid out. The *cursus honorum*, open to those of senatorial rank, enumerated various public offices one could aspire to as well as setting the minimum age required by the candidate. Before entering office one had to complete ten years of military service as an *equites* in the cavalry. While the term of office was usually limited to a set period this was often flagrantly ignored. A set of honorific titles such as *vir illustris*, *vir clarissimus* and *vir spectabilis*, were conferred as men rose through the ranks. This stratification created a patronage system based on masters and clients which is still endemic in Italian society. While Jesus admonished his disciples not to see worldly honours or titles, his words were largely ignored by the developing priestly class in the early Christian era.

When the emperor Constantine established himself as sole ruler of the Western and Eastern parts of the Roman Empire, he granted considerable privileges to the Christian community. In particular, he gave imperial support to a beleaguered Church and ended decades of sporadic persecution. He endowed churches and promoted bishops, granting them the same travel rights and other privileges enjoyed by senators. In particular his pecuniary gifts allowed the influence of the Roman Church to increase.

The medieval popes expanded their Curia according to the needs of the diocese and the expanding papal court. The papal administration expanded as the Roman pontiff claimed papal superiority over other bishops. By the ninth century the papacy had an extensive network issuing documents and granting privileges. Much of these were connected with the granting of lucrative benefices.

Connected with this expansion was the growth in the prestige of the College of Cardinals. In 1274, with the promulgation of the bull *Ubi Periculum* by Gregory X (1271–6) the cardinals became the exclusive electors of the Roman pontiffs. Their power increased considerably during the second millennium and cardinals came to occupy key positions in the Roman Curia and important European Sees.

In the late sixteenth century, Pope Sixtus V (1585–90) reorganised the papal administration into sixteen offices or congregations according to suggestions made at the Council of Trent (1545–63). Over the centuries successive pontiffs modified or expanded the Curia. The most recent development was the modification required following the Second Vatican Council (1962–5) executed by Pope Paul VI (1962–78) in the apostolic constitution *Regimini Ecclesiae* in 1967. Further changes and updates were carried out according to the reforms of the apostolic constitution *Pastor Bonus* by Pope John Paul II (1978–2005) in 1988. Importantly, a cardinal prefect oversaw the most important Vatican offices.

From its ancient Roman origins the administration has been based on patronage, clientalism and extraordinary discretion. This is deeply engrained in the Italian mentality and culture. While many members of the Roman Curia come from different parts of the world, they are expected to adopt a particular code of practice and manners. This is often referred to by the word 'Romanitas'. The third century theologian, Tertullian, coined the term in his work *De Pallio* when he criticised people in Carthage for aping Roman mannerisms.

Five days after his election to the papacy, Francis told Cardinal Óscar Andrés Rodríguez Maradiaga of Honduras that he wished to set up a small group of cardinals on whom he could call to assist in the governance of the Church. Francis was clearly drawing on his experience in the Society of Jesus where the Superior General and Provincials are assisted by a small group of counsellors. Although Francis had not decided how many cardinals he would use or their provenance, he placed Maradiaga in charge.

One month later, Francis had made up his mind and on 13 April the list of eight was published. The only Vatican official was Cardinal Giuseppe Bertello, President of the Commission of Cardinals which governs Vatican City State. The other cardinals came from each of the five continents. Cardinal Seán Patrick O' Malley of Boston, the Australian Cardinal George Pell of Sidney, Cardinal Oswald Gracias of Mumbai, India, Cardinal Laurent Monsengwo Pasinya of Kinshasa, Congo, the retired Chilean Archbishop of Santiago, Cardinal Francisco Javier Errázuriz Ossa, and the German Cardinal Reinhard Marx of Munich and Freising.

The first task Francis set the group was the reform of the Roman Curia. As Archbishop of Buenos Aires, Bergoglio had served as a visiting consultant on five of the offices of the Curia and thus had first-hand experience. The eight cardinals had both global experience and were well acquainted with the bureaucracy of the Roman Curia. Although the commission was an advisory council, it was clear that Francis intended granting its members a certain amount of autonomy. Cardinal Maradiaga confirmed that the reform would not simply be tinkering with *Pastor Bonus* but a complete rewrite in the light of modern administrative models. The first three-day meeting was set for early October and a second exactly two months later, 3–5 December. Without waiting for the cardinals' commission to assemble, Francis tackled difficulties at the Institute for the Works of Religion (in Italian, *Instituto per le Opere di Religione* – IOR), commonly but mistakenly referred to as the Vatican Bank.

In 1942, at the height of the Second World War, Pope Pius XII founded the Institute to facilitate the global movement of funds for religious Orders. By the end of the century the Institute was in financial difficulty. A scandal involving loans to the Ambrosian Bank involved the suspicious death of the financier Roberto Calvi and an Italian state investigation centred on the Institute's president, Archbishop Paul Casimir Marcinkus.

In 1990, Pope John Paul II ordered a review of the finances of the Holy See. During the pontificate of Benedict XVI (2005–13), scandals at the bank proliferated and on 30 December 2010 the Pope established the Financial Information Authority to regulate the commercial and monetary movements of Vatican offices, and the administration of Vatican City State and the Patrimony of the Apostolic See. In large part the juridical group was designed to prevent money laundering, reminiscent of Sommerset Maugham's comment about the French Riviera as 'a sunny place for shady people'.

Francis had thought about closing the IOR where Catholic institutions, clerics and lay employees of Vatican City and those with pension and salary accounts, embassy officials and staff keep the money. In the event he decided at first to attempt reform even if permanent closure was not ruled out at a later stage. Francis moved rapidly to improve the administration of the finances and, on 24 June 2012, he published a chirograph establishing a commission of five to ensure that the IOR was in harmony with the social teaching of the Church.

With extraordinary timing, just three days later, a priest working at the Vatican office for the administration of the finances of the Holy See was arrested. Monsignor Nunzio Scarano, a native of Salerno, was detained at Rome's *Regina Caeli* prison by Italy's secret financial services on suspicion of trying to smuggle twenty million euro from Switzerland to Italy. On 1 July, the Director of the IOR, Paolo Cipriani, and his deputy, Massimo Tulli, announced their surprise resignations. The President of the Institute, Ernest von Freyberg, who had been appointed by Pope Benedict XVI in February 2013, dryly noted: 'It is clear that today we need new leadership.'

Over one month later, on 8 August, Pope Francis issued more regulations which broadened the finance laws to cover all the offices of the Roman Curia, including non-profit charitable organisations such as *Caritas International* and *Aid to the Church in Need*. In particular the Pope decided that his commission would oversee the works of the IOR and the Administration of the Patrimony of the Apostolic See, where Scarano had served prior to his suspension. In particular, the Pope was determined to stamp out the prevalent problem of money laundering. The Holy See was committed to meeting the requirements of the Committee of Experts on the Evaluation of Money Laundering Measures and the Financing of Terrorism (Moneyval). This is the financial monitoring committee of the Council of Europe.

In October, the Institute took the unprecedented step of publishing accounts and, in December, closed hundreds of suspicious accounts.

A report published by the IOR in January claimed that fifty-five per cent of the 18,900 client accounts had been checked by the financial group Promontory, which had been hired to assist in the financial overhaul. By late January 2014 the IOR asked the Italian banks to restore full transactions which had been suspended in 2010. At the same time Pope Francis replaced four of the five cardinals who had been appointed eleven months earlier to the commission of cardinals to oversee the Institute. Thus Francis installed four new cardinals whom he trusted to bring about his desired reform.

Most people working in the Curia are well aware of the limitations of the unwieldy bureaucracy. Because the various congregations and councils grew piecemeal, there is a certain lack of co-ordination. Although the Secretariat of State tries to oversee them, most offices act independently. Thus, for example, the Congregation of Bishops might publish a document which would not have been seen by or approved of by other congregations prior to publication. This can cause confusion at best, and aggressive tension at worst.

The Roman pontiff makes all the appointments to the Curia although obviously he seeks advice from competent councillors. The papacy is the oldest surviving non-hereditary monarchy in the world. It is something akin to a benign dictatorship. Francis replaced Benedict's Secretary of State, Cardinal Tarcisio Bertone, with a Vatican-trained diplomat, Archbishop Pietro Parolin. In a surprise move, Francis carried out a series of appointments in late 2013 and early 2014 which saw the termination of a number of Benedict's appointees. Among those leaving was Cardinal Raymond L. Burke, Prefect of the Supreme Tribunal of the Apostolic Signatura, the legal High Court who was not appointed for a second term of five years. Burke was not the only cardinal not to serve a new term. Cardinal Justin Rigali, former Archbishop of Philadelphia, also concluded his five-year term in which he had once served as Secretary.

In reality the changes were not pivotal. Already *Pastor Bonus* provided for terms of office which were to last only five years and were only renewable in exceptional circumstances. In the latter part of John Paul II's pontificate and during Benedict's papacy, these terms were repeated as, for example, Archbishop Piero Marini, Master of Pontifical Ceremonies, who served twenty years in office.

The air of curial uncertainty clearly irritated some figures. Archbishop Georg Gänswein, Prefect of the Papal Household, commented with barely concealed exasperation that he waited each day to see what innovation would come to the Vatican. In an interview with the American cable network, EWTN, Cardinal Burke noted that it was 'not altogether clear what the results of the reform will be' and that there was 'a kind of unpredictability about life in Rome in these days'. In an attempt to overhaul the Curia, the Holy See engaged a number of international professional managerial firms to offer discreet advice on how best the cardinals and Pope might achieve the desired reform.

One of the contributions of the Second Vatican Council was the promotion of the concept of collegiality. This requires the bishops of the world to work in harmony. It also entails the principle of subsidiarity, whereby issues which should be administered in a local diocese are not referred to Rome. When this is the case the Roman Curia becomes the overall arbitrator. It also, perhaps unintentionally, deprives the local church of its rightful autonomy.

But Francis has an uncanny knack of delivering reform in small bites. His daily homilies at Mass celebrated in his residence attract a huge audience beyond the walls of the small chapel. His pithy sayings strike a chord in people's hearts. The appointment of nineteen cardinals at his first consistory held on 22 February 2014 brought the number of cardinal electors to one hundred and twenty-two, just two over the one hundred and twenty limit of under eighty year olds. The Pope chose the first cardinal from Haiti, the poorest place in the Northern hemisphere, while bypassing Turin and Venice, sees which traditionally carried the cardinal's biretta. He also created the Secretary General of the Synod of Bishops a cardinal, Lorenzo Baldisseri. Francis also summoned an extraordinary meeting of the Synod of Bishops to be held at the Vatican in October 2014 to discuss the family. This has given rise to hopes that the Pontiff might give the synod more importance in the Curia and administration of the Church.

Public opinion, largely shaped by the international media, is broadly favourable to Francis. He is perceived as a saintly Robin Hood, cheerfully despoiling the rich to give to the poor. His benign statements rarely condemn and appear in stark contrast to the admonitions of John Paul and Benedict. His spontaneous gestures, warm smile and sense of mischief are welcomed by many. In reality, however, it is wise to admit that the mood music has changed, but the album is still the same.

Pope Francis and the Dictatorship of Tolerance

John Waters

Something strange has happened with the change of popes that occurred in the spring of 2013. At the time of writing, almost a year later in the late winter of 2014, this strangeness has not been dispelled.

The inevitable result of recent changes in media culture is a tendency towards manipulation, a kind of 'Hollywoodisation' of journalism. Instead of simply reporting what happens, media seek to tweak real-life events so they acquire storylines in the manner of soap operas or popular novels. Increasingly, editors *sotto voce* insist that every 'story' conform to a script, with a storyline which must become amenable to a process of resolution in terms outlined more or less at the outset.

An example of this syndrome is the 'narrative' offered to the world concerning Pope Francis. The 'story' was essentially that we had somehow – miraculously, it was suggested by one Irish priest on the *Late Late Show* – jettisoned an unsympathetic and conservative pope in favour of a radical, democratic-minded and 'caring' one – a 'people's pope' to replace the excessively cerebral 'God's Rottweiler'. Although this 'new pope, new hope' narrative flew in the face of all the facts, nothing seemed capable of derailing it.

In the first year of his pontificate, Pope Francis announced no new doctrinal initiatives, nor was his emphasis significantly different to that of his predecessor, who had, in the eight years he spent as head of the Catholic Church, accrued no credits at all with the kind of people who lionised Francis as the saviour of Catholicism and the liberator of its dissenting elements. Yet, the stories kept on coming. Pope Francis was named Person of the Year by *Time* magazine, which praised him for his rejection of Church dogma. Not to be outdone, *The*

Advocate, an American magazine for homosexuals, also named Francis its 2013 Person of the Year, for the compassion he had shown to gay people. (The Pope, in several interviews, had merely emphasised that, when God looks at a gay person, he 'endorses the existence of this person with love', rather than rejecting and condemning that person.)

For anyone with even the most rudimentary understanding of Catholicism, there was something deeply perplexing about all this. For a start, of course, the idea of a 'people's pope' was a contradiction in terms, since the pope exists to convey an understanding of God to mankind, not the other way around. The idea of Pope Francis representing some kind of radical shift towards a more 'democratic' Church was fatuous in the extreme. Secular cultures have come to take as axiomatic that the word 'democratic' signifies the purest conceivable values and aspirations, but this assumption operates – when or if it does – in the political realm only. In the realm of the infinite, 'democracy' is neither here nor there.

Inevitably, great attention was paid to every statement made by the new pope, so when he spoke about homosexuals, women, divorced Catholics or atheists, his words were always going to end up in the lead headlines on newspapers and news bulletins. In the immediate wake of his election, too, much was made of the different style of the new pope, as compared to Pope Benedict XVI – the fact that he insisted upon taking the bus or driving his old Ford Focus, wore his own black shoes and lived not in the papal apartment but continued to stay in the guest house, Casa Santa Marta, where visiting clerics are accommodated when they have business in the Vatican.

The impression was slyly conveyed – mainly by people who no more believe in Jesus Christ than in the Tooth Fairy – that Pope Francis was more 'humble', that is, more Christlike, than his predecessor. All this added to the sense of an impending revolution – the unravelling of, what was frequently interpreted as, the thirty-five years of traditionalist retrenchment that began with the election of Pope John Paul II in 1978.

To an extent, this took up and reversed a more subtle narrative that had begun in April 2005, with the election of Joseph Ratzinger, an event that took many journalists by surprise and filled 'liberal' Catholics with dismay. Although there could have been little doubt about his determination to take the Church back to fundamentals, Pope John Paul II had been a highly charismatic and avuncular figure,

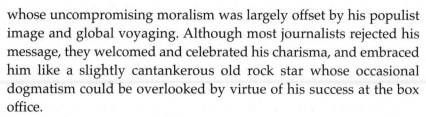

whose uncompromising moralism was largely offset by his populist image and global voyaging. Although most journalists rejected his message, they welcomed and celebrated his charisma, and embraced him like a slightly cantankerous old rock star whose occasional dogmatism could be overlooked by virtue of his success at the box office.

Pope Benedict, however, offered a different proposition. A long-time loyal lieutenant of Pope John Paul II, he was widely regarded as the most brilliant theologian of his time, but this cut little ice with media commentators. A reserved and gentle man, he offered journalists nothing of the same 'rock star' potential of his predecessor. In truth, journalists regarded him as the worst of all possible popes: traditionalist, reticent, soft-spoken, given to long and complex sentences, and utterly rejecting of their view of the world.

The 'story' about Benedict from the outset, therefore, was of a regression from the days of John Paul II. Although nothing could have been further from the actual message articulated by Benedict XVI, the narrative that emerged was of an even more determined 'con-servative' who eschewed the modern world and all its works and pomps. Although Pope Benedict almost weekly issued erudite analyses of the nature of human reality in the modern moment, the message pumped out by journalists was that the Church had slipped further back towards the Middle Ages.

His rigidities forgotten, Pope John Paul II was 'remembered' as a kind and benevolent figure, whereas his successor was presented as little short of a despotic intransigent, obsessed with evil and sin. Few of those who praised John Paul and sought to bury Benedict could have named a single point of theological difference between them, but this did nothing to curtail the new narrative.

Far from the ogre of popular media mythology, Benedict XVI quietly revealed himself as a totally new kind of voice in modern culture, speaking with clarity and enormous depth about the constitution of mankind in a world seeking to live without Christ. His great gift was his capacity to analyse the deep condition of the modern world, to describe with extraordinary facility how its drifts and tendencies were impacting upon the human person in the most authentic recesses of the heart. Among the qualities that made him so uncongenial to journalists was what often seemed his almost obsessive determination to pursue arguments from beginning to conclusion, through many loops of attentive reasoning, setting out his case as though every word was required to reach both God and men.

With a firm insistence, the Pope reminded humankind of the dangers of misunderstanding human desiring, of pursuing too narrow a definition of freedom, of misusing reason in ways that would make such errors unavoidable. He consistently characterised the condition of modern society as defined by a futile pursuit of things that do not exist. But his adherence to the core content of Christianity and his detailed critiques of modern reality were – to say the least – of no interest to those peddling the very agendas he was trying to finger and name.

Almost anything he wrote or said was reported – if it was reported – as an attack on secularism, promiscuity or homosexuality, with journalists poring over his texts to find the word that would trip them into one of the handful of familiar narrative loops they had established. Hence, Benedict's every word was drowned out by clichés from the gatekeepers of modern culture. He remained 'God's Rottweiler', a renegade liberal who had become an implacable enemy of progress.

In this behaviour of the media there was an odd mixture of ideological activism and professional peevishness. Most journalists, especially the Catholic ones, are hostile to the Church. Being essentially the promulgators of the 'progressive' mindset, they inevitably seek to use their positions to mould events in a manner calculated to promote what is termed a 'more liberal' dispensation. Pope John Paul II, though regarded as a 'reactionary' was in part forgiven because he was a star who could put bums on pews just about anywhere – and deliver audiences, and revenues, for the media. Pope Benedict XVI was celebrated largely by thinking Catholics, who loved him with a passion possibly unprecedented in the recent history of the papacy, but this was of little use or interest to those reporting on Church affairs from the outside.

None of this should surprise us. All over the crime scene of the crisis that engulfs Western society are to be found the fingerprints of the media which, behind the façade of objective reporting of reality, pursue an ideological mission inextricably entangled with an economic one. The objective is to make the world free for human desiring understood in its most immediate, crudest form, thereby maximising income for both media and their advertisers. Seen in this light, it is unsurprising that virtually every word of Pope Benedict was twisted beyond recognition.

But it remains important to reiterate: in spite of the persistent attempts to insinuate that every speech and statement of his concerned homosexuality, contraception or abortion, the great themes of Benedict's papacy were: love, charity, hope, faith, reason and beauty. Nobody in the previous first decade of the third millennium had described the contemporary condition of mankind with anything approaching his penetration and eloquence – perhaps most powerfully in his September 2011 speech in the Bundestag in Berlin, when he spoke of the 'bunker' that man has built for himself to live in, shutting out light, mystery and truth.

In his announcement of his resignation, Pope Benedict gave his critics their definitive answer, demonstrating in the most dramatic way that his life as pope had been lived in service – not power – and that all the time he had been in the hands of Another. In his gesture of surrender, this most radical of men reminded us that the ultimate radicalism does not rest in the human being who exhibits it, but in the transcendent and eternal 'radicalism' of the Creator of all things and the Redeemer who entered history to save mankind.

Benedict was alert at all times to the inevitable consequences of a world seeking to amend itself to its own demands. In particular he warned against the tendency to adapt Christianity to such demands. One of the greatest threats to the Church, he had said as Cardinal Ratzinger – in *God and the World*, a book-length interview with the journalist Peter Sewald – is public pressure for a watered-down, appeasing Christianity: 'And I think the situation may absolutely develop here in which there must be resistance against the dictatorship of this apparent tolerance, which eliminates the scandal of the faith by declaring it intolerant.'

The change that occurred with the shift from Benedict to Francis is difficult to define because it largely depends on what position you approach it from. From within the Church itself, the change was minimal. Nothing that had been said by the man who had just become pope – as cardinal, bishop or priest – had suggested him as a liberal. On the contrary, he had been at war with politicians in his native Argentina over their determination to liberalise laws to provide for abortion and gay marriage. What unfolded can be understood only in terms of the dynamic of the world's media – their needs, demands and driving philosophy. For reasons of both ideology and commercial advantage, the world's media required the Pope to offer, in effect, the 'watered-down, appeasing Christianity' his predecessor had warned against. It is undeniable that, in as far as his published interventions are concerned, he allowed himself to be presented as offering precisely that.

There was something remarkable, in the first instance, about the manner of some of his interventions. Whereas previous popes had tended to issue communications to the world through encyclicals and weekly homilies, Pope Francis pursued the kind of engagement more readily identified with a politician – and rather unconventional ones at that. Sometimes, he made his most newsworthy statements apparently off-the-cuff, at least once on a long plane journey, when he approached the media section unannounced. In September 2013, he appeared to issue a number of rapid-fire pronouncements in a series of interviews, one conducted with an atheist journalist at the Pope's own invitation. Taken together, these interventions were presented as encapsulating Pope Francis' outlook on a range of important doctrinal matters.

In one case, the Pope apparently simply picked up the telephone and called the left-wing, atheist journalist, Eugenio Scalfari, a co-founder of the socialist newspaper *La Repubblica*, who had requested an interview. In the wide-ranging exchange that ensued, the Pope had spoken *inter alia* about the nature of good and evil, provoking fears and whispered accusations of relativism from many surprised hearers within the Church: 'Everyone has his own idea of good and evil and must choose to follow the good and fight evil as he conceives them,' he told Scalfari. 'That would be enough to make the world a better place.' Without naming names, the Pope accused many of his predecessors of narcissism, and condemned clericalism as inimical to Christianity.

Some weeks earlier, in an interview with Fr Spadaro, the editor of *La Civiltà Cattolica*, the Pope had spoken in what appeared to be an equally non-judgemental manner about a number of the headline 'moral' issues which had been the flashpoints of Catholic-liberal conflict for many years. That interview, subsequently published in English in *America* magazine, was hailed as the manifesto of a pope who had 'broken with the past' by announcing new doctrinal initiatives on matters like homosexuality, atheism and women priests.

Here is the core of what the Pope said on these matters in that interview:

> We cannot insist only on issues related to abortion, gay marriage and the use of contraceptive methods. This is not possible. I have not spoken much about these things, and I was reprimanded for that. But when we speak about these issues, we have to talk about them in a context. The teaching of the Church, for that matter, is clear and I am a son of the Church, but it is not necessary to talk about these issues all the time.

In fact, there is no deviation here from the Church's position, merely an observation that it is 'not necessary' to speak about these issues all the time. The Church cannot insist 'only' on these issues, but must speak about them 'in a context'. Pope Francis' point here appeared to relate to the possibility of an emphasis on moralism serving to suffocate the deeper message of Christianity. Yet, as with some of his earlier off-the-cuff statements, there did appear to be an at least unconscious attempt to communicate a degree of relaxation in respect of certain headline aspects of Church teaching, and these hints were happily passed on to the world by a media delighted to report that the Pope had finally come around to agree with what journalists had been saying all along.

In Ireland, a spokesman for the (generally liberally-inclined) Association of Catholic Priests said he was 'absolutely exhilarated' by the Pope's words. He complained that his association had been criticised for not being more publicly supportive of the bishops during a recent controversy about abortion in Ireland. He said that the Catholic bishops, who had criticised the Irish Government's proposal to liberalise anti-abortion legislation, had 'overegged their case'. 'Now', he said, 'I see that Pope Francis is saying something similar [to the ACP].'

An important question, then, which has remained largely unaddressed, relates to the role Pope Francis himself may have played in the creation of the false narrative which has attached itself to his papacy. At times, it has appeared that the Pope was being, at best, naive in failing to realise that the media would selectively report and manipulate his words. It also seemed that, in his emphasis on controversial issues, and his selection of sceptical, if not hostile, journalists to communicate with the public, Pope Francis seemed to be flirting with the media's obsession with issues like atheism, homo-sexuality and women priests.

In fact, even while his remarks on these matters were being digested, events occurred, and were reported *sotto voce*, that appeared to convey an entirely different impression concerning Pope Francis' approach and intentions. During a papal audience with MaterCare International as part of the group's tenth international conference in September 2013, Pope Francis spoke clearly on abortion to a group of obstetricians and genealogists. The Pope told these doctors that they had a responsibility to make known the 'transcendent dimension, the imprint of God's creative work, in human life from the first instant of conception'.

'Every child that isn't born, but is unjustly condemned to be aborted,' he said, 'has the face of Jesus Christ, has the face of the Lord.' He urged them to abide by Church teachings, saying: 'Things have a price and can be for sale, but people have a dignity that is priceless and worth far more than things … In all its phases and at every age, human life is always sacred and always of quality. And not as a matter of faith, but of reason and science.'

That same month, Pope Francis was also reported – though not in the usual banner headlines – as having excommunicated an Australian priest, Fr Greg Reynolds, for speaking in favour of the ordination of women. The excommunication was conveyed in a letter from the Archbishop of Melbourne, Denis Hart, stating that

> the decision by Pope Francis to dismiss Fr Reynolds from the clerical state and to declare his automatic excommunication has been made because of his public teaching on the ordination of women contrary to the teaching of the Church and his public celebration of the Eucharist when he did not hold faculties to act publicly as a priest.

Fr Reynolds was also known to be a supporter of same-sex marriage, had founded Inclusive Catholics, a pro-female ordination and gay marriage group, and was known to have attended rallies in favour of changing the definition of marriage. He told the *National Catholic Reporter*: 'I am very surprised that this order has come under [Pope Francis'] watch; it seems so inconsistent with everything else he has said and done.'

There was then, on the face of things at least, a contradiction. On the one hand, Pope Francis was preaching a new dispensation of radicalism and, apparently, relativism. On the other, it was business as usual.

In January 2014, an interesting insight into the disposition of the Pope was provided in an article in *The Tablet*, in which a close confidante of Francis, Cardinal Joachim Meisner of Cologne, was quoted as offering a somewhat different understanding of things. The particular example was the question of Communion being permitted for remarried divorcees, a proposal with which Pope Francis had on a number of occasions hinted his agreement. Cardinal Meisner, however, insisted that the Pope remained firmly opposed to permitting remarried divorcees to receive Communion. 'When I last visited Pope Francis recently,' he said, 'I was able to speak to him very openly about all and sundry. I drew his attention to the fact that some of what he had said in interviews and short addresses had left certain questions open to debate which really needed explaining further for those not in the know. The Pope opened his eyes wide and asked me to give him an example. I pointed to his remark about remarried divorcees on the plane back from Rio de Janeiro [when the Pope had said, 'I believe this is the time of mercy']. Whereupon the Pope said quite simply: 'Divorcees can go to Communion – remarried divorcees cannot.'

'And then he spoke of mercy,' Cardinal Meisner continued. I told him that in our country [Germany] mercy is always interpreted as a stand-in for all sorts of human errors. Whereupon the Pope very forcefully insisted that he was a son of the Church and had not said anything that the Church did not teach. 'Mercy must be identical with the truth otherwise it did not deserve to be called mercy,' he emphasised. 'And by the way,' he specifically underlined, 'if theological questions remain open, then the Congregation for the Doctrine of the Faith (CDF) is there to clarify and formulate such matters in detail.'

So there, as journalists are wont to say, you appear to have it. On this issue, the Pope remained a Catholic. Indeed, on all issues, he remained 'a son of the Church' and had not said anything the Church does not teach. In fact, when you get right down to it, Pope Francis has not said anything of any significance that his predecessor, Pope Benedict XVI, had not said just as clearly, albeit sometimes more elaborately.

What really marks out Francis from Benedict is his personality, more garrulous and spontaneous, and his style of speaking, which is based on stories and images rather than reasoned argument and logic. This aspect, however, has not proved interesting enough for those who seek to use every outing on the topic of Catholicism to mould their Church into their own way of thinking. Hence, Benedict was deemed a 'reactionary' choice and almost everything he said ignored or dismissed by the same people who suddenly trumpeted Pope Francis as 'a breath of fresh air'.

Pope Francis is neither a rigorist nor a loose minister. He seeks to reconcile those inside the Church with those who have fallen away, but also the necessary dogmatism that goes with truth and the fluidity essential to a living, breathing faith. He is indeed a 'breath of fresh air', but not in the sense that journalists tend to report, or in the way those who oppose virtually everything the Church stands for would lead us to believe.

The most astonishing thing about Pope Francis is the extent to which he shares and continues Pope Benedict's depiction of the state of the world. In this there is no distinction between them. Francis, like his predecessor, sees the human person in society as floundering in a mess of relativism and hopelessness, besieged by ideology and disinformation, driven away from the authentic course of the authentic human journey. Francis presents his explanations in the form of anecdote and analogy, placing the listener into a context where the meaning becomes clear on the basis of personal experience and the deep structural appetite for story that resides in every human heart.

On Saturday, 18 May 2013, I stood alongside Pope Francis on the steps of St Peter's. I was greatly moved by the power of simply watching him, observing the profundity of his physical skills in communicating. I was struck in particular by his physicality – the way his whole body seems to be summoned towards the act of communication, and also by the way he spoke to these two hundred thousand people as though he was speaking to one. Having his words translated later on, I was transported by his description of the necessity for the Church to move out of its stuffy room and take the risk of meeting the rest of humanity. 'When the Church becomes closed, it becomes sick.'

This, for me, is Pope Francis in his essence: a man who has absorbed everything that is vital in Christianity and now offers it back as his personal witness to this moment.

The media have chosen to turn the change of popes into a different kind of story – one that will sell newspapers or advertising space with a narrative of revolution and democratisation. But there is no point of severance or breach between the two popes, merely a continuum manifesting a dramatic but timely shift in style. Benedict had done his work, which remains in the countless words he wrote and published as pope and, before that, as Cardinal Ratzinger. Now it is time to translate this for communication through the megaphone controlled by some of the Catholic Church's most implacable enemies.

Those who love the Church know now, as they always have, that the 'changes' being clamoured for in the world's media are neither well-advised nor necessary. What is required, as always, is an ear attuned to the heartbeat of the world in time. This must remain the hope of sane people for the pontificate of Pope Francis. The question is: can the Pope stand firm in front of the truth, against the dictatorship of apparent tolerance?

Borrowing an Idea from the Pope

Aidan Troy, CP

From the moment he stepped out onto the balcony of St Peter's Basilica in March 2013 and asked the faithful below to pray for him, Pope Francis has stressed in word and deed that he wants his to be an interactive papacy. He lives with others at Casa Santa Marta, meets with all sorts of people and gives surprisingly open interviews. He's in regular contact by telephone, e-mail and occasional meetings with his 'kitchen cabinet' of eight cardinals advising him on Vatican reform. In a new departure for the Vatican, he sent out a questionnaire on Church policies to dioceses around the world to be used to prepare the synod of bishops on the family in October.

The example he sets got me to thinking that a bit of interactivity might be an interesting way to gauge the impact the Pope has had in this parish of St Joseph, a Passionist parish since 1869 in the shadow of the Arc de Triomphe in Paris. Parishioners of about forty different nationalities fill five weekend Masses, all celebrated in English (and in Irish on St Patrick's Day!). I've been the parish priest here for six years. Following Francis' lead, I decided to seek opinions among this rich diversity. In addition to face-to-face talks, my appeal in the parish bulletin for contributions also brought in comments from abroad because former parishioners saw it posted on the parish website. The response was greater than I expected, as everybody seemed to have an opinion. Many were positive, even enthusiastic, while some were cautiously critical.

Diverse opinions
An American mother studying canon law in Paris responded immediately in writing and with enthusiasm:

Beyond the absolute media ridiculousness that is occurring, his conversations with people truly show the desire of Francis to change the dynamics of dialogue and adapt the Gospel message to the modern world. It is not 'Michael row the boat ashore' theology, anti-traditionalist, anti-institutional Church in tone, but truly shows an adaptation of the Gospel message to the reality of life in the modern world. This is the conversation for which I have been searching for a very long time, the Gospel message in the vernacular of everyday life.

She followed up her comment by visiting me to explain her scepticism about the image of the new Pope in the mainstream media, where he seems to do almost no wrong. She's positive about him, without doubt, but is looking deeper into what he says and does. Somehow I suspect her approach is one the Pope himself would encourage. It's good to see that parishioners are thinking beyond what they see on the nightly news.

Beyond that initial impression, this lady articulates well a search that many others may have been on for a long while. She talks about a pope who preaches a Gospel message that is adapted for today but doesn't fall into a 'Michael row the boat ashore' theology. She says she has been searching for this for 'a very long time'. Readers who didn't live through the 1960s might not even know the song she's referring to. Those of us who did can think back to when we heard it and feel how long that wait must have been for her.

This lady has an eighteen-year-old son, a regular attendee at Mass, who is finishing up his schooling at a French lycée and has applied to Notre Dame University in the USA. His 'take' on Pope Francis:

While I am a very young Catholic, I have seen churches from Azerbaijan to France come together to support their new Pope twice … Benedict XVI and now Pope Francis. I cannot forget my Facebook exploding with articles and opinions about the newly-elected Pope Francis. Many of these comments were from Catholics but still more were from Muslims, Protestants and atheists. What was written negated entirely my expectations; these young people, my non-Catholic peers, were rejoicing at the new pope's election. Since his election, online forums known for their savagely atheist communities have sung the praises of Pope Francis and his willingness to make significant changes to the office of the Holy See. My friends have talked to me several times about Pope Francis' activities, more often in his favour than not. I believe that the Pope's personal sacrifices speak volumes of the kind of men who make up the Church and his actions will speak louder than any words that could possibly be said against the Church.

We're a multicultural parish, known in French as *'Mission Anglophone'*, with many expatriate families who've travelled far and wide, so it's not surprising this young man would know many non-Catholics. But this kind of openness, which older generations of us didn't have as much, is quite normal for many young Catholics in western countries now. That makes it even more important that Pope Francis so naturally reaches out to others, such as at the Holy Thursday 'Washing of the Feet' of young women and men – one of them a Muslim – at a Rome detention centre. Or his kissing of that man whose head was covered with sores. Images of simple acts like these go around the world and touch hearts across barriers of language, faith and nationality. As St Francis of Assisi said: 'Always preach the Gospel, use words if necessary.'

Virtual parishioners

Not all the responses came from Paris residents. Each week, reaction to the weekly bulletin comes from many 'virtual parishioners' through the parish website. One of these, a seventy-year-old man in the United States wrote:

> Pope Francis is resetting the focus. We are children of God, encouraged by Christ's example, inspired by the Holy Spirit and destined to use our gifts in a revolution of love and thanksgiving. The rules and bureaucracy of the Church may be important, but they can obscure the essence.

A retired religious sister living in Scotland is a regular correspondent:

> In Christ there is no condemnation. Each morning at Mass in Rome Francis proclaims the Good News of Jesus, the love of God for *all* he has created. He listens as a fellow pilgrim, a sinner who rejoices greatly in the saving grace of God, sharing with us simply and clearly all that Scripture demands of us. He condemns no one but tells everyone, no matter who they are or what they have done, of God's unending love for them. Pope Francis reminds us again and again that all we need to do is turn towards God and ask him. Francis never stops reminding us that the call to follow Jesus is sheer grace, a gift we have received.

Young people respond

The French are very proud of their secular system called *laïcité*, rooted in the separation of Church and State in 1905, and one aspect of it is that there is no religious instruction in state schools. Parents who send their children to the local schools and want catechism for them look to us to provide it. Up to two hundred children from all over the Paris region attend class here each Sunday.

Forty candidates will be presented for the sacrament of confirmation on Pentecost Sunday this year. Preparation includes a retreat day in a neighbouring Paris church and starts with all of us walking from St Joseph's Church through the streets to this neighbouring church whilst praying the Rosary. This is quite unusual for Paris but the young people give witness in an unselfconscious way. Watching them as we walk along reminds me of Pope Francis recently quoting his predecessor, Benedict XVI:

> The Church grows through witness, not proselytism. The witness that can really attract is that associated with attitudes which are uncommon: generosity, detachment, sacrifice, self-forgetfulness in order to care for others.[1]

During this confirmation retreat, a discussion on Pope Francis got varied reactions from these twelve- to fourteen-year-olds. One young man was not convinced that anything had really changed since Francis was elected: 'He has promised a lot for the Church but little has changed.' A girl said she is impressed by the way 'he reaches out to all people and is clear in what he is saying'. She added: 'He is unique; there is an aura about him.'

What impressed me was the energy and enthusiasm generated in the retreat group by this topic. The fact that France has not had the same concentration on the clerical and religious abuse crimes may have given these young people a more positive starting point than in some other countries.

Personal memories of past years

The year since the election of Pope Francis reminds me of my own enthusiasm fifty years ago when I entered the Passionist novitiate at

---

[1] Benedict XVI, Homily at Inaugural Mass of General Episcopal Conference Latin America and the Caribbean, 13 May 2007.

eighteen years of age. Vatican II was underway and Facebook was decades away from being invented. After the novitiate, university was a breath of fresh air and the texts of the Second Vatican Council were devoured in theology studies. At ordination in December 1970, I was filled with hope and enthusiasm believing that this could only get better.

The words of Paul VI's *Evangelii Nuntiandi* (1975) inspired me: 'Above all the Gospel must be proclaimed by witness ... The wordless witness of Christians stirs up irrepressible questions in the hearts of those who see how they live' (*Evangelii Nuntiandi*, n. 21). Interestingly, in *Evangelii Gaudium* Francis quotes *Evangelii Nuntiandi* at least thirteen times.

But my 'dream' didn't last as I felt the brakes being applied in church life, with fear and caution replacing hope and risk. Abuse scandals revealed evil as well as the many inadequacies in human and religious formation. Have we yet learned lessons from these scandals that enable us to offer to God's people priesthood and religious life fit for purpose?

Uncomfortable economics

An elderly Argentinian with a legal and business background, a devout and long-time parishioner here, has doubts about the papal delight that he sees all around him. Though he has profound respect for Pope Francis, he adds:

> I fear that his high media profile with daily papal 'sound bites' is leading to false expectations. For instance, even though Pope Francis has not altered any of the beliefs of the Church, the emphasis he places on the poor may give hard-working people a sense that they are not equally treasured by God.

Evangelii Gaudium dealing with 'the economy and the distribution of income' (nn. 202–8) worries him. It is the one area in which he has most difficulty in being positive towards Francis.

The 'Francis effect'

It is said that more people are participating in Mass and worship since Francis became Bishop of Rome. An annual Mass attendance census here in January 2014 indicates that this may be so. Congregations at some of the weekend Masses have begun spilling into the adjoining hall to use a TV link originally installed for Sunday morning catechism classes. I've also seen something of this 'Francis Effect' in a very personal and touching way. One Sunday in January, a lady from Kenya who has been living for the past few years in Paris asked that her five children, ranging in age from infancy to eighteen years, be baptised. Though baptised herself, she had married in Africa outside the Catholic Church. 'So I felt that I could not ask that my child, as each was born, be admitted to a community of faith that I was outside of', she said. Hearing the words of Pope Francis led her and her husband to have their marriage validated by the Church. Now the whole family are preparing for the baptism of their five children with an excitement that is wonderful to behold.

Nobody can quantify the part played by Francis in this and other situations – the reopening of the Irish Embassy to the Holy See has even been attributed to the Francis Effect. An Irish lady living in Paris for fifty years told me of the comment of her local pharmacist: 'You know, Pope Francis is really Christ on earth.' She added: 'What is particularly interesting is that the pharmacist is a practicing Buddhist!'

The 'second chance fisherman'

This same lady has her own description of Francis:

> He could be renamed 'the second chance fisherman' because I can't count the number of people I've heard saying, 'Pope Francis actually tempts me to go back to practicing my religion again', and several have started doing so.

I came across an instance of a French lady, a parishioner for six years who is finding her way back to Mass from reading and observing Francis. She wrote:

> I am not the type of person who becomes anyone's fan, not even of a pope. I had a special fondness for Benedict XVI. I was shocked when media attempted to oppose the two. To me the renunciation was inspired by the Holy Spirit to allow Francis step in. The coherence between the type of person he was in Argentina and what he does now is very soothing. What I appreciate most is the text of *Evangelii Gaudium* because I am a Catholic who has grown estranged from the

Church and had to begin again. Paragraph 34 acknowledges that most people have no background knowledge to understand what the Church teaches. I like his words in paragraph 70 about the difficulty of Christians incorporating into their lives what the Church teaches.

The vast majority of parishioners here have probably not read the text of *Evangelii Gaudium*, but apparently some have sat down with it and gone through it carefully. In the home of a parishioner during a pastoral visit, I was delighted to see a copy of the exhortation. At a Catholic school where I serve as chaplain some parents are arranging sessions so that they can learn more about the text.

A Sri Lankan parishioner, a grandmother living a long time in Paris, had tears in her eyes as she told me of her own conversion because of Francis:

> When the Pope said he was a sinner, I was shocked. I was brought up to detest sin but now realise that I thought of myself as holier than people around me whom I looked down on. When the Pope asked, 'Who am I to judge?', I knew that I had to change my attitude to others. I know in my heart that I am now a better Catholic.

Many parishioners here are from the Philippines and mostly young. One of them, a man, remarked that in Pope Francis: 'The light of Christ has come into the world. His humility, devotion to Mary and encouraging confession impress me a lot.'

Women's place in the Church
Among the adults preparing for the sacraments of initiation (RCIA) are five young women from late teens to a mother in her thirties. They acknowledge that they see women in our liturgical ministries and service of the community. A nineteen-year-old, however, tells of her sadness regarding the place of women in the Catholic Church: 'My friend now studying theology in the USA will soon be "Reverend Annie", while I as a Catholic cannot aspire to this. I don't see why not.' A teacher in her twenties sees a disconnection between the place of Mary and the restricted role of women in the Church: 'I will be baptised this Easter but I fail to understand the treatment of women in the Church after all that I have learned of the role of Mary in the plan of salvation.' An older lady on our RCIA team admitted: 'I have no answers for you.' These women see their place in the Church as

one of the biggest challenges facing Pope Francis, especially since he seems ready to change some things but is so clear about not having women priests.

Conclusion

In a recent homily[2] Pope Francis spoke of dialogue which is at the heart of his interactive approach to the papacy. He said:

> We need to draw near in dialogue, because time makes walls grow. Once walls have grown, reconciliation is so difficult; it is so difficult … As the Berlin Wall had been an element of division for many years, the possibility also exists in our hearts of becoming like Berlin, of putting up walls against others.

One of our cantors is a well-travelled American who saw the Berlin Wall fall in 1989. When I asked him for his thoughts about the Pope's remarks, he said:

> This is a great encouragement. I like the way he's telling us to be confident and move out of the confines of an inward-looking church. Rome has grown quite 'self-referential', as Francis likes to call it, and now he's saying to reach out to other Christians, to Muslims and Jews, to atheists – and he's doing it too. This is the global world we live in today, not the Catholic ghettos many of us older Catholics grew up in. This also goes for inside the Church. Francis has placed himself beyond the liberal-versus-conservative struggles over the Council that we've seen in recent decades. He's breaking down the wall too by focusing on the Gospel message, not this or that rule, or whether we use Latin or not. This makes him a real pontifex, a bridge-builder.

Having lived a decade in Holy Cross, Ardoyne, Belfast, Northern Ireland, I know something about 'peace walls' that stay up because of walls in our hearts and minds. As Pope Francis completes one year as Bishop of Rome, I hope he continues 'untying the knots'[3] and keeps encouraging all people to go to the table of dialogue so that we may eventually dismantle the walls of division in Ireland and in all places around the world where they keep people apart.

---

[2]   Feast of St Francis de Sales, 24 January 2014.

[3]   The phrase comes from Paul Vallely's insightful book, *Pope Francis: Untying the Knots* (London: Bloomsbury, 2013).

Setting Us Free:
A Personal View of Pope Francis

Willie Walsh

There appears to be a freedom about this man, a freedom which all of us seek, but few of us find and enjoy. Certainly few of us attain that fullness which he speaks of: 'those who accept his offer of salvation are set free from sin, sorrow, inner emptiness and loneliness' (*EG*, n. 1).[1] Pope Francis' freedom is obviously rooted in his deep trust in a loving and forgiving God. I suspect that it is also further rooted in his total acceptance of himself. He strikes me as a man at peace with himself and at peace with his God. It is this peacefulness of his that presents to me as freedom.

Freedom from the outset
Albert Nolan, in his book, *Jesus Today*, speaks of the 'radical freedom' which Jesus experienced in his own life. He suggests that Jesus' freedom 'knew no limits because his trust in God knew no limits'.[2] Jesus was free from fear, or rather he never allowed his fears to prevent him from doing his Father's will. Even in the hour of his greatest fear, he prayed, 'not my will but yours be done' (Lk 22:42). He felt free to challenge courageously the religious leaders of his time regarding their strict adherence to rules and regulations.

From the very beginning of his papacy, Pope Francis felt free to challenge many of the traditional rules or customs surrounding the office of pope. We are familiar with the new approaches he took:

---

[1]   Pope Francis, *Evangelii Gaudium* (The Joy of the Gospel), Apostolic Exhortation on the Proclamation of the Gospel in Today's World, 2013. Subsequent references will be denoted by *EG*, followed by the paragraph number(s).

[2]   Albert Nolan, *Jesus Today: A Spirituality of Radical Freedom* (New York: Orbis Books, 2006), p. 161.

choosing to live in a simple apartment in Casa Santa Marta and leaving aside some of the more elaborate vestments associated with previous popes. These were small though highly significant gestures of a man who felt free enough within himself not to be held captive by tradition for tradition's sake.

Sensitivity of expression

Even more striking about his freedom is the gentle manner in which he presents the teachings of the Church. He hasn't changed any teachings, but he presents them in a manner that is non-judgemental and in keeping with the Christian values of mercy and love. His comments on the issue of homosexuality have received much publicity – 'if someone is gay and searches for the Lord and has goodwill, who am I to judge?' Likewise, the way he has spoken about our overemphasis on single issues such as abortion, contraception and gay marriage is far more nuanced than what we have been accustomed to hearing from Church authorities. In his now famous interview for Jesuit publications, he observed:

> We cannot insist only on issues related to abortion, gay marriage and the use of contraceptive methods. I have not spoken much about these issues and have been reprimanded for that … when we speak about these issues we have to talk about them in context.

I believe that many of us, especially those of us who are or were in positions of responsibility in our Church, did not enjoy the kind of personal freedom Pope Francis has that allows him such freedom of expression. Many of us felt the fear of responsibility that caused us to be torn between what was expected of us by others and what our hearts called us to do, or say. I have in mind a tension that often existed between our sense of loyalty to Church teaching and what we felt in our hearts. I am speaking also of the tension that is caused when a Roman Congregation insists that some matters such as compulsory clerical celibacy, or exclusion of people in second unions from some of the sacraments, are not up for discussion.

Our hearts were speaking to us of mercy, forgiveness and love, but we couldn't always allow ourselves to bring these values or qualities to our expression of Church teaching. For some reason, we felt that these values and Church teaching were not synonymous with one another. I think that overnight Pope Francis healed that tension between the head and heart in the Church. He has restored our freedom to put 'heart' at the centre of the Christian life. It is now up to us to preach the Gospel of Christ with sensitivity, gentleness and compassion.

The priority of the poor

For a number of years priests of the Killaloe diocese had a mission outreach to Africa and later to South America. I had the privilege of visiting my fellow priests in both places. One of the things that impressed me most on those visits was that the people, who lived in serious poverty by our standards, seemed to be perfectly happy if they managed to have enough food for the present day. I can honestly say that I saw more smiling, warm and welcoming faces in the shanty towns of Lima and in the slums of Nairobi than I see when walking the streets of the average Irish town.

My limited experience of such serious poverty I found mirrored in the words of Pope Francis: 'I can say that the most beautiful and natural expressions of joy which I have seen in my life were in the poor people who have nothing to hold on to' (*EG*, n. 7). As pope, Francis is freer than most to bring the plight of the poor to centre stage in the life of the Church. Many of us in the Western Church have not had the authentic experience of poverty that he has had in his lifetime to date. Again, he is heightening our awareness of the poor and freeing us to be voices for the poor in our own countries, dioceses and parishes.

As Christian bishops, priests, religious men and women and with our lay sisters and brothers, we too can learn to be a Church of the poor by following the example of Pope Francis. I think of the lifestyle he adopted in Buenos Aires – living in a simple apartment, using public transport, a habit he has continued in Rome, in his living accommodation and use of an older and smaller car to get about. He is leading by example and even though his gestures may seem small, one might say that they are grand-scale gestures because they are Christ-centred.

Pope Francis' own detachment from worldly goods is an example to all of us, but like all good example, it is founded on solid ground. He has a real love for the poor, the sick and the vulnerable – one can even see it in his body language – and in his first year he has moved the questions of justice and the unacceptable gulf between rich and poor further up on the international agenda. He put it there in language that is caring but also stark and unrelenting when he said that an economy of exclusion and inequality kills. Again, the concern for the poor reflects Christ's own freedom to love without condition. Jesus' love of the poor, the sick and the outcasts was a scandal to many people at the time, but his love was unconditional and free, and could not be held back by the customs of the time. Pope Francis seems to have that same sense of freedom that will not allow him to renege on the Gospel of unconditional love.

The truth frees

I have the clear impression listening to and seeing Pope Francis that there is an openness about him that has no fear of the truth; he displays, in fact, an obvious love of the truth. There is a gentle boldness (if such be possible) in the way he speaks. One detects no evasion, no reluctance to say what he believes. At times, he speaks in a manner that seems to make the traditional teaching of the Church more palatable to today's world. In particular, I think of his response to the issue of sexual orientation, or the comment that the God in whom he believes is not 'a Catholic God'. At other times, he says things which may seem less acceptable to modern thought such as his response to the admission of women to the ordained ministry. One finds oneself almost content to agree to disagree with him because of his honesty and clarity which, again, speaks to me of a great personal freedom.

This courage to face the truth was, I feel, learned through his personal experience of past failure in his life. In his now famous interview with a Jesuit confrere, he was asked to say who he was and he replied: 'I am a sinner.' Which of us would give such a spontaneous answer? Of course, we all acknowledge that we are sinners, but few of us would give it as our first answer. Yet Pope Francis recognises his own frailty. He has lived with the knowledge of personal failure in his life.

In particular, he has expressed his pain and regret in relation to his time as Jesuit Provincial in Argentina and his failure to act more strongly in the protection of priests who worked among the poor. At a memorial Mass for the reburial of one of those priests, Fr Mugica, he prayed for pardon: 'for the times as members of the Church we did not have the courage to denounce his assassination'.[3]

This capacity to recognise our failures in humility and to learn from them is a sign of real maturity. When we add to that the deep faith in a loving God who is always ready to forgive us, we are on a journey of transformation and of self-acceptance. I think that Pope Francis is on that Christ-centred journey and he invites us to join him as individuals and as a Church.

Where is he leading us?
Francis projects a call to personal freedom in his words and deeds. As bishops, priests and religious, we may find it hard to free ourselves from all the comfort zones of our lives. Pope Francis projects a call to personal freedom in his words and deeds. We need to stir ourselves if we are to follow the example that he is showing us. There are some things that we need to address with urgency:

- To make a conscious effort to preach by example, and remember to be gentle when we preach by word.

- To find a personal inner peace through reflection on the love of the Gospel Christ.

- To be tolerant towards those whose opinions and lifestyles are at variance with our own.

- To make room for the marginalised in the life of the local Church.

- To lead by example and to encourage people who are struggling.

- To take many leaves out of Francis' book when it comes to the poor in our society.

- To seek out and honour the truth even when it pains us to do so.

Where is Pope Francis leading us? One would like to think that he will lead us back to Christ. It will be a long road back for many of us. Some of us may feel tired and disillusioned and too old to care about a new direction for the Church. Younger people may look to the Church for more certainty than Francis offers and may be unwilling

---

3   Cited in Paul Vallely, *Pope Francis: Untying the Knots* (London: Bloomsbury, 2013), p. 96.

to embrace fully the challenges that the journey of the heart will demand of us. To all of us (old and young), Pope Francis' example is pointing to hope for the future of the Church. It is the hope that Christ gave to all humanity through his life, death and resurrection.

Pope Francis speaks of the joy of the Gospel; so too, these are joyful times. They are liberating times. They are, in my opinion, a return to the Church that I and many of my generation welcomed after the Second Vatican Council and to which I hope I never lost my allegiance. However, somewhere along the way we may have lessened in our enthusiasm for and love of the Gospel message. We may have given up our freedom to the enslavements of rules and regulations, and we allowed Christ's radical message of love and compassion to be imprisoned in compromises, untruths and worldly attachments.

Now, a man has come to us from 'almost the ends of the earth' and he is reminding us that Christ came to bring the Good News to the poor and to set captives free. It is my hope that we will be freed from whatever form captivity has taken in our lives.

Pope Francis:
Living the Call to Kenosis

Sarah Mac Donald

He must increase, but I must decrease. (Jn 3:30)

A year into the Francis pontificate, the Pope of Surprises continues to challenge and confound. His teachings and leadership eschew easy categorisation and so little consensus has emerged on who Pope Francis is, what he stands for and where he is leading the Church. Does he represent a new departure or merely a shift in tone? When his predecessor was elected in 2005, his viewpoints and emphases on a range of issues were already well documented thanks to his role as Prefect of the Congregation for the Doctrine of the Faith. In contrast, when the Argentinian Jesuit stepped out onto the balcony of St Peter's on 13 March 2013, he was pretty much an unknown quantity beyond his homeland. But there were telltale signs in this first short encounter: he had dispensed with the traditional papal mozzetta cape, his engaging manner, and his humble request for prayers from the assembled pilgrims, to whom he bowed; perhaps the most potent gesture of this introduction.

Over the past twelve months, his steadying hand and charismatic 'man of the people' style of leadership has gained the confidence of the faithful despite scandals, careerism, rivalries and revelations of corruption at the heart of the Holy See. What could have been a public relations disaster for a Church already tarnished by clerical abuse scandals, has been minimised by a pontiff willing to acknowledge the problems and grasp the nettle on long overdue reform of Vatican institutions such as the Vatican Bank and the Curia. By declaring that the Church needs to be 'a poor Church for the poor', and by choosing to live modestly in the Vatican guest house, the Casa Santa Marta, he has sent a strong signal that there will be no papal court, and the channel through which influence was previously exercised will no longer operate. In his interview with Eugenio Scalfari,[1] the Pope reportedly admitted: 'Heads of the Church have often been narcissists, flattered and thrilled by their courtiers. The court is the leprosy of the papacy.' Lamenting the Vatican-centric view of the Curia and its preoccupation with temporal interests, he told Scalfari: 'I do not share this view and I'll do everything I can to change it. The Church is or should go back to being a community of God's people, and priests, pastors and bishops who have the care of souls, are at the service of the People of God.'

In tandem with his drive for greater integrity and transparency, Francis has radically sought to devolve power away from the papacy towards a more collegial and decentralised leadership. This shift was signalled by his appointment of an advisory group of eight cardinals and his suggestion that local episcopacies should be dealing with issues like dissident priests rather than referring everything back to Rome. His less judgemental tone and strong emphasis on social justice, as well as his simple apparel, in marked contrast with the perceived excesses of the Benedictine papacy, have struck a chord with many of the faithful at a time of economic recession. They have also assuaged some of the frustration voiced in the final months of Benedict's pontificate by priest and lay reform groups such as the Association of Catholic Priests, the Association of Catholics in Ireland and We Are Church Ireland, who were vocal in demanding that there should be no 'big hats' at the 2012 International Eucharistic Congress in Dublin. Under Francis, bishops' mitres have diminished appreciably in height, and the threatened comeback of the cappa magna, which prelates like Cardinal Raymond Leo Burke had donned with increasing frequency, now looks more like a quirk than a trend.

The popularity of Francis in the media is another new phenomenon for the Church and a boon to the faithful, still grappling with the fact that their pope is liked and therefore as liable to grace the cover of *Rolling Stone* as *America* magazine. But it would be wrong to believe that Francis was universally acclaimed on election. Dark hints and insinuations about his record as Jesuit Provincial in Argentina during the Dirty War threatened, in those first days and weeks, to undermine

---

[1] Eugenio Scalfari, 'The Pope: How the Church will Change', *La Repubblica*, 1 October 2013, trans. from Italian to English by Kathryn Wallace.

fatally the new pontiff. In his book, *Pope Francis: Untying the Knots*, Paul Vallely deals with the journey the future pope made from a divisive figure within the Argentinian province of the Society of Jesus, where some recall him as an authoritarian and conservative leader, to a bishop of the slums, prepared to take on economic and political elites.[2] George Bernard Shaw once opined, 'Progress is impossible without change, and those who cannot change their minds cannot change anything.' The contradictions apparent in Francis' life story are an indication of how living the journey has changed him. A Gorbachev-type figure bringing *Glasnost* and *Perestroika* to his own outlook as well as the musty corridors of power in the Vatican. For Francis, it has been a personal journey of *kenosis* (self-emptying).

In a recent article in *The Tablet*, John Borelli suggested that Pope Francis was 'incorporating an Ignatian style of leadership into the office of Peter'. But it is his other great influence, St Francis of Assisi, who has inspired his ongoing *kenosis*. As Capuchin Fr Raniero Cantalamessa, preacher to the pontifical household, explained in his Advent 2013 reflection, St Francis did not 'choose between wealth and poverty, nor between the rich and the poor, or belonging to one class rather than to another' but he chose 'between himself and God, between saving his life or losing it for the Gospel'.[3] The main goal of Francis of Assisi was not reforming the Church, according to Fr Cantalamessa; it was living the Gospel. St Francis 'carried on the reform in himself, and he silently indicated to the Church the only way out of the crisis: embracing again the Gospel and men, particularly the humble and the poor'.

Whether by design or due to his preoccupation with more the immediate concerns of Vatican reform, Pope Francis has mostly steered clear of those thorny issues of sexual morality which are so deeply divisive, and which preoccupy the media and agenda-driven faith. By talking a lot about mercy, the more compassionate tone of the Francis papacy thus far has enabled the Church's first Latin American pope to remain all things to all people. Twelve months on, as the figures for attendances at papal events soar, all sides are anxious

---

2 Paul Vallely, *Pope Francis: Untying the Knots* (London: Continuum, 2013).

3 Fr Raniero Cantalamessa on Francis of Assisi's Method for Church Reform; First Advent Homily: 'to prepare ourselves for Christmas in the company of Francis of Assisi' (Rome, 6 December 2013), http://www.zenit.org/en/articles/father-cantalamessa-on-francis-of-assisi-s-method-for-church-reform [accessed, 11 February 2014].

to claim him as their own. A prime example of this is the two understandings of Pope Francis articulated by leading Catholic commentators at the meeting of the American Academy of Religion and the Society of Biblical Literature in Baltimore in November 2013. On the one side, George Weigel, biographer of John Paul II and distinguished Senior Fellow at the Ethics and Public Policy Centre in Washington DC and, on the other, Richard Gaillardetz, Joseph Professor of Catholic Systematic Theology at Boston College and President of the Catholic Theological Society of America. In the perception of the latter, Francis is a potential catalyst for reform, whose approach to the papacy so far represents 'a significant change in trajectory', while Weigel, in contrast, perceives continuity between Francis and his two immediate predecessors. How is Francis able to keep these diametrically opposed wings in the Church onside?

It has helped that the Church's progressive wing has been supportive and hasn't given vent to its frustration that significant changes in the teachings on divorce and remarriage, homosexuality, women priests and contraception remain off the agenda. But that may not last for long. In an article titled, 'Liberals Should Stop Eulogising this Reactionary Pope', James Bloodworth rounds on Pope Francis' 'reactionary politics' which he says have been 'played down by liberal Catholics in favour of his musings on social justice and global capitalism'.[4] Warning that 'little of substance has actually changed' under Francis, he says the Church 'stands on roughly the same political terrain as it did under the leadership of Pope Benedict'. In contrast, in an aside to *Zeit Online*, the traditionalist Archbishop Georg Gänswein, prefect of the papal household and secretary to Pope Emeritus, Benedict XVI, articulated his concerns over the pace of change, in an observation likely to resonate with those who wish to maintain the status quo. Of Francis, he observed, 'I wait every day for another innovation, what will be different?'[5] Such undercurrents of unease must produce a current of resistance to Francis' reform plans. The reconfirmation of Archbishop Gerhard Müller as head of the Congregation for the Doctrine of the Faith was undoubtedly aimed at appeasing this camp.

---

[4] James Bloodworth, 'Liberals Should Stop Eulogising this Reactionary Pope', *New Statesman*, 20 December 2013.

[5] 'Benedikts Privatsekretär hadert mit Papst-Rücktritt', *Zeit Online*, 4 December 2013.

Every new pontificate brings with it hopes for change in a myriad of areas. If, as some believe, the papacy of Francis heralds a new springtime in the Church, then his handling of demands for an expanded role for women in the Church will be keenly watched as a litmus test. It is an area in which he potentially could make a lasting impact and quench some of the mounting frustration within the rank and file. But this voyage won't be plain sailing, as Francis navigates between the Scylla of liberals' demand for women's ordination and the Charybdis of magisterial teachings on the matter, such as John Paul II's declaration that 'the Church has no authority whatsoever to confer priestly ordination on women' and that this judgement is 'to be definitively held by all the Church's faithful'.[6] Francis himself has moved to dampen down expectations by forthrightly ruling out any possibility of women being ordained to the priesthood. In *Evangelii Gaudium*, he stated: 'The reservation of the priesthood to males, as a sign of Christ the Spouse who gives himself in the Eucharist, is not a question open to discussion' (*EG*, n. 104). He has also rejected the possibility of women cardinals, telling Andrea Tornielli in his interview 'Never be Afraid of Tenderness', 'I don't know where this idea sprang from. Women in the Church must be valued not clericalised. Whoever thinks of women as cardinals suffers a bit from clericalism.'[7] It was an astute way of shelving the issue as most women and men would baulk at the prospect of women being clericalised, particularly because clericalism was cited as a factor in the Church's sexual abuse scandals.

From the outset of his papacy, Francis has, nevertheless, given strong signals of his intention to recognise the contribution of women. Just a couple of weeks into his pontificate, on 28 March 2013, he visited the Casal del Marmo detention centre in Rome for Holy Thursday ceremonies. Among those whose feet he washed were two young women, one of whom was a Muslim. There was some disquiet from traditionalist Catholics who questioned why, if the rite is a re-enactment of Jesus' washing of the feet of the twelve apostles, a woman should be included. Edward Peters of Sacred Heart Major Seminary in Detroit described this gesture as 'questionable' and referred to a 1988 letter from the Vatican's Congregation for Divine

---

6   Pope John Paul II, *Ordinatio Sacerdotalis*, Apostolic Letter on Reserving Priestly Ordination to Men Alone.

7   Andrea Tornielli, 'Never be Afraid of Tenderness', Vatican Insider/*La Stampa*, 14 December 2013.

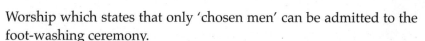
Worship which states that only 'chosen men' can be admitted to the foot-washing ceremony.

Pope Francis talks about women's 'sensitivity, intuition and other distinctive skill sets which they, more than men, tend to possess'. He mentions 'the special concern which women show to others, which finds a particular, even if not exclusive, expression in motherhood' (*EG*, n. 103). In another sentence, he talks about the 'feminine genius'. However, his call for the development of a 'profound theology of the woman' wins few laurels from Jon O'Brien of Catholics for Choice, who perceives it as 'condescending'.[8] The call for a theology of the woman also raised concerns for Sr Joan Chittister who expressed her reservations at the meeting of the American Academy of Religion and the Society of Biblical Literature in Baltimore in November 2013. In his interview with Fr Antonio Spadaro, the Jesuit editor of *La Civiltà Cattolica*,[9] Francis suggested that only through a theology of the woman 'will it be possible to better reflect on women's function within the Church. The feminine genius is needed wherever we make important decisions. The challenge today is this: to think about the specific place of women also in those places where the authority of the Church is exercised for various areas of the Church.' But for Sr Chittister, a former leader of the Leadership Conference of Women Religious, what concerns her is who will do this proposed theological study: 'The same clerical, patriarchal types who have been doing it for the last 2,000 years when the Church Fathers first said that women "have the malice of both dragons and asps" among other things,' she wondered. The Benedictine Sister also laments the fact that a Vatican document can rail against 'forms of feminism hostile to the Church' but 'never mention male chauvinism' or the structures of patriarchy as a matter of concern.

Francis seeks to allay women's disappointment over their exclusion from the priesthood by stating that in the Church, functions 'do not favour the superiority of some vis-à-vis the others', and adds: 'Indeed, a woman, Mary, is more important than the bishops' (*EG*, n. 104). This is high praise from a pope known for his strong personal devotion to Mary. To those who perceive the ministerial priesthood as hierarchical, Francis reminds them that it is in fact 'totally ordered

8   Barbie Latza Nadeau, 'Does Pope Francis Have a Woman Problem?', *The Daily Beast*, 20 December 2013.

9   Antonio Spadaro, SJ, 'A Big Heart Open to God', *America*, 20 September 2013.

to the holiness of Christ's members'. 'Its key and axis is not power understood as domination, but the power to administer the sacrament of the Eucharist; this is the origin of its authority, which is always a service to God's people' (*EG*, n. 104). One of the questions Pope Francis put to participants attending the seminar 'God Entrusts the Human Being to Woman', which was organised by the Pontifical Council for the Laity (October 2013) to mark the twenty-fifth anniversary of Blessed John Paul II's apostolic letter, *Mulieris Dignitatem*, was 'What presence does woman have in the Church?' Pope Francis' question is not easily answered, as the vocation and mission of women in the Church is both a vexed question and a changing reality. Expressing his concern that 'woman's role of service' can slide towards a role of *'servitude'*, he commented 'When I see women doing things of servitude, it is because what a woman should do is not understood. What presence does woman have in the Church? Can she be largely appreciated? It is a reality that I have very much at heart.'[10] He also recognises that

> the hour is coming, in fact has come, when the vocation of women is being acknowledged in its fullness, the hour in which women acquire in the world an influence, an effect and a power never hitherto achieved. That is why, at this moment when the human race is undergoing so deep a transformation, women imbued with a spirit of the Gospel can do so much to aid humanity in not falling.

This willingness to consider new frontiers for women coupled with his regard for 'boldness'[11] as a virtue, suggest that this Pope could affect some radical change though not in the way those lobbying for women's ordination or cardinals might expect.

---

[10] Address of Pope Francis to Participants in a seminar organised by the Pontifical Council for the Laity on the occasion of the twenty-fifth anniversary of *Mulieris Dignitatem*, Vatican, 12 October 2013. http://www.vatican.va/holy_father/francesco/speeches/2013/october/documents/papa-francesco_20131012_seminario-xxv-mulieris-dignitatem_en.html [accessed, 11 February 2014].

[11] Andrea Tornielli, 'Never be Afraid of Tenderness', Vatican Insider/*La Stampa*, 14 December 2013. He explains that when he speaks of prudence 'I do not think of it in terms of an attitude that paralyses but as the virtue of a leader. Prudence is a virtue of government. So is boldness. One must govern with boldness and prudence.' He continues: 'We must try to facilitate people's faith, rather than control it. Last year in Argentina I condemned the attitude of some priests who did not baptise the children of unmarried mothers. This is a sick mentality.'

There are two areas in which Francis could make a bold statement of solidarity with women. The first concerns the Leadership Conference of Women Religious in the US. In April 2013, the Pope affirmed the line adopted by Pope Benedict and his advisors. Ahead of the year dedicated to consecrated life, which opens in November 2014, the Pope could make a strong statement of solidarity and affirmation with US women religious communities. There is so much ground this pope, with his commitment to social justice, shares with the group's 57,000-strong membership. One symbolic gesture Francis could use to rebuild the trust lost concerns the fate of Cardinal Bernard Law, who was a prime mover against the nuns, as Robert Mickens of *The Tablet* revealed.[12] Isn't it time to send him back to Boston as a gesture not just to the women religious but also the victims of clerical abuse?

The second suggestion is a more long term one and has its genesis in an article in *Doctrine and Life* by theologian, Fr Seán Fagan.[13] In it, he questioned the Church's need to maintain thousands of ordained priests bound to administrative tasks with no significant ministerial relationship with any Christian community. These Vatican functionaries say Mass alone or for a few domestic servants.[14] 'Why do the members of the Pope's diplomatic service representing the Vatican to countries around the world need episcopal or priestly ordination?', Fr Fagan asked. If Pope Francis wants to begin a process of true reform within the Church and at the same time recognise the gifts and contributions women can make to the Church, perhaps this is where he could begin, with the Holy See's diplomatic service. As Francis himself has said: 'we need to create still broader opportunities for a more incisive female presence in the Church' (*EG*, n. 103). A bold strike in solidarity with the 'feminine genius' would be to select a woman as the Vatican's first lay diplomat. Let the planning begin.

---

[12]   Robert Mickens, *The Tablet*, 3 May 2012.
[13]   Seán Fagan, 'Church Renewal or Church Reform', in *Doctrine and Life*, 57(5), May/June 2007, p. 48.
[14]   *Ibid.*

Where is Pope Francis Leading Us?

Timothy Radcliffe, OP

One year after his election, Pope Francis continues to receive an astonishingly positive reception. We are moved by his gestures. He went to the prison and washed the feet of the inmates, men and women, Christian and Muslim; the world sat up. He embraced the man whose face was covered with terrible tumours; the world went wild. These are wonderful gestures of compassion, but will they really change the Church so that it becomes a more radiant witness to Christ's love?

At the heart of Catholicism is the belief that words and gestures may be sacramental and so transformative. They are not merely 'symbolic'. On the night before he died, when his community of disciples was disintegrating and hope seemed lost, Jesus performed a gesture of unimaginable creativity, taking the bread, blessing, breaking and sharing it: 'This is my body given for you.' The Church lives from such signs of hope. John Paul II had a gift for superb gestures which shook the world, as when he went to pray with the Jews at the Wailing Wall in Jerusalem. These gestures of Pope Francis are not mere show. Gestures are one of the ways in which we begin to shape a future which is as yet beyond our understanding.

What is this new Church to which Francis' gestures point? When he was interviewed for the Jesuit periodicals, he began with Caravaggio's picture of Jesus gazing at Matthew. 'Here, this is me, a sinner on whom the Lord has turned his gaze.' Israel longed for the Lord to smile on her: 'Let your face shine, that we may be saved' (Ps 80:19). This smile became flesh in Jesus. Francis says, 'If he [Jesus] speaks to someone, he looks into their eyes with deep love and concern: "Jesus, looking upon him, loved him"' (*Evangelii Gaudium*, n. 269).[1] We are ministers of his loving gaze.

---

[1] Pope Francis, *Evangelii Gaudium* (The Joy of the Gospel), Apostolic Exhortation on the Proclamation of the Gospel in Today's World, 2013, n. 269. All subsequent references will be denoted by *EG* in parentheses, followed by the paragraph number(s).

Whatever they have done, God is in all human beings. 'Appearances notwithstanding, every person is immensely holy and deserves our love.' It is only in being drawn out of ourselves and our self-obsession that we become human. Pope Francis makes an astonishing assertion, which is at the heart of his understanding of being human and of the nature of the Church: 'I am a mission on this earth' (*EG*, n. 273). Each of us only truly exists in reaching out to others, just as the Son and the Holy Spirit exist in proceeding from the Father.

This loving gaze is at the heart of his vision of the Church. The Church must get out of the sacristy and be with people where they are, with their sufferings, their troubles. She 'is called to come out of herself and to go to the peripheries, not only geographically, but also the existential peripheries: the mystery of sin, of pain, of injustice, of ignorance and indifference to religion, of intellectual currents, and of all misery'.[2] The priest must have the smell of his sheep. It's risky but 'I prefer a Church which is bruised, hurting and dirty because it has been out on the streets, rather than a Church which is unhealthy from being confined and from clinging to its own security' (*EG*, n. 49). This is why he detests clericalism, the priesthood as a caste apart, turned inward, and obsessed with its own privileges and status. It is better that we leave the sacristy, get involved with people and make mistakes, even sin, than that we sit gazing at our ecclesiastical navels. We must take that risk otherwise we shall die.

The phrase, 'the People of God', was widely used at the Second Vatican Council, but then fell out of favour. Pope Francis has put it back at the centre. He said that the word of God invites us to recognise that we are a people: 'Once you were not a people, but now you are God's people' (1 Pet 2:10). We need the hierarchy to preserve the unity of God's people, but it must not to squeeze us into a suffocating pyramid or make us functionaries of an institution. The institution exists for the sake of the people, and not the people for the sake of the institution.

How can the Pope achieve this radical transformation of the Church? Does he have a plan? Is there a blueprint on his desk? I think not. He wants to start a process and is content not to know how it will evolve. In a slightly obscure passage in *Evangelii Gaudium*, he says that we must respect time rather than space: 'Giving priority to time means

---

[2] Cardinal Bergoglio's statement to the congregation of cardinals, prior to his election, according to Cardinal Jaime Lucas Ortega y Alamino.

being concerned about *initiating processes rather than possessing spaces'* (*EG*, n. 223, emphasis added). We start on a journey not knowing where the Holy Spirit leads us: 'There is no greater freedom than that of allowing oneself to be guided by the Holy Spirit, renouncing the attempt to plan and control everything to the last detail, and instead letting him enlighten, guide and direct us, leading us wherever he wills' (*EG*, n. 280).

At the heart of Francis' spirituality is the desire to undo the mechanisms of control. In *A Secular Age*,[3] Charles Taylor argues that one of the foundations of contemporary secularism is the culture of control. Everything must be administered, checked, and monitored. This leads to the rise of the modern state with its control of every aspect of our lives. Taylor asserts that this obsession with control developed in the sixteenth century, when confidence weakened in God's providential government of the world. If God no longer runs the show, we must.

So the Church should be an oasis of liberty in a nightmare of bureaucratic management. It should cherish 'the unruly freedom' of God's word (*EG*, n. 22). Alas, the Church has often been infected by this same secular obsession with control. Curial officials spent a lot of time checking up on people, fretting about theologians who were suspected of departing from the official line, nervous that everything will get out of control.

But the Pope believes that the Spirit blows where she wills. The government of the Church ought to be at the service of God's surprising rule. The rule of the bishops should ensure that no one else rules: the bullies must not rule nor the fearful. The latest fashion must not manipulate us; nor the media, nor people who threaten to report others to Rome. God's rule works through the Holy Spirit which is poured into every member of the Body of Christ. The bishop's government should help the timid to speak up, the minority to have their word, the despised to be heard with respect and especially those who disagree with him. The bishop's government should open the space for God's surprising rule.

When Francis was a young Jesuit provincial, he was rather authoritarian. He was not popular with his brethren. He admits that he got a lot of things wrong. Before he became a bishop, he went through some sort of spiritual crisis which transformed his understanding of

---

3   Charles Taylor, *A Secular Age* (London: The Belknap Press of Harvard University, 2007).

the Church. In prayer he learned to hand things over to God: 'I have the sense of being in someone else's hands, as though God were taking me by the hand.'[4] 'Prayer is an act of freedom but sometimes it emerges as an attempt at control, which is the same as wanting to control God.'[5] When I had the privilege of a long private audience with him, I met a man who was free and who let others be free in his presence. This is rooted in the centrality of prayer in his life.

This rejection of control goes with a theology of mess! We must be unafraid to get involved in a messy world, which does not conform to the tidy categories of much church discipline. The Church has a beautiful and wise theology of marriage, but Francis worked in barrios in Buenos Aires where the married were a tiny minority. If we plunge into a messy world, we shall get our hands dirty. He said during the World Youth Day in Rio de Janeiro, after the downpours of rain, 'I expect a messy World Youth Day. But I want things messy and stirred up in the congregations.' The Holy Spirit hovered over the messy chaos in the beginning and the world was born. We should dare to wade into the mess of this world, trusting in the fertility of the Spirit, who is hatching the new creation. This is alarming for tidy-minded people.

So the Pope has a sense of where the Church should go but he probably does not want to have an exact blueprint as to exactly what this future Church should be like or how it will come about. He is initiating a process that opens us to the unpredictability of God's grace. All this will take time. Francis says that his first idea of what is to be done is often wrong. He has learned not to rush: 'I have learned not to trust my first reaction. When I'm calmer, after passing through the crucible of solitude, I come closer to understanding what is to be done.'[6]

Media reports on popes usually portray them as heads of government who impose their own party policies. But Francis is not a man with a party political agenda. He seeks to be obedient to the Holy Spirit, opening the space for what is new and unexpected to happen. Here one notices a difference between Benedict and Francis. Both have a humble understanding of the papacy. Neither sees himself as free to do what he wants. But Benedict stressed fidelity to

---

[4]   Paul Vallely, *Untying the Knots* (London: Bloomsbury, 2013), p. 144.
[5]   *Ibid.*
[6]   *Ibid.*

the tradition. He wrote that 'the true meaning of the teaching authority of the Pope is that he is the advocate of Christian memory'.[7] He must be faithful to what has been given whereas Francis stresses obedience to the new impulses of the Spirit. He quotes Irenaeus of Lyon, of the second century: 'By his coming, Christ brought with him all newness.' 'Every form of authentic evangelisation is always new' (*EG*, n. 11). There is no absolute contradiction between their positions: the memory of the past opens us to the surprises of the future. Rather there is a difference of sensibility.

How then is Pope Francis opening the Church to the new impulse of the Holy Spirit? From the moment that he stepped onto the balcony after his election, he showed that he wanted to be, above all, the Bishop of Rome and not a monarch. He referred to Benedict as the emeritus Bishop of Rome. He refused the papal mozetta, the short cape usually worn by popes. He quoted St Ignatius of Antioch, that Rome is the Church which presides 'in love'. He pointed us back to the beginnings of the Church, when the Pope was seen as the bishop of a local church which had a unique role within the communion of churches.

The Church has fought the domination of monarchs for centuries – from Constantine, the Holy Roman Emperor, Henry VIII, Napoleon, to the Communist dictators of the twentieth century. Perhaps it was inevitable that she should come to look like her opponents. There was no other way to preserve her freedom. But papal monarchy is like a medieval suit of armour, necessary if one is fighting other knights in armour. But today the challenge is to get out onto the streets, to engage in conversation. If one is staggering around with a heavy helmet and a big shield, it is hard to have easy chats with one's neighbours and befriend them. So Francis wants to liberate the papacy from the burden of monarchy and put the Bishop of Rome back into the college of bishops, the guardian of the unity of the Church.

This means that the control of the Church by the Vatican must be eased. In an interview with *La Republica* he was amazingly frank. The Curia

> manages the services that serve the Holy See. But it has one defect: it is Vatican-centric. It sees and looks after the interests of the Vatican, which are still, for the most part, temporal interests. This Vatican-centric view

---

[7] Pope Benedict XVI, *Values in a Time of Upheaval* (New York: The Crossroad Publishing Company, 2006), p. 95.

neglects the world around us. I do not share this view and I'll do everything I can to change it. The Church is or should go back to being a community of God's people, and priests, pastors and bishops who have the care of souls, are at the service of the People of God.[8]

When he was the Archbishop of Buenos Aires, he was fed up with receiving instructions from the Vatican, with, as one of his assistants said, 'Italians with emptying churches, telling bishops in countries with growing congregations what they should or should not be doing.'[9] Cardinal Basil Hume said that the Vatican should serve the government of the Church by the pope and bishops, and not the bishops serve the pope and the Vatican.

Many people in the Vatican would agree with him wholeheartedly. Even so, institutions do not surrender power easily. Old habits are deeply ingrained. Francis has taken three steps to loosen things up. He moved out of the papal apartments into a guest house, the Casa Santa Marta. This was certainly because he wanted a simpler lifestyle. It also helps him to have freedom from the Vatican gatekeepers.

Secondly he appointed a commission of eight cardinals, all of whom were critical of the Vatican. This gives him the necessary support base in his transformation of the Vatican.

Thirdly, and most significantly, he wishes the synods of bishops to have a real share in the government of the Church. He told the Dutch bishops: 'We have been implementing the Council only halfway. Half of the work has still to be done.'[10] The fathers of the Vatican Council wanted real collegiality. Paul VI looked as if he was implementing this with the establishment of the synod of bishops,[11] but it lacked any teeth. It was just an advisory body. I attended three synods, which mainly consisted of people reciting eight minute speeches they had composed before coming. We voted propositions which disappeared into the archives of the Vatican and had not much to do with the pope's following exhortation. Benedict made cautious moves towards more free debate.

Francis has called for an extraordinary synod of bishops this coming October, dealing with the family. This is a smaller group to begin reflection on the challenges facing the family, in preparation for

8   1 October 2013.
9   Vallely, p. 141.
10   Joshua McElwee, 'The Dutch Bishop Says', *National Catholic Reporter*, 6 December 2013.
11   John O'Malley, *What Happened at Vatican II* (London: The Belknap Press of Harvard University, 2008), p. 252.

a larger synod in 2015. The Pope has asked the bishops to consult with their people and see what they believe. The Holy Spirit is poured upon them. The People of God cannot be ignored.

But how will these local discussions work? Who will come to the synod? How will it make decisions? Who will vote? What weight will its decisions have? Francis insists that the Church is not a clerical elite. It is the community of the baptised. The whole people must have a voice. But how? It cannot just passively receive decisions from above. Nor can it simply be a democracy, with decisions taken by majority vote. The Church is the community of the living and the dead. Past councils and popes made affirmations about our faith which must stand. G. K. Chesterton wrote:

> Tradition means giving votes to the most obscure of all classes, our ancestors. It is the democracy of the dead. Tradition refuses to submit to the small and arrogant oligarchy of those who merely happen to be walking about. All democrats object to men being disqualified by the accident of birth; tradition objects to their being disqualified by the accident of death.[12]

So the most intriguing question of this papacy is this: What sort of conversations will enable the laity to have a voice in the life of the Church? I imagine that the Pope sees himself as initiating a process of discovery rather than as having the answer in his back pocket.

It is in this context that we should put what is perhaps the urgent question for the Church: the voice of women. Francis believes that women must have a strong voice in the decision-making of the Church, but maintains that the ordination of women is not on the agenda. He wants to declericalise the Church and not clericalise women.

What can this mean? Francis thinks that the crux of the problem is that power in the Church has become closely identified with sacramental power, the ordained priesthood. The bishops and priests make all the important decisions. Francis writes that confining priestly ordination to men 'can prove especially divisive if sacramental power is too closely identified with power in general'. So we have to think about 'the possible role of women in decision-making in different areas of the Church's life' (EG, n. 104).

---

12 G. K. Chesterton, *Orthodoxy* (London: Hodder and Stoughton, 1996), p. 63.

How might this happen? My own intuition is that we need to nurture other institutions in the Church besides the hierarchy. A healthy society has multiple institutions which give voice and authority to various people. In the Middle Ages, the Church was animated by counterbalancing institutions: the hierarchy, the religious orders, the universities, the fraternities, the nobility, and so on. Each gave a part of the People of God a voice. We need to strengthen and invent other institutions to give a voice to the whole People of God. We need to be a bit messier.

Pope Benedict wrote:

> The Trinity is truly perfect communion! How the world would change if in families, in parishes and in all other communities relationships were lived following always the example of the three Divine Persons, where each one lives not for themselves but with the other, for the other and in the other.[13]

What would parishes, dioceses, and the Church look like if we lived with a Trinitarian love: a love that is equal and without domination? What would it be like if we all had freedom to speak and no one felt pushed to the margins or marginalised themselves? Imagine if we listened to the word of God together, attended faithfully to the tradition, and opened ourselves to the new. What would such a Church be like? Maybe we are on the way to discovering it.

---

[13]   Michael H. Crosby, *Repair My House: Becoming a Kingdom Catholic* (New York: Orbis, 2012), pp. 105–6.

Up from the Underground

Donald Cozzens

At 8:22 p.m., on the evening of 13 March 2013, an Argentinian prelate stepped out of the shadows into the spotlight of the world's stage. Simply vested in the Dominican-inspired white cassock of his office, Jorge Mario Bergoglio did what no pope of recent or ancient memory, I suspect, ever had done – he bowed his head to the mass of cheering faithful below the balcony of St Peter's Basilica. In this slight yet exquisite gesture, he bowed not only to the thousands gathered in St Peter's Square, but also to the world. And the Catholic world collectively caught its breath.

To the waving throng below, Francis asked – the voice gentle but steady – that before he blessed them they might pray for him ... that they might bless him:

> And now I would like to give the blessing, but first – first I ask a favour of you: before the bishop blesses his people, I ask you to pray to the Lord that he will bless me: the prayer of the people asking the blessing for their bishop. Let us make, in silence, this prayer: your prayer *over* me.

Along with millions of others glued to television screens, I asked myself what this humble gesture and this disarming request for a prayer blessing might mean. And what did it signal?

In an instant, the seconds of silent prayer drew the Pope, the thousands in the square, and the millions watching into a wondrous communion. Yes, of course there was spectacle and high religious drama, but the man from Argentina in a matter of minutes transformed the spectacle into a sacrament. I still wonder how anyone, standing on the balcony of St Peter's Basilica, stage-centre of Catholicism's triumphalism and grandeur, could radiate such humility and authenticity. How, in God's name, could Bergoglio so easily and spontaneously turn the glow of the world's spotlight from himself to the people below? He had turned the spotlight from the shepherd onto the Church itself. 'Pray over me, bless me, I am standing here', he seemed to say, 'as the Bishop of Rome, for you, the People of God. I'm here to give you hope, to walk with you into the new life promised by Jesus the Christ.'

Also in March 2013, on an infinitely minor scale of significance, my book, *Notes from the Underground: The Spiritual Journal of a Secular Priest*, was published.[1] With a nod to Dostoyevsky, the title captured my experience of Church and priesthood for more than four decades – I was living in a virtual underground. Above ground, I saw a Church that tried to teach without listening, that tried to govern without concern for the human condition, that tried to turn the light of the Gospel on the world's brokenness without turning that same light on itself. The Second Vatican Council had taught me that the legalism and moralism so central to the Catholic Church for centuries was a distortion of what was at the heart of Christianity. Yet the Church I was ordained into seemed more concerned about sin and sexual misbehaviour than about the spiritual freedom and new life of the Gospel. As a priest and, as such, an official spokesperson for my Church, I felt conflicted and confused, like a traveller in a foreign land who didn't speak the language.

My seminary training seemed to reinforce the idea that the Church's mission was to keep people from sinning – and that sinners abounded. I was to teach that the use of artificial means of birth control was a serious sin, that missing Mass on Sunday was a serious sin, that sexual thoughts, desires, and behaviours outside of marriage were, likewise, serious sins. I felt like a moral policeman. And one day when I came across William Blake's poem, 'The Garden of Love,' and read its closing lines, I wanted to weep:

> And Priests in black gowns were walking their rounds,
> and binding with briers my joys and desires.

Moral policeman, indeed. Of course morality and right belief are foundational to Christianity. But Christ, we know, was not first and foremost a moral teacher or even a dogmatic teacher. His mission was to show us a new way of living and that a divine spark rested in the

---

[1] Donald Cozzens, *Notes from the Underground: The Spiritual Journey of a Secular Priest* (New York: Orbis Books, 2013).

deep recesses of every human heart. Over the years I've come to see that we priests are not ordained to bind or restrict human joys and desires, but instead to name God's grace in a cracked and bleeding world. It is clear that Francis understands this. He knows that priests who teach a rock-hard dogmatism and an ironclad moralism often do more harm than good. He has asked his bishops and priests to be shepherds rather than moral enforcers, to leave their sacristies and move among the throngs of ordinary people doing ordinary things. We are to be wounded healers, encouraging those we meet to trust in God's hidden presence and transforming love.

Now, a year later, Francis continues to connect not only to the world's Catholics but also to many of the world's wary and suspicious. And it's been a year now since I'm up from the underground and perhaps I too should be wary and suspicious. I'm still adjusting to the light and fresh air. In these heady days of Francis' pontificate, I think of the light and fresh air that followed Vatican II and the tragic closing down of its vision and message that soon followed. But this new pope rings true to me. So with each breath my lungs fill with hope and the promise of a new day of healing for our wounded Church and world. But that hope and promise certainly will be tested. Francis knows well that the Church is embedded in the world, embedded in history. The forces of greed and power have built their own mighty fortress. Moreover, the Church is encrusted in its own medieval, feudal bureaucracy that has prevailed over the reforming efforts of previous popes. Francis' mettle will surely be tested, and tested soon.

What we have seen in his first year as pope prompts me to believe Francis will measure up. He has the strength and noble courage of a man of God. And he knows how to look into his own soul. To Antonio Spadaro, SJ, the editor-in-chief of *La Civiltà Cattolica*, the Italian Jesuit journal, he said without nuance, 'I am a sinner.' That kind of transparent honesty should give us hope that in spite of the daunting, complex challenges facing our new pope, this sinner from Argentina has been blessed with the strength, courage and wisdom to renew the Church from the inside out.

During the first year of Francis' ministry as Bishop of Rome and Servant of the Servants of God, the tattered credibility of the Church showed signs of mending. And to the surprise of many, the Pope's authenticity and humility have caught the attention of the world's media masters. Here in the United States, Pope Francis was *Time* magazine's Person of the Year for 2013. And, in Rome, Francis created a new mode of papal communication – what we might call the apostolic interview – freeing him to engage in real, unscripted conversation. His interviews remind me of scripture scholar Walter Brueggemann's pithy insight: 'What we are about is serious conversation leading to blessed communion.' Journalists and Vatican watchers report that, since the election of Francis, simplicity has trumped triumphal display and humility has softened the regal accretions of the Vatican Curia. His very manner of being pope is shaking the long unchallenged foundations of the papal court where, until recently, princely clericalism was deemed fashionable.

> God is greater than religion, faith is greater than dogma.
> (Rabbi Abraham Heschel)

We now have a pope whose humility and simplicity have captured the Catholic imagination. We also have, as we've seen, a pope of remarkable candour. When, in an open letter to the Italian journalist and atheist, Eugenio Scalfari, Francis said, 'I would not speak of absolute truths, even for believers … Truth is a relationship …', Rabbi Heschel must have smiled. If God remains ultimately unknowable, Francis has put our doctrinal beliefs and teachings in perspective. They are but our best efforts at approaching and responding to the great mystery we call God. I suspect Francis is familiar with the work of the South African theologian, Albert Nolan, who writes:

> Upsetting for some people is the undermining of their long held certainties … As we move into a world where many of the things that we took for granted in the past are now being questioned … we can cope only by being truly detached from our own ideas and certainties. Obsession with absolute certainty is yet another form of slavery. It is a way of finding security without having to put all our trust in God.[2]

Both Francis and Nolan understand that the Church is not a broker of God's grace, as if grace were somehow 'Catholic', as if grace were a Catholic spiritual commodity to be awarded to those who practice their faith. Francis writes:

---

[2]   Albert Nolan, *Jesus Today: A Spirituality of Radical Freedom* (New York: Orbis Books, 2006), p. 132.

> The Eucharist … is not a prize for the perfect but a powerful medicine and nourishment for the weak … Frequently, we act as arbiters of grace rather than its facilitators. But the Church is not a tollhouse; it is the house of the Father, where there is a place for everyone, with all their problems (*EG*, n. 47).[3]

In this line of thought, the Catholic Church doesn't hold the copyright on Jesus Christ. The ecumenical implications here are obvious and significant.

Neither does the Church control the manifestations and inspirations of the Holy Spirit. The Spirit, to the befuddlement of some, is loose in the world. She is free to roam where she will. Francis' meetings and correspondence with religious leaders and non-believers underscore this point. Herein lies his readiness to enter 'serious conversation leading to blessed communion'. From what we've seen in the first year of Francis' papacy, we can expect substantive, perhaps dramatic, advances in the Catholic Church's relations with the world's major religions.

> If the church does not subject itself to the judgment
> which is pronounced by the church,
> it becomes idolatrous towards itself.
> Such idolatry is its permanent temptation …
> A church which tries to exclude itself
> from such a judgment loses its right to judge the world
> and is rightly judged by the world.
> This is the tragedy of the Roman Catholic Church.
>
> (Paul Tillich)[4]

Lutheran theologian Paul Tillich's trenchant observation is as true today as it was a half century ago. The Church has rightly turned the light of the Gospel on the dignity of all human life; on the mind-numbing, ever-expanding financial gap between the world's super rich and the world's middle and lower classes; on the appalling hunger and destitution of literally countless millions of children and adults; on the real danger of nuclear violence and war; on the dark

---

[3] Pope Francis, *Evangelii Gaudium* (The Joy of the Gospel), Apostolic Exhortation on the Proclamation of the Gospel in Today's World, 2013. References will be denoted by *EG*, followed by the paragraph number.

[4] Paul Tillich and F. Forrester Church, *The Essential Tillich: An Anthropology of the Writings of Paul Tillich* (New York: Macmillan, 1987), p. 102.

evils of sexual abuse of children and minors; and on the equally dark world of trafficking of women and children. And the Church, as Pope Francis has acknowledged, has done an enormous amount of good to meet and right these deep wounds in the human family.

But what the Church hasn't done is turn the light of the Gospel on itself. I believe Francis understands this. Out of fear of harm to the Church's teaching authority, to its perceived reputation among ordinary Catholics, and to the Church's financial resources, it has misjudged its own sacred integrity and until recently has excused itself from the Gospel's searing judgement and light. What is so disturbing to traditionalist prelates and see-no-evil believers is Francis' readiness to submit the Church – and even the papacy – to the judgement of the Gospel. If Francis can admit that he's a sinner, then the Church itself can admit that it, too, has sinned. What healing balm this would be to the countless victims of clergy sexual abuse.

I hope that Francis will soon meet with abuse victims, listen to their stories of rebuff and accusations of disloyalty by Church authorities when they tried to report their seductions. I hope his recently appointed commission to address this evil will finally lift the heavy curtains of denial, deflection and lies that have exacerbated this systemic and worldwide ecclesial scandal. And I hope Francis will turn the light of the Gospel on the bishops who placed their loyalty to the institution, the reputation of the clergy, and their regard for the Church's treasures ahead of their pastoral concern for the most vulnerable of their flocks. For centuries, the Church has thought of itself as a perfect society accountable to no authority on earth save that of the Supreme Pontiff. Vatican II changed all that in theory. It remains for Francis to move us from theory to practice.

To his great credit, Pope Francis has already taken creative, promising steps towards reform and renew the Vatican Curia. Still, the centuries-old ecclesial court is damp and musty with not a few self-serving, career-minded prelates who think of themselves as princes rather than servants. These prelates see privilege as their due. They are, and have been for ages, the Church's aristocracy. And more than a few love their royal regalia, their cappa magna (long trailing cape), their lace and water silk robes, their jewelled rings and pectoral crosses. These prince-prelates must find Francis' example of humility and simplicity unsettling.

There is an Episcopal church, St Bartholomew, just outside my home city of Cleveland, Ohio that has a striking sign above the main entrance. The sign reads: 'Servants' Entrance'. It's already clear that Francis has a lively imagination. What would his brother bishops think if they saw such a sign above the sacristy doors where they solemnly vest for the sacred liturgy? And what would we priests think if Francis proposed that signs reading 'Servants' Entrance' were placed above the sacristy doors of parish churches throughout the world?

In the months and years ahead, I hope Francis will turn the empowering light of the Gospel on the limited role of women in the Church. Their time surely has come. Believers need to hear the word of God preached in voices both male and female. And because Francis has learned how to listen, I expect he will understand the need for serious conversation about the thwarted, unused charisms evident in the lives of many Catholic women. Discerning the rightful leadership role of women in the Church is central to Francis' efforts to restructure the Vatican Curia. They are not separate issues.

I'm certain that many of today's Latin Rite priests continue to wonder how the Church can hold that celibacy is a gift, a charism of the Spirit and then, without blushing at its arrogance, insist that this charism will be bestowed on anyone called to the priesthood. Does the Church have that kind of influence over the Holy Spirit? The plight of the priesthood, we priests trust, is high on Francis' list of priorities.

> Beauty will save the world.
> (Fyodor Dostoyevsky)

My hunch is that Pope Francis agrees with Dostoyevsky's enigmatic claim. His deep submersion in theology, his broad knowledge of the fine and performing arts, of poetry, fiction and film all have conspired to fire his imagination. The uniting and saving power of the honoured trinity of Truth, Good and Beauty have refined Francis' soul. His widely read interview with Fr Spadaro unveiled his rich cultural background as well as his refreshing earthiness. So, Francis, I believe, is very much at home with the elusive phrase, 'beauty will save the world'.

But Francis' first apostolic exhortation, *Evangelii Gaudium* (The Joy of the Gospel), suggests he would also claim that 'joy will save the world'. 'Without the joy of beauty', Francis has written, 'any work for the good becomes a gloomy concern for efficiency ...'[5] And he understands there is no real joy without humility. So, we have a pope who refuses to be clad in the robes of a sovereign, who refuses to live in a palace, who refuses the comfort of a limousine. We have a pope, on the other hand, who chooses to live as simply as possible, who understands his need for the common touch and for the comfort of community.

If preaching is fundamentally 'naming grace', how can joyless proclamations of the word of God be successful? Neither can a joyless evangelisation touch hearts or heal souls. Francis knows that joy is no easy quality of soul. It is grounded first of all in faith, in the trust that God walks with his people. And this at times demands almost everything. We might speak of 'courage to rejoice'. As a community of disciples, we encourage one another to stay the course and, no matter what, to rejoice. That's precisely what Francis is doing in *Evangelii Gaudium*; he's encouraging the Church to live joyfully in the power of Christ's presence, open to the wisdom of the Spirit. Francis, following the insights of St Ignatius, understands that living joyfully means savouring the blessings of life.

And we learn to savour, to literally 'savour the joy of Christ', by contemplative living. Francis writes, 'true love is always contemplative, and permits us to serve the other not of necessity or vanity, but rather because he or she is beautiful above and beyond mere appearances ...' (*EG*, n. 199). It follows then that true joy is always contemplative. We see now in our new Jesuit pope, a 'contemplative in action', a man who invites us to come and see and taste the life-giving, joyful, way of Jesus Christ.

So we priests and Catholic faithful have a pope whose joy, authenticity, and humility inspire and challenge us at the same time. He's calling us to Gospel simplicity and to genuine concern for the poor. He wants bishops and priests who ring true, who are willing to risk the comforts of the rectory for the insecurity of the streets. And,

---

5   Jorge Mario Bergoglio, 'Anointed with the Oil of Gladness', Homily at the Chrism Mass, Buenos Aires, 21 April 2011, in *Encountering Christ: Homilies, Letters, and Addresses of Cardinal Jorge Bergoglio* (New York: Scepter Publishing, 2013), p. 105.

following his lead, I want to measure up. I want to remain up from the underground where there's healing light and fresh air.

My more sceptical brothers aren't so sure. They remind me that Francis hasn't 'changed the words, but he's changed the music'.[6] And the music might change again. 'Don't get your hopes up', they say. 'He's only been pope for a year. Let's wait and see … You might be back in the underground before you know it.' Perhaps. But I'd rather listen to my brother priests and lay friends who sense something extraordinary is afoot. Thanks to Francis, I'm up from the underground and breathing fresh air. What a joy.

---

6   Nancy Gibbs, *Time*, 3 January 2014, p. 44.

Recommended Reading

(A) By Pope Francis

BERGOGLIO, Jorge Mario, *Encountering Christ: Homilies, Letters, and Addresses of Cardinal Jorge Bergoglio* (New Rochelle, NY: Scepter Publishers, Inc., 2013).

_____, *Open Mind, Faithful Heart: Reflections on Following Jesus*, trans. by Joseph V. Owens (New York: Herder & Herder, 2013).

_____, *Fighting Corruption and Sin* (London: Catholic Truth Society, 2013).

_____, *On the Examination of Oneself* (Nairobi: Paulines Publications Africa, 2013).

_____, *The Way of Humility* (London: Catholic Truth Society, 2013).

BERGOGLIO, Jorge Mario and SKORKA, Abraham, *On Heaven and Earth: Pope Francis on Faith, Family, and the Church in the Twenty-First Century*, trans. by Alejandro Bermudez and Howard Goodman (London: Bloomsbury, 2013).

Pope Francis, *Lumen Fidei* (The Light of Faith), Encyclical Letter (Dublin: Veritas Publications, 2013).

_____, *Evangelii Gaudium* (The Joy of the Gospel), Apostolic Exhortation on the Proclamation of the Gospel in Today's World (Dublin: Veritas Publications, 2013).

_____, *Why My Name is Francis* (Milano: Figlie di San Paolo, 2013).

_____, *Words of Mercy and Joy* (Dublin: Veritas Publications, 2013).

_____, *Lenten Message 2014* (Rome: Libreria Editrice Vaticana, 2014).

(B) ABOUT POPE FRANCIS

BERMÚDEZ, Alejandro (ed.), *Pope Francis: Our Brother, Our Friend* (San Francisco: Ignatius Press, 2013).

BUNSON, Matthew E., *Pope Francis* (Huntington, IN: Our Sunday Visitor, Inc., 2013).

COLLINS, Michael, *Francis, Bishop of Rome: A Short Biography* (Dublin: The Columba Press, 2013).

COOL, Michael, *Francis: A New World Pope*, trans. by Regan Kramer (Grand Rapids, Michigan: William B. Eerdmans Publishing Company, 2013).

COTTER, Kevin (ed.), *Through the Year with Pope Francis: Daily Reflections* (Huntington, IN: Our Sunday Visitor, Inc., 2013).

CRAUGHWELL, Thomas J., *Pope Francis: The Pope from the End of the Earth* (Charlotte, North Carolina: St Benedict Press, 2013).

CROOS, Dushan, *Pope Francis* (London: Catholic Truth Society, 2013).

DONNELLY, Nick, *Stations of the Cross with Pope Francis* (London: Catholic Truth Society, 2014).

ERUPPAKKATT, Joe, *Pope Francis* (Mumbai: St Pauls, 2013).

FAZIO, Mariano, *Pope Francis: Keys to His Thoughts* (New Rochelle, NY: Scepter Publishers, Inc., 2013).

GROGAN, Brian, *Pope Francis: The Jesuit Pope and What We Can Expect From Him* (Dublin: Veritas Publications, 2013).

LOWNEY, Chris, *Pope Francis – Why He Leads the Way He Leads: Lessons from the First Jesuit Pope* (Chicago: Loyola Press, 2013).

MOYNIHAN, Robert, *Pray for Me: The Life and Spiritual Vision of Pope Francis* (London: Ryder, 2013).

TORNIELLI, Andrea, *Francis: Pope of a New World*, trans. by William J. Melcher (San Francisco: Ignatius Press, 2013).

ROSSA, Alberto (ed.), *A Year with Pope Francis: Daily Reflections from His Writings* (Macao, Chine: Claretian Publications, 2013).

RUBIN, Sergio and AMBROGETTI, Francesca, *Pope Francis: Conversations with Jorge Bergoglio* (London: Hodder & Stoughton, 2013).

SCHWIETERT COLLAZO, Julie and ROGAK, Lisa, *Pope Francis in His Own Words* (London: William Collins, 2013).

VALLELY, Paul, *Pope Francis: Untying the Knots* (London: Bloomsbury, 2013).

VALENTE, Gianni, *Interviews with a Future Pope* (London: Catholic Truth Society, 2013).